Madison County, Tennessee

Marriages

1838 – 1871

Byron and Barbara Sistler

JANAWAY PUBLISHING, INC.
Santa Maria, California

Originally Published:
Nashville, Tennessee
1983

Reprinted by

Janaway Publishing, Inc.
732 Kelsey Ct.
Santa Maria, California 93454
(805) 925-1038
www.JanawayGenealogy.com

2009, 2012

ISBN: 978-1-59641-060-2

MADISON COUNTY, TENNESSEE MARRIAGES

1838-1871

Where two dates appear on an entry, the first one is the date license was issued, the second (in parentheses) the date marriage was solemnized. If only one date, either the marriage did not take place or at least there was no return to the courthouse.

A word of caution. These marriages were not copied directly from the originals but from WPA books prepared in the 1930s and 1940s from those originals. They include a number of errors, either in the reading or transcribing of the records. They should therefore be used with care, and confirmation through examining microfilm of the original is well advised.

Byron Sistler
Barbara Sistler

Nashville, TN
July 1983

Acre, Lewis to Anna Lambert 1-3-1839 (1-6-1839)
Acre, Michie to Susan Copher 7-1-1843 (7-2-1843)
Acree, Wesley S. to Harriet A. Peters 1-4-1870 (1-6-1870)
Acres, James N. to Mary (Mrs.) Melley 6-6-1857
Adam, Tapley to Margaret A. Butler 8-24-1853 (8-25-1853)
Adams, Chester T. to Nancy Oliver 10-30-1860 (11-1-1860)
Adams, James to Mary E. Rollins 9-20-1854 (12-21-1854)
Adams, Minus O. to Frances C. Butler 1-10-1859 (1-11-1859)
Adams, Robert G. to Susan Davis 3-17-1862
Adams, Robt. H. to Susie (Mrs.) McFarland 8-22-1871 (8-22-1871)
Adams, Whitmill P. to Rachel Pierce 11-16-1853
Adams, William Henry to Miranda Jane Massey 2-10-1859 (2-17-1859)
Adkins, William to Sally Oliver 11-26-1860 (11-27-1860)
Adkins, William to Sarah E. F. Gannaway 11-24-1866 (11-25-1866)
Albritton, John H. to Elizabeth Spring 3-31-1852
Alexander, Dudley to Mary Pierce 5-5-1858
Alexander, Duncan L. to Hannah Chandler 1-31-1854
Alexander, Edward F. to Julia A. Dodds 6-22-1870
Alexander, Elijah to Sarah E. Guinn 12-22-1868 (12-23-1868)
Alexander, Harvey M. to Malinda Maynard 12-16-1869 (12-17-1869)
Alexander, James M. to Mary Elizabeth Rollings 3-15-1855
Alexander, James M. to Mary Jane Cobb 11-17-1871
Alexander, James M. to Narcissa D. Harris 8-29-1844
Alexander, James to Peninah Teague 12-25-1856
Alexander, Jimms P. to Nancy P. Kell 10-24-1871 (10-25-1871)
Alexander, John B. to Margaret Allison 7-14-1866 (7-15-1866)
Alexander, Joseph F. to Frances (Mrs.) Frieles 12-10-1868 (12-13-1868)
Alexander, Martin D. to Mary Jane Alexander 5-14-1853
Alexander, Philip D. to Jane Guinn 12-22-1869 (12-23-1869)
Alexander, William A. to Suzy Ann Irvin 3-21-1843 (3-23-1843)
Alexander, William to Nancy N. Guinn 3-18-1868
Alford, James to Jane Vantrence 3-9-1841
Alford, Leander to Nancy Davis 1-30-1844
Algee, Robert C. to Margaret C. Mooring 12-27-1855
Allen, Andrew J. to Mary A. Russell 1-25-1870
Allen, John H. to Martha Nelson 12-10-1839 (12-12-1839)
Allen, Moses S. to Elizabeth C. Teague 4-17-1856
Allen, Peter J. to Nettie Phillips 9-8-1866 (9-9-1866)
Allen, S. Lafayette to Margaret Estes 7-9-1862
Allen, T. Walker to Martha Appleby 5-20-1869 (5-23-1869)
Allen, Thomas to Adaline Sanders 11-21-1870 (11-23-1870)
Allen, Tomlin P. to Rhoda Ann Nelson 12-22-1840 (12-24-1840)
Allen, W. T. to Frances Nelson 4-16-1853
Allen, William M. to Amanda Hodgson 6-15-1839 (6-18-1839)
Allen, William M. to Hulda Hicks 3-15-1870 (3-16-1870)
Allen, William T. to Eliza J. Nelson 12-30-1844
Allen, William to Jane Belton 3-12-1850 (3-14-1850)
Allison, Daniel M. to Amanda Mills 2-19-1870 (2-20-1870)
Allison, Daniel R. to Nancy Watson 6-29-1843
Allison, Henry T. to Sallie J. Duncan 10-12-1871
Allison, John W. to Martha A. Betty 10-24-1859
Allison, Joseph to Mary Frances Johnson 7-16-1839
Allison, William Malichi to Agasy Caroline Adams 11-18-1857
Allison, William to Sarah A. E. Robinson 8-20-1848
Alston, Augustus B. to Judith F. Holt 3-14-1854 (3-15-1854)
Altman, Joel W. to Rachel A. Maddox 2-19-1849 (12-20-1849)
Altom, Elisha to Hannah Williamson 4-16-1849 (4-6?-1849)
Amos, Jas. T. to Sudie Newel 11-14-1871 (11-15-1871)
Amos, T. F. to Mary A. T. Johnson 12-2-1867 (12-5-1867)
Amos, William L. to M. J. Wallis 12-2-1867 (12-5-1867)
Anderson, Beverly to Nancy Smith 1-6-1844
Anderson, Fredrick to Bertha H. Britton 2-23-1846 (2-26-1846)
Anderson, Hugh N. to Mary C. Waters 1-30-1845
Anderson, James M. to Nancy J. Black 7-13-1840
Anderson, James R. to Virginia Estes 10-8-1870 (10-13-1870)
Anderson, James W. to Ellen B. Dunaway 5-8-1861
Anderson, Jefferson to Narcissa Dew 5-11-1855
Anderson, John J. to Matilda W. Fussell 9-8-1847
Anderson, John T. to Martha P. Johnson 7-15-1850
Anderson, John Tyler to Julia Ann Brown 10-9-1860
Anderson, John to Mary Ann Snowden 6-18-1846
Anderson, Logan J. to Susan E. Franklin 12-8-1862 (12-9-1862)
Anderson, Marma D. to Sarah E. Oliver 12-23-1850

Anderson, Montgomery to Alpha Webb 1-10-1844
Anderson, Montgomery to Cynthia E. Steward 8-8-1849 (8-16-1849)
Anderson, Robt. D. to Sarah A. Womack 3-10-1868 (3-20-1868)
Anderson, Thomas to Eliza Jane Harrison 8-7-1854
Anderson, Turner M. to Eliza Jane McNaion 8-3-1869
Anderson, Wesley to Sarah Manley 1-27-1858
Anderson, William L. to Amanda D. Vick 4-29-1848
Anderson, William to Rebecca McGroom 6-22-1852
Anderson, Wm. J. to M. Caroline Dickinson 1-29-1867 (1-31-1867)
Anderson, Wm. P. to Frances Cox 1-15-1870 (1-16-1870)
Anderson, Wm. R. to Fanny Pace 9-12-1866 (9-13-1866)
Anthony, William A. to Julia S. (Mrs.) Boner 3-1-1858 (3-8-1858)
Anthony, Wm. D. to Mary E. K. Crist 8-7-1867 (8-8-1867)
Appleton, John S. to Elizabeth t. Gregory 3-11-1870
Archa, Thomas to Susan Delda 11-15-1838
Armstead, Geo. E. to Mary Jane Glass 2-8-1870 (2-9-1870)
Armstrong, Robert E. to Ann E. Hathaway 8-4-1858
Armstrong, William to Elizabeth Forsythe 2-21-1850
Arnold, Francis N. to Mahala Thomas 9-29-1858
Arnold, James D. to Eliza Thomas 12-17-1849 (12-17-1850?)
Arnold, John N. to Sarah Thomas Henning 1-5-1844 (1-2?-1844)
Arnold, Littleberry to Elizabeth F. Barnett 12-15-1862 (12-17-1862)
Arnold, Theo. to Rebecca Walker 8-27-1839 (9-4-1839)
Arnold, Thomas G. to Margaret J. Humphreys 9-14-1853 (9-15-1853)
Arnold, Thos. G. to Margaret J. Humphreys 9-4-1853
Ashford, George W. to Eliza Jane Shuford 11-29-1856 (12-2-1856)
Askew, Joseph D. to Rutha J. Doherty 12-19-1857
Askew, Thomas to Sarah Cash 6-22-1857
Atkinson, Jno. R. (Dr.) to Bettie Lanier 12-6-1869 (12-8-1869)
Atkison, Robert A. to Levina Donald 10-30-1840
Aubrey, James H. to Mary Boon 8-23-1845 (8-25-1845)
Austin, Henry J. to Mary Ann Howell 9-30-1857 (10-1-1857)
Austin, John A. to Mary P. Stout 5-25-1866 (5-27-1866)
Avery, William M. to America E. Hardgraves 8-26-1867
Avery, Wm. A. G. to Sarah N. Rosamon 9-3-1866 (9-9-1866)
Ayers, George C. to Temperance A. Patterson 11-25-1868
Baber, Francis J. to Janetta J. Day 10-6-1859
Bagley, George A. (of Miss.) to Jemima Johnson 7-16-1861
Bagnell, Isaac to Mary A. Butts 1-24-1849
Bailey, Anderson to Angeline Frances Stewart 1-7-1867 (1-8-1867)
Bailey, Andrew I. to Elizabeth Goodrich 2-8-1842
Bailey, Elijah to Martha C. Bailey 12-28-1866 (12-31-1866)
Bailey, Jeremiah to Dizia Ann Bailey 6-22-1857 (6-23-1857)
Bailey, Joseph to Harriet M. Jackson 12-18-1847 (12-20-1847)
Bailey, Nathe. C. to Martha M. Thomas 12-26-1870 (12-27-1870)
Baily, William W. to Paralee Wadley 8-18-1855 (8-19-1855)
Bain, Wm. W. to Julia B. Haynes 12-18-1866 (12-20-1866)
Baker, Fetus to Judith Phelps 11-8-1842 (11-9-1842)
Baker, George W. to Arabella Barrett 8-15-1846 (8-17-1846)
Baker, Henry C. to Sarah A. Graves 6-23-1866 (6-24-1866)
Baker, Henry to Elizabeth Read 8-3-1858 (8-12-1858)
Baker, Jacob to Rebecca Jackson 11-4-1850
Baker, James F. to Amanda C. Deaton 7-26-1869 (7-28-1869)
Baker, James H. to Elizabeth Glenn 12-27-1849 (12-29-1849)
Baker, James J. to Martha A. D. Wilson 12-14-1847 (3-26-1848)
Baker, John W. to Elizabeth F. Toones 9-16-1867 (9-18-1867)
Baker, John W. to Mary E. Little 7-3-1852 (7-8-1852)
Baker, Joshua to Lucretia Perry 5-11-1839
Baker, Shadrich to Mary Piercifull 1-14-1850 (1-17-1849?)
Baker, Thomas to Elizabeth Cook 3-4-1839 (3-5-1839)
Baker, William R. to Martha Ann Percy 12-13-1843 (12-15-1843)
Baker, William to Margarett Wilkins 7-28-1846
Baker, Wm. C. to Frances A. E. Reeves 8-9-1869 (8-12-1869)
Baldridge, William Thomas to Mary C. Hickman 12-24-1853 (12-27-1853)
Balentine, James to Margaret Ann Burrow 2-19-1857
Ball, Charles S. to Mary Goodwin 7-30-1860
Ballard, Isaac W. to Talitha C. O'Neal 11-7-1866
Baly, Elisha to Martha C. Jackson 1-14-1852 (1-15-1852)
Bancroft, Daniel to Elizabeth Senter 8-22-1840 (8-23-1840)
Barber, Thomas to Mary Jane Horn 1-11-1849
Barclay, James W. to Nancy Minerva Henderson 3-10-1857 (3-11-1857)
Barham, I. H. to June Christian 2-14-1840 (2-16-1840)
Barham, Thomas C. to Louisa S. Orgain 2-28-1848 (3-1-1848)

Barnes, Edward to Matilda Anderson 5-1-1849 (5-3-1849)
Barnes, Thomas to Elizabeth Nevill 8-20-1852
Barnes, Timothy J. to Laura L. Kirby 10-5-1869 (10-6-1869)
Barnet, John M. to Jackey J. Harp 2-21-1855 (2-27-1855)
Barnett, Elias D. to Almira N. Key 3-22-1848 (3-28-1848)
Barnett, Elizabeth J.? to Martha Houghton 10-20-1845 (10-21-1845)
Barnett, Enos H. to Lucinda J. Henderson 8-17-1846 (8-20-1846)
Barnett, John J. to Margaret E. Thompson 4-6-1867 (4-9-1867)
Barnett, Leroy to Naomi Gordon 9-25-1850 (10-1-1850)
Barnett, Matthew B. to Louisa Malinda Allen 3-19-1870 (3-22-1870)
Barnett, Peter B. to Mahala V. E. Garrett 12-3-1860 (12-5-1860)
Barnett, Peter B. to Susan J. Barnett 9-2-1859 (9-8-1859)
Barnett, Samuel D. to Mary L. Fogg 5-25-1857
Barnett, Theron B. to Mary E. Nelson 4-15-1861 (4-18-1861)
Barnett, Thomas to Eliza McLeary 2-8-1843
Barnhill, Wm. A. to Caroline (Mrs.) Goodrich 2-16-1871
Barr, Benjamin to Sarah R. Elrod 1-4-1843
Barr, William M. to Sarah J. Russell 9-12-1859 (9-13-1859)
Barrier, Lafayette to Amanda Bingham 12-4-1860
Barron, Amos W. to Sarah Jane Munn 10-25-1859 (11-1-1859)
Barton, Thomas F. to Nancy Black 12-28-1847 (12-30-1847)
Barton, William R. to Harrie A. Provine 11-4-1850 (11-6-1850)
Bates, Chalres T. to Pattie Barr 8-16-1871 (8-19-1871)
Battle, Lewis to Frances Sorrell 8-11-1860 (8-16-1860)
Baxter, James M. to Nancy A. Dougan 10-2-1850 (10-3-1850)
Baxter, James to Margarett Humphreys 7-20-1849
Bayley, Henry to Arcady F. Jones 6-12-1848
Beadles, Duke J. to Ann C. Harris 11-18-1857
Beal, Simon to Jane Wilkinson 12-25-1843
Behns, John to Mary Ann Gibson 2-5-1870
Bell, Cit L. to Sallie Webb 3-8-1871
Bell, David D. to Martha G. Gibbs 4-9-1846
Bell, John G. to Mary C. Taylor 11-10-1856
Bell, John H. to Lucy A. Smith 10-9-1866
Bell, Joseph to Mary Jane Montgomery 12-28-1840
Bell, Peyton S. to Matilda (Mrs.) Oliver 8-4-1862 (8-10-1862)
Bell, Ransom H. to Zelphia J. Brigance 1-24-1870 (1-25-1870)
Bell, Samuel J. to Frances B. Montgomery 1-16-1849
Bell, William J. to Nancy Roseman 9-19-1855 (9-20-1855)
Belote, Charles R. to Nancy E. White 8-31-1854
Belue, George to Sarah E. Dollar 6-7-1854 (6-8-1854)
Benjamin, S. C. to Harriet D. May 12-9-1857 (12-10-1857)
Bennet, Elijah to Mlda? B. Grant 7-3-1855 (7-4-1855)
Bennett, George M. to Mary Kirby 4-15-1857 (4-16-1857)
Bennett, Powhatton P. to Sue Matthews 12-16-1868 (12-19-1868)
Bennett, Richard to Matilda Bass 7-31-1839
Bennett, William K. to Eliza A. Read 3-1-1849 (3-5-1849)
Benson, William A. to E. I. Blackmon 9-22-1842
Benton, Nathaniel to Nancy A. Stribling 9-12-1848 (9-13-1848)
Berry, Thomas F. to Mary Pearson 3-10-1870
Bess, Richard to Eleanor (Mrs.) McCrory 4-30-1857
Bethshares, George to Louisa Thomas 3-19-1870
Betty, Joseph A. to Sarah E. Alexander 2-2-1852 (2-10-1852)
Beveridge, John T. to Amanda M. Bledsoe 12-20-1854 (12-21-1854)
Bevill, Andrew H. to Mollie Kirby 12-13-1866
Bevill, Marcus L. to Emily Brown 10-4-1860
Bevill, Wesley B. to Susan A. Roberts 10-9-1856
Bickers, Lewis A. to Susan Thompson 11-1-1848
Bickers, Robert to Isabella Thompson 11-1-1847 (11-18-1847)
Bickerstaff, Sandford M. to California Lovell 4-13-1869 (4-14-1869)
Biddle, William A. to Sarah E. Gillum 10-22-1866 (10-30-1866)
Biggs, Jesse to Sophia J. Rutherford 7-18-1867
Bigloe, Alfred to Mary Ann Burnam 11-13-1854 (11-16-1854)
Billingsly, Robert to Frances R. Thomas 12-8-1846
Billington, John H. to Nancy Gaston 10-29-1866 (10-31-1866)
Bingham, Jabez to Martha S. Patterson 10-1-1855
Binkley, Rufus N. to Mary E. (Mrs.) Willett 2-18-1869
Birch, George W. to Catherine Swan 12-13-1858 (12-16-1858)
Bird, Bartlett F. to Sophronia Bostrick 12-18-1850
Bird, Dempsey to Sarah Jane Emerson 7-15-1848 (7-20-1848)
Birdsong, Henry F. to Mary E. Sanders 3-19-1866
Birdsong, John C. to Gemina Thedford 11-23-1841
Birdsong, William J. G. to Virginia M. Sims 7-26-1862 (7-30-1862)
Birmingham, Daniel F. to Ann D. W. Cate 5-19-1846
Birmingham, Danl. J. (Gibson Co) to Sarah J. (Mrs.) Sykes 8-19-1869

Birmingham, Edward L. to Caroline Frederick 7-6-1859 (7-7-1859)
Bishop, George to Isabella Cooper 3-3-1857 (3-4-1857)
Bishop, George to Margaret Revely 1-17-1853 (1-18-1853)
Bivins, David w. to Jane Parker 2-2-1846 (2-6-1846)
Black, Amos to Jane M. Stephens 10-26-1857
Black, Geo. B. to Sarah E. Harrison 12-22-1868 (12-24-1868)
Black, John C. to Amanda Stewart 2-6-1854
Black, Thomas to Amanda Allison 12-2-1846 (12-3-1846)
Black, Thomas to Loset M. York 2-21-1843
Black, William G. to Martha Hotchkiss 1-10-1850
Blackard, Wiley F. to Terrissa M. Wyley 12-22-1855 (12-24-1855)
Blackard, William T. to Martha J. Holt 2-11-1850
Blackburn, Wesly to Sarah Brooks 12-29-1846 (12-31-1846)
Blackman, Burwell to Mary E. Watson 9-8-1846 (9-10-1846)
Blackman, James to Miriam L. Anderson 1-4-1843 (1-5-1843)
Blackmon, John to Eliza Reid 9-21-1842 (9-22-1842)
Blacknall, Charles H. to Eliza K. Edmondson 11-23-1852 (11-25-1852)
Blackwell, Joseph to Mary Delph 12-2-1856 (12-7-1856)
Blair, George D. to Martha McGuire 2-9-1846
Blair, John R. to Deborah Haltom 11-21-1855
Blair, John to Eliza Stone 9-19-1845
Blair, John to Sarah Brown 1-22-1839
Blair, Thomas to Nancy Barton 1-1-1868 (1-2-1868)
Blake, Frederick to Nancy Jane Mays 4-21-1870 (4-24-1870)
Blanchet, Thomas D. to Martha Jane Fagg 11-4-1850
Bland, Arthur to Elizabeth Mangrum 5-8-1841 (5-9-1841)
Bland, Charles A. to Louis S. Morrell 4-11-1846 (4-12-1846)
Blankenship, Raymond A. to Martha Thompson 7-17-1855
Blankinship, James P. to Frances A. Hollingsworth 11-12-1866 (11-13-1866)
Blaydes, Samuel H. to Mary N. McLemore 11-23-1852 (11-25-1852)
Bledsoe, Anthony to Drusilla Griffin 7-4-1842 (7-7-1842)
Bledsoe, Jamerson to Mary Nance 1-31-1843
Bledsoe, Joseph M. to Tabitha J. Thomas 12-29-1868 (12-31-1868)
Bledsoe, Marcus S. to Frances Ventreese 3-15-1856
Bledsoe, Marcus to Lucy Young 3-20-1850 (3-21-1850)
Blevins, Hugh to Sarah Coopender 1-18-1840 (1-19-1840)
Blume, Benj. H. to Hannah O. (Mrs.) Simmons 3-20-1867
Blurton, John W. to Catherine Faulkner 12-16-1870 (12-18-1870)
Boals, George W. to Nancy J. Hathaway 7-19-1859 (7-21-1859)
Boals, John R. to Ann Eliza Jones 12-17-1860 (12-19-1860)
Bobbit, Samuel to Jane Croom 12-8-1841 (12-9-1841)
Bobbitt, Matthew G. to Martha Williams 12-14-1846 (12-15-1846)
Bolen, Lewis Z. T. to Emma Moore 11-16-1870 (11-17-1870)
Bolin, George A. to Nancy Parker 6-23-1856 (6-24-1856)
Bolton, Richard T. to Malissa Boals 1-9-1849 (1-10-1849)
Boman, James to Frances Sumner 4-24-1860 (4-25-1860)
Bona, Ben Franklin to Elizabeth Nelson 9-11-1838
Bond, Benj. F. to Martha Bone 2-19-1861
Bond, Benjamin F. to Biddy (Mrs.) Scott 10-20-1858 (10-21-1858)
Bond, Francis A. to Martha L. Young 12-3-1850
Bond, George W. to Mary J. Chester 10-6-1845 (10-7-1845)
Bond, James W. to Martha N. C. Wilkes 1-16-1856 (1-22-1856)
Bond, Lewis B. to L. R. Hawkins 7-3-1860 (7-4-1860)
Bond, Robert W. to Sallie F. Henning 2-17-1869
Bond, Theophilus to Laura Warlick 4-1-1852
Bond, Whitmell T. to Hannah O. Bond 5-3-1852 (5-4-1852)
Bond, William L. to Eliza Chapman 12-2-1844 (12-4-1844)
Bond, Wm. W. to L. S. Harbert 4-27-1854 (5-3-1854)
Bond, jr., Eaton to Bell Penn 12-9-1867
Booe, Radford to Sarah Elizabeth Jenkins 1-24-1857
Boon, Charles F. to M. E. Henderson 8-24-1869
Boon, John J. to Lucretia L. Lacy 3-28-1866 (3-29-1866)
Boon, John J. to Martha E Johnson 7-10-1850
Boon, Milton to Mollie Richardson 3-25-1868 (3-31-1868)
Boon, Robert D. to Martha A. Senter 10-20-1856
Boon, Robert H. to Ann A. Mitchell 11-1-1858 (11-4-1858)
Boon, Sion to Mary Louisa Pyles 4-17-1856 (4-8?-1856)
Boon, William M. to Sarah Todd 11-19-1866 (11-22-1866)
Boone, Jordon B. to Elizabeth L. Short 1-8-1844 (1-11-1844)
Boren, James W. to Elizabeth Fussell 12-12-1867
Boren, Wm. A. to Permelia J. Jeffries 12-12-1870 (12-13-1870)
Bosheers, Ben Franklin to Louisa Patterson 8-14-1869 (3?-15-1869)
Bostick, John to Mary Carrington 12-30-1845 (12-31-1845)
Bostick, John to Susanna B. Hudson 2-22-1841 (2-24-1841)

Bostick, Levi to Caroline Carring 10-15-1846
Boswell, Jonathan to Elizabeth Horne 10-30-1849
Botts, Jno. T. to Lyde Tomlin 12-1-1868
Bourland, James R. to Olivia J. (Mrs.) Lewis 2-20-1871 (2-21-1871)
Bowles, John R. to Betsy Ann McIver 1-30-1856 (2-5-1856)
Bowling, Alexander to Sarah J. Davie 11-29-1850
Bowman, Joshua M. to Mary (Mrs.) Bowman 12-14-1867 (12-15-1867)
Box, Jess to Martha E. (Mrs.) Stewart 3-11-1870 (3-13-1870)
Boyd, Archibald to Mary Ann Emerson 9-22-1858 (9-23-1858)
Boyd, Hugh to Mary Lemons 2-5-1855 (2-7-1855)
Boyd, James W. to Caroline A. Malone 2-6-1845 (2-8-1845)
Boyd, John E. to Dora E. McLemore 5-12-1870 *
Boyd, Milton B. to Mary L. W. Becton 10-26-1850 (10-27-1850)
Boyet, William W. to Elizabeth T. Grant 10-6-1851 (10-9-1851)
Boyett, Ezekiel to Eliza Jane Massey 5-6-1848 (5-18-1848)
Boyett, Thomas to Elizabeth Harris 12-15-1839 (12-19-1839)
Boykin, Carren E. to Mary E. Matthews 4-17-1854 (4-18-1854)
Boykin, James M. to Eliza E. Cox 12-6-1861 (12-8-1861)
Boykin, John E. to Rosalie A. Wilson 11-6-1855 (11-7-1855)
Boykin, Samuel B. to Mattie U. Ferrel 12-12-1870 (12-14-1870)
Boykin, William O. to Martha J. Lane 11-17-1852
Bradbury, John M. to Martha F. Moore 3-16-1857 (3-18-1857)
Bradford, James C. to Ann Reeves 7-24-1855
Bradford, James C. to Lucy Usery 10-5-1844
Bradford, William to Martila Sturdevant 2-18-1868 (2-20-1868)
Bradford, Young to Catherine E. Wilkins 4-3-1860 (4-5-1860)
Bradford, Young to Elizabeth Cox 11-24-1846 (11-25-1846)
Bradley, William to Kate Marks 3-8-1870 (3-9-1870)
Bradley, Williams H. to Mary E. Henderson 1-15-1850 (1-17-1850)
Branch, Benj. F. to Nancy Ann McKnight 10-13-1858 (10-14-1858)
Branch, Bogan to Elizabeth Branch 9-10-1842 (9-20-1842)
Branch, Jesse B. to Elizabeth Vinson 10-6-1842
Brasfield, George R. to Mary J. Roger 10-6-1848 (10-17-1848)
Brasfield, John J. to Margaret Young 8-17-1850 (8-22-1850)
Brassfield, Albert to Francis Lucinda Oliver 3-2-1857 (3-5-1857)
Brassfield, Joshua E. to Amanda M. Oliver 1-2-1854
Bratton, William H. to Martha J. Ross 2-8-1853 (2-10-1853)
Bratton, William J. to Martha J. Phifer 6-27-1852
Bray, Henry L. to Mary Elizabeth Day 3-15-1859 (not executed)
Bray, James H. to Fanny A. Spence 8-14-1869
Bray, Wm. H. to Margaret A. Hunter 5-15-1866
Brent, William L. to Nancy E. Steward 12-9-1849
Bridges, Rowan to Mary E. Ford 11-20-1866
Brigance, William D. to Mary T. Spratt 3-14-1842
Brimingham, John to Jane Massey 9-8-1852
Brimingham, Liberty W. to Mary S. Boaz 10-18-1859 (10-20-1859)
Brinson, John to Julia Ann Nevils 2-10-1850
Brinson, Robert W. to Caroline C. Neville 3-22-1845
Brinson, Robert to Sarah Neville 10-20-1853
Britt, Nathaniel to Amanda Jane Williams 8-26-1857 (8-27-1857)
Britten, Adolpha to Sarah Sweeny 8-26-1841
Britton, Adolphus to Anne Sweeny 11-30-1852 (12-2-1852)
Britton, Adolphus to Mary Barrier 9-27-1848 (11-27-1848)
Britton, Bartholomew C. to Eliza Jane (Mrs.) Fawcett 7-27-1870 (7-28-1870)
Britton, Bartholomew C. to Margaret E. Gilliland 4-11-1861
Britton, Thomas to Frances Briton 4-1-1850
Brock, Franklin to Sophronia Anderson 7-12-1853 (7-14-1853)
Brock, Josephine to Logan Hopkins 11-16-1857
Brogden, George to Margaret Belton 12-26-1854 (12-27-1854)
Brogdon, George M. to Louisa F. Manus 6-17-1868 (12-3-1868)
Brogdon, James L. to Minerva Spencer 3-20-1839
Brooks, Benjamin S. to Adaline Perry 5-23-1850
Brooks, George K. to Lizzie H. Brooks 11-13-1866
Brooks, John P. to Lucretia W. Watson 9-20-1845 (9-25-1845)
Brooks, John to Sarah L. Action 12-7-1848
Brooks, Joseph A. to Sarah A. (Mrs.) Stanley 8-1-1860 (8-2-1860)
Brooks, Robert M. to Margaret E. Langston 9-6-1866
Brooks, Stephen to Matilda Lackey 2-8-1840 (2-16-1840)
Brooks, William to Fannie Brooks 11-13-1866
Brookshire, William to Nancy Mary 12-29-1841 (12-30-1841)
Browder, John W. to Martha J. Simmons 9-3-1853 (9-5-1853)
Browder, Pitt C. to Nancy Susan Davis 12-9-1867 (12-10-1868?)
Browder, Washington R. to Sarah T. Davis 10-17-1857 (10-18-1857)
Browder, William T. to Martha A. Franklin 10-29-1860 (10-30-1860)

Brower, Isham H. to Elvira Catherine Johnson 12-28-1855 (12-29-1855)
Brown, Andrew T. to Adeline E. Lock 12-2-1850 (12-5-1850)
Brown, Andrew T. to Caroline M. Nobles 11-2-1846
Brown, Benjamin F. to Emily C. Ray 11-14-1846 (11-15-1846)
Brown, Charles H. to Sarah C. Kyle 8-9-1854
Brown, Eli to Lucim Askew 3-13-1866
Brown, George W. to Mary A. Anderson 4-23-1860 (4-25-1860)
Brown, Henry C. to Maie Glenn 5-19-1871 (5-22-1871)
Brown, Henry H. to Sarah E. Wrenn 5-23-1842 (5-26-1842)
Brown, James M. to Mary W. Boon 5-3-1856 (5-4-1856)
Brown, John I. to Mary F. Whitenton 11-16-1869
Brown, John T. to Ann E. Butler 11-23-1859 (11-24-1859)
Brown, John W. to Sarah A. Johnson 7-9-1846
Brown, Josiah W. to Sallie Knott 8-20-1867 (8-22-1867)
Brown, Lacy L. to Elizabeth J. Davie 12-4-1857 (12-6-1857)
Brown, Lacy L. to Nannie E. Wells 11-28-1866
Brown, Milton A. to Mary Hathaway 10-4-1866 (10-9-1866)
Brown, Robert F. to Sarah A. Locke 7-12-1855
Brown, Samuel B. to Nancy Micheal 7-31-1847 (8-4-1847)
Brown, William to Judie B. Cook 7-18-1855 (7-19-1855)
Browning, Francis O. to Mollie Beal 12-9-1867
Bruce, Allen A. to Martha Hays 11-4-1850
Bruce, William A. to Mary Vandouser 11-25-1862
Bruton, Lenoir to Harriett E. Jones 11-16-1843
Bruton, William H. to Mollie F. Gill 12-18-1866 (12-20-1866)
Bryan, Enoch to Margaret J. Boone 7-29-1840
Bryan, Finis E. to Elizabeth A. Jett 12-7-1868
Bryan, Hinton to Sarah Freeling 4-4-1842 (4-7-1842)
Bryan, Ransom A. to May Ann Cook 12-17-1838 (12-18-1838)
Bryan, Robert I. to Ann E. Winston 12-17-1867 (12-19-1867)
Bryan, Stephen R. to Barbara A. Harston 12-8-1856 (12-10-1856)
Bryan, William H. to Penelope Byrn 1-21-1843 (1-24-1843)
Bryant, Allen to Peninah Williams 4-15-1850 (4-18-1850)
Bryant, B. O. to Nancy L. Muse 8-27-1870 (9-4-1870)
Bryant, Caleb D. to Margaret C. Stone 4-10-1854 (4-18-1854)
Bryant, James H. to Mary Ann Wilkins 4-9-1852 (4-16-1852)
Bryant, Matthew S. to Armanda Jane Woods 10-4-1847 (9-6-1848)
Bryant, William H. to Alsa J. Parrish 12-30-1846
Bryant, William R. to Frances C. Snodgrass 8-3-1861 (8-5-1861)
Bryant, William to Eveline Hedleburg 11-4-1840
Buchanan, John T. to Eliza Jane York 8-22-1866 (8-26-1866)
Buckingham, George J. to Elizabeth S. Arnis 12-18-1866 (12-19-1866)
Buckner, Edward to Mary L. Coggins 8-14-1860 (8-15-1860)
Buffalow, George D. to Udora J. Clements 2-20-1871 (2-21-1871)
Bullock, Meciagah to Susan A. M. Brown 9-29-1841
Bumpass, Alex. A. to Elizabeth T. Frazier 9-4-1848
Bumpass, James M. to Lucinda Hopper 8-9-1853 (8-10-1853)
Bumpus, Alpha R. to Margarett M. Henry 1-3-1843
Bumpus, James M. to Marcha A. Frazier 3-15-1842 (3-17-1842)
Bunten, Daniel W. to Nancy P. Britton 5-12-1860 (5-?-1860)
Buntin, Asa to Emma Montgomery 4-28-1866
Buntin, Council to Susan T. Davis 1-28-1867
Buntin, James H. to Susan A. B. Wilie 2-8-1870
Buntin, Joel to Nannie M. Hart 1-18-1871 (1-19-1871)
Buntin, Reubin to Mary E. Davis 12-16-1850 (1-1-1851)
Burge, Andrew to Sarah Gordon 4-27-1838
Burkes, Barney to George Ann Norton 2-18-1844 (12-24-1844)
Burkett, John M. to Eugenia Roberson 10-13-1869 (10-14-1869)
Burkett, Wm. M. to Lucy A. Saners 1-25-1870 (1-26-1870)
Burkhead, A. Hamilton to Mary F. Walsh 1-28-1869
Burn, Bennett to Charlotte Taylor 11-15-1844 (11-19-1844)
Burn, Daniel R. to Martha J. Lambert 12-31-1849 (12-16?-1849)
Burns, Robert H. to Mary Jane Dungan 12-11-1862
Burns, Robert W. to Ruth Gibson 7-17-1839 (7-19-1839)
Burns, Thomas V. to Matilda A. Darby 4-28-1868
Burrow, Albert L. to Jane V. Bugg 11-28-1842 (11-22?-1842)
Burrow, Handsel W. to Fannie E. Gill 10-12-1857 (10-13-1857)
Burrow, Isham to Elvira Chandler 2-14-1838
Burrow, James R. to Amanda T. Wilson 2-?-1845
Burrow, John S. to Betsy Ann Ledbetter 12-21-1842
Burrow, Washington M. to Mary C. Tigert 8-18-1844
Burrow, William to Emeline Smith 12-12-1848 (12-13-1848)
Burrus, John to Elizabeth M. Goodrich 1-9-1849
Bursh, James to Theresa Thom 4-13-1840 (4-1-1840)

Burton, Daniel W. to Sarah A. Ferris 12-9-1854 (12-10-1854)
Burton, Frank A. W. to Elizabeth C. Willis 10-31-1844
Burton, Iverson to Martha C. Dick 10-16-1850 (10-17-1850)
Burton, James L. to M. E. A. Taylor 8-1-1871 (8-2-1871)
Burton, James to Caroline Love 10-1-1855
Burton, Jefferson to Elizabeth C. Crop 11-17-1840
Burton, Samuel to Emeline Volentine 6-5-1855
Burton, William to Charity Valentine 3-23-1854
Busick, Owen J. to Martha Kirby 9-25-1847
Busick, Thos. C. to Mary A. Boce 10-30-1844
Butes, Newton to Julian Irvin 7-5-1841
Butler, Daniel to Hannah Bains 10-29-1860
Butler, Elias T. to Mary Jane McVey 7-10-1848 (7-13-1848)
Butler, Henry to Martha E. Revely 2-12-1845
Butler, Jackson G. to Elizabeth M. Butler 12-4-1852 (12-8-1852)
Butler, Jasper N. to Sarah Alexander 2-17-1857 (2-26-1857)
Butler, John to May Parmer 11-5-1838
Butler, Lawrence to Susan Seats 11-15-1860 (11-18-1860)
Butler, Oliver to Mary Ann Hulsey 8-5-1848
Butler, Thomas J. to Mary C. Swink 1-19-1869 (1-21-1869)
Butler, Thos. T. to Eugenia Gates 6-1-1870 (6-11-1870)
Butt, William N. to Elizabeth H. Harris 6-20-1856
Butts, Halsted to Elizabeth Worrell 11-18-1850 (11-20-1850)
Butts, James R. to Martha Mahalda Yarbrough 8-23-1870 (8-25-1870)
Butts, Richard F. to Cornelia A. Snowden 1-1-1855
Butts, William N. to Helen Harris 7-15-1852
Byner, Andrew J. to Sarah Brook 9-1-1841
Byrd, Wm. Thomas to Eliza Catharine Wallace 8-28-1867 (8-29-1867)
Byrum, Jestice to Mary T. Fitzhugh 12-15-1852
Byrum, John T. to Lydia Glenn 11-1-1866
Byrum, Wade to Martha M. Dick 5-9-1861
Caffrey, Thomas to Belinda Chaney 12-10-1850
Cain, George W. to Amanda J. Bell 9-9-1871 (9-10-1871)
Cain, Robert F. to Margaret R. Haltom 5-18-1858 (5-19-1858)
Caldwell, Alex C. to Lizzie L. Taylor 8-20-1868
Caldwell, Alexr. C. to Mary W. Alexander 11-7-1860
Caldwell, Samuel P. to Sarah Jane Taylor 5-29-1855 (5-30-1855)
Calloway, Benj. R. to E. J. (Mrs.) McDaniel 1-25-1869 (1-27-1869)
Calloway, Chas. J. to Sarah J. Bond 12-13-1869 (12-14-1869)
Calloway, William J. to Emma C. Kirk 10-8-1867
Calloway, William S. to Elizabeth N. Brown 1-22-1840
Campbell, Eugene to Emily Ann Lambert 10-27-1866 (10-30-1866)
Campbell, Francis W. to Mariah A. Womack 12-19-1859 (12-20-1859)
Campbell, Geo. E. to Callie Williamson 10-18-1871
Campbell, Narcus R. to Caroline Massey 7-28-1852
Campbell, Robert A. to Mary Ann Davis 8-11-1847 (8-12-1847)
Campbell, Thomas to Lucinda Hardy 12-13-1852
Canaven, James to Telitha Piercy 12-17-1856 (12-18-1856)
Cannady, Allen to Mary Jane Cook 11-16-1870 (11-17-1870)
Capell, Hans to Susan Taylor 1-18-1843
Capher, James to Emeline Boals 8-11-1847 (8-12-1847)
Caradine, Andrew to America ____ 12-16-1846
Caradine, James to Frances Dent 12-27-1843 (12-28-1843)
Cardwell, William G. to Joannah Dew 5-4-1860
Carey, Everett to Nancy Williams 11-11-1841 (11-12-1841)
Carlington, Jas. to Mary Jane Ross 12-23-1846
Carly, Philip D. to Nancy Dickson 10-27-1840 (10-29-1840)
Carnatzan, Charles E. to Mary E. D. Perry 9-9-1857 (9-10-1857)
Carnatzer, James to Ellen Ferguson 12-26-1860
Carnetzer, William D. to Malvina Brimingham 12-29-1859
Carpenter, John C. to Maria L. Taylor 12-23-1857 (12-24-1857)
Carpenter, Nathaniel C. to Mary D. Smith 10-29-1849 (11-1-1849)
Carpenter, O. K. to Sarah A. Hopper 12-10-1855 (12-11-1855)
Carr, Allen to Lucety Bools 1-4-1859 (1-5-1859)
Carr, Thomas to Mary M. Tatum 12-3-1853 (12-4?-1853)
Carrington, Charles W. to Eliza Hardin 3-12-1868
Carrington, Neal to Elizabeth E. Johnson 4-24-1852
Carrington, William to Julia P. Harton 6-4-1842
Carroll, Chas. D. to Maudy Perry 6-2-1869
Carroll, John to Louisa N. W. Manley 12-30-1847
Carroll, Thomas B. to Martha D. Linton 11-1-1866 (11-8-1866)
Carruthers, James N. to Elizabeth J. A. Benton 1-1-1845
Carruthers, James W. to Mary Ann Morrow 5-28-1846
Carson, William to Mary Ann Gholson 12-10-1839 (12-12-1839)
Carter, Augustine to Mary Halliburton 9-28-1848 (10-10-1848)

Carter, Chas. W. to Martha J. Young 1-27-1862 (1-28-1862)
Carter, De L. to Martha Norton 2-24-1859 (2-25-1859)
Carter, Drury (Fayette Co.) to Bella Shepard 8-19-1848 (8-21-1848)
Carter, Elijah H. to Martha Ann Bailey 6-15-1867 (6-16-1867)
Carter, James to Malvina Armstrong 12-22-1846 (12-24-1846)
Carter, John to Elizabeth McKnight 1-3-1848 (1-6-1848)
Carter, Perry G. to Emma W. Shaw 11-9-1843 (11-14-1843)
Carter, Thomas L. to Bettie Lackie 12-24-1867 (12-25-1867)
Carter, Thomas L. to Mary Ann Carter 6-2-1869
Carter, William Y. to Mary Ann Lackey 3-12-1859
Carthel, John T. to Minnie Neely 5-13-1857
Cartwright, W. C. to Sarah Jane Brandon 4-1-1850
Caruthers, James W. to Margaret A. Sharp 12-15-1856 (12-16-1856)
Caruthers, William to Mary Jane Stoddert 6-6-1859 (6-7-1859)
Case, Ezekiel to Margaret Nanny 7-14-1856 (7-15-1856)
Casey, James C. to Tennessee Casey 8-15-1870 (8-17-1870)
Casey, Thomas B. to Elizabeth R. Benson 10-11-1858 (10-13-1858)
Casey, William L. to Mary E. Neal 1-11-1867 (1-15-1867)
Cash, John J. to Julia A. Lyon 12-28-1859
Cash, Lorenza D. to Mary Wyatt 4-4-1843 (4-6-1843)
Cash, Watt to Sarah Ann Stone 6-29-1850 (7-1-1850)
Caskins, Henry to Elizabeth E. Jones 7-29-1844
Cason, William C. to Mary Jane Hamilton 6-26-1860 (6-27-1860)
Cass, Elijah to Caroline C. Alexander 12-29-1846
Cassels, Henry C. to Martha Jane Boyd 1-7-1867
Cassels, William H. to Polly A. N. E. Draper 8-24-1853 (8-25-1853)
Castles, Green to Frances J. Holyfield 9-3-1846 (8?-3-1846)
Cate, Atlas J. to Eliza F. Davidson 8-7-1866 (8-9-1866)
Cate, Charles W. to Sarah Tyson 12-16-1845 (12-10?-1845)
Cathey, Alexander H. to Sarah J. Watson 2-9-1853
Cathey, Robert A. to Rebecca A. Exum 11-12-1856
Causler, Jas. C. W. to Sarah Ashworth 1-4-1869 (1-7-1869)
Cazort, Anthony Haywood to Rebecca Kerby 3-8-1848 (3-9-1848)
Chamberlain, Charles D. to Sarah C. Cupp 10-9-1855
Chamberlin, Alonzo M. to Margarett A. Henderson 4-14-1842
Chamberlin, Charles W. to Susan Chamberlin 1-13-1841 (1-14-1841)
Chamberlin, Charles to Huldy Brinkley 12-27-1841
Chamberlin, Charles to Thera Harris 1-7-1847 (1-10-1847)
Chamberlin, Has. to Mary Woodard 1-3-1842
Chandler, Eli C. to Hannah Irvine 6-5-1850
Chandler, Gabriel to Elizabeth B. Gizzard 1-22-1855 (1-25-1855)
Chandler, James C. to Mary Maginis 11-22-1842 (11-23-1842)
Chandler, Jno. W. to Emily E. Guinn 3-14-1871
Chandler, Martin L. to Martha A. Holland 2-9-1869 (2-11-1869)
Chandler, Miles P. to Mary J. Denny 10-18-1842
Chandler, Ryland to Mary I. Wiggs 5-17-1838
Chandler, William R. to Mary Thomas 7-21-1857 (7-2?-1857)
Chapman, C. A. (Dr.) to Bettie D. Wood 12-17-1866 (12-18-1866)
Chapman, Williams to Caroline Todd 3-26-1850
Chappel, George W. to Mary A. (Mrs.) Wiseman 2-22-1870
Chappell, Claudius E. to Mollie Hamerly 5-22-1867
Chappell, Joel R. to A. W. Conger 9-23-1839 (9-24-1839)
Chappell, John L. to Elmina Parrott 12-18-1838
Chappell, Wm. Thomas to Paralee Cole 4-11-1870 (4-5?-1870)
Chatten, Thomas to Mary Grant 8-7-1853 (9-8-1853)
Cherry, John T. to Martha Sarah Johnson 1-28-1858
Cherry, Lemuel L. to Susan R. Thompson 1-8-1859 (1-13-1859)
Chester, John to Apphia A. Taylor 10-24-1848
Chester, Robert H. to Mary J. Long 11-1-1853
Childress, Preston L. to Jane R. Panst 3-6-1841 (3-7-1841)
Childress, William C. to Nancy Gateley 4-7-1856 (4-10-1856)
Chipman, Frederick to Mary Ann Prendergrast 4-19-1852 (4-20-1853)
Chipman, George to Mary Ann Jones 12-18-1852
Chisum, James L. to Caroline Henry 12-2-1867
Chisum, William W. to Mariah Olivia Caruthers 3-11-1867
Chisum, William to Caroline Vinson 1-3-1848
Chrisp, John W. to Elizabeth P. Mitchell 12-23-1847 (12-25-1847)
Christian, Gilbert T. to Sallie Snodgrass 4-9-1866
Christian, Harry B. to Mary America Moore 7-22-1839 (7-23-1839)
Christian, John to E. P. Thomas 3-5-1838
Christian, Thomas to Sarah B. Logan 8-25-1841 (8-26-1841)
Christian, William A. to Mary R. Sherman 1-15-1859 (1-20-1859)
Claiborne, Wallace C. to Ellen N. Haskell 11-12-1853
Clanton, John J. to Susan T. Hicks 5-11-1870 (5-12-1870)
Clanton, Josiah F. to Martha Deloach 9-6-1847 (9-9-1847)

Claridge, Alexander H. to Mary Jane Stephens 8-21-1854
Claridge, Henry B. to Rebecca J. Dyer 9-8-1853
Clark, Andrew H. to Mary Ann Thompson 11-4-1871 (11-6-1871)
Clark, Edwin to Martha Childress 8-17-1852
Clark, Henry F. to Rhoda M. Rodgers 4-30-1870 (5-1-1870)
Clark, James W. to Mary E. Thomas 1-2-1866 (1-3-1867?)
Clark, Jefferson to Elizabeth G. Samuel 11-24-1841
Clark, John E. to Mary Jane Doake 1-25-1849 (1-30-1849)
Clark, John H. to Malinda C. Prewitt 4-12-1860
Clark, John R. to Elizabeth May 2-13-1844 (2-15-1844)
Clark, Mary I. to Willis Overton 11-28-1842
Clark, Robert to Delia Bradberry 10-8-1870
Clark, Thomas to Frances Patterson 8-19-1845
Clark, Thomas to Lamira Ann Littlepage 12-8-1866 (12-16-1866)
Clark, William D. to Kate L. Scurlock 5-24-1869
Clarke, H. M. to Mary Irene Read 12-23-1839 (12-25-1839)
Clay, John H. to Mary E. Garrett 1-30-1868
Clayton, James H. to M. Alice Harris 3-6-1866 (3-7-1866)
Cleaves, William H. to Margarett Verser 3-8-1843
Cleavis, William to Martha Ann Mason 6-1-1842 (6-9-1842)
Clement (Weakley Co), Thos. P. to Jane T. (Mrs.) Smith 3-16-1870
Clement, Benjamin W. to Catherine E. Matthews 12-21-1858 (12-22-1858)
Clement, Calvin C. to Mary E. Lewis 7-10-1866
Clement, Edward R. to Mary A. T. McCullough 8-10-1859
Clements (Gibson Co), Calvin C. to Mary A. Fly 11-10-1849 (11-13-1849)
Clements, F. S. to America Catherine Bevill 8-26-1868 (8-27-1868)
Clifton, Lemuel K. to Sarah J. Lyon 11-6-1845
Climer, John W. to Gracy Simpson 11-27-1843
Climer, Milton to Barbara A. Oliver 12-22-1854 (12-25-1854)
Clinard, Alexander to Arcenia Reddick 4-5-1860 (4-6-1860)
Cline, Jacob Daniel to Sarah Cline 3-30-1841
Cline, Marcus H. to Emoline Mitchell 9-14-1839 (9-15-1839)
Cloud, Samuel to Lucy Jane Underwood 5-13-1858
Coates, James S. to Elizabeth Mooring 11-9-1852 (11-11-1852)
Coates, John to Eliza Jane Neely 2-26-1857
Coats, John to Mary E. Jayne 6-21-1849
Coats, John to Susan E. (Mrs.) Nipper 1-12-1867 (1-13-1867)
Coats, William C. to Ella V. Moore 1-7-1867 (1-8-1866?)
Cobb, James M. to Mary Thom 10-23-1842 (10-25-1842)
Cobb, John B. to Mary Ann Guthrie 5-27-1862
Cobel, Thomas J. to Susan (Mrs.) Williams 9-7-1867 (9-10-1867)
Cobourn, James to Irene Turley 2-24-1857 (2-25-1857)
Cock, Caswell C. to Mary M. Goodrick 11-4-1857 (11-5-1857)
Cock, Edward to Harriett May 12-9-1858
Cock, John L. to Mary Jane Shumate 2-26-1857
Cock, M. T. to Mary Ann Lassiter 9-21-1852 (9-22-1852)
Cock, Thomas A. to Julia A. E. King 5-14-1849 (5-15-1849)
Cocke, George W. to Laura A. Boon 1-15-1856
Cockrill, William G. to Amanda P. McMillen 7-1-1857
Cofer, John to Mary Ann Acre 6-29-1839 (7-2-1839)
Cole, Alexander T. to Evelina Cook 10-26-1850 (10-28-1850)
Cole, George W. to Susan Thompson 12-3-1849
Cole, James R. to Phinela Whitlow 2-17-1842
Cole, Phillip to Mollie V. Turner 2-1-1868
Cole, Thomas B. to Nannie D. McLemore 5-13-1856 (5-14-1856)
Cole, Wm. R. (Dr.) to Sallie E. Dunnaway 11-12-1870 (11-17-1870)
Coleburn, William N. to Francis A. Perry 8-14-1854 (8-15-1854)
Coleman, John T. to Celicia Perry 7-30-1855 (7-31-1855)
Collingsworth, James M. to Martha H. Sawrie 11-20-1855 (11-22-1855)
Collins, Franklin E. to Susan E. (Mrs.) Coats 6-26-1869 (6-27-1869)
Collins, George W. to Mattie E. Kirby 12-14-1870 (12-15-1870)
Collins, James A. to Sallie Bivens 12-6-1866
Collins, John J. to Julia A. Stewart 3-3-1866 (3-8-1866)
Collins, Oscar F. to M. E. Thompson 3-20-1867 (3-28-1867)
Collins, Simon A. to Sallie Yarbrough 9-12-1870
Combs, Alfred to May Ann Rasons 9-24-1838 (9-25-1838)
Combs, Peter to Mattie Ingram 10-10-1871 (10-14-1871)
Compton, J. B. to Ann E. Brantley 1-31-1854 (2-2-1854)
Compton, Robert M. to Rebecca Moore 11-26-1840
Compton, William A. to Miria L. Wilson 1-5-1853
Conger, John S. to Harriet Caroline Hampton 5-20-1861

Conger, Philander D. W. to Eliza Jane Chambers 12-14-1842 (12-15-1842)
Connell, James R. to Martha Jane Blan 1-15-1843
Conner, Andrew to Nancy Chapman 6-21-1845 (6-24-1845)
Conner, Henry to Eveline Bryant 12-16-1845 (12-18-1845)
Conner, J. T. to Sarah Lucinda Lee 2-8-1871
Connor, John Thomas to Sarah Frances Valentine 12-22-1856 (12-23-1856)
Connor, John to Lucy A. Verser 12-1-1856 (12-17-1856)
Connor, Joseph F. to Mary J. Volentine 12-12-1868
Cook, Elias G. B. to Celia Johnson 10-26-1840
Cook, Elias to Sibella A. Darby 5-22-1843 (5-24-1843)
Cook, James M. to Mary Elvira Darnell 10-12-1841 (10-13-1841)
Cook, Milos C. to Martha Ann Bumpass 1-16-1842
Cook, Milton to Sophie Ellington 7-28-1838 (7-29-1838)
Cook, Shim to Emelin Parrish 2-19-1867 (2-21-1867)
Cooper, Daniel B. to Rebecca E. Haltom 11-20-1866 (11-21-1866)
Cooper, George W. to Mary A. Horton 11-12-1866 (11-13-1866)
Cooper, J. N. to Margaret E. Fanner 11-16-1859 (11-17-1859)
Cooper, James L. to Delphina E. Wilson 12-7-1861
Cooper, Joseph H. to Kaziah T. Owen 3-15-1867 (3-16-1867)
Cooper, Joseph J. to Elizabet L. Gladney 11-20-1845
Cooper, Thaddeus D. to Sarah Jane Strayhorn 10-12-1859
Cooper, William H. to Lucrita A. Anderson 12-14-1838
Cooper, Wilson to Mary C. Weaver 9-12-1853 (9-15-1853)
Copeland, William L. to Mary E. J. Dick 3-19-1853
Coppedge, John to Mary A. Alexander 8-29-1855 (9-4-1855)
Corbitt, George C. to Ella V. Hafflabower 11-17-1869 (11-18-1869)
Corum, Tilman D. to Matilda A. Maxwell 11-19-1847 (11-21-1847)
Cotter, jr., H. W. to Mary Johnson 6-5-1867 (6-6-1867)
Cotton, H. P. (Dr.) to Ella V. Smith 10-3-1870 (10-5-1870)
Covington, Edward to Vicey Patterson 5-18-1859
Covington, Joseph A. to Edney J. Adcock 8-11-1866 (8-12-1866)
Cox, Dempsey to Elvira Bradford 11-14-1866 (11-15-1866)
Cox, Lewis C. to Martha Parthenia Sewell 11-16-1867 (11-27-1867)
Cox, Lewis I. to Mary E. Young 11-10-1869 (11-11-1869)
Cox, P. G. to Mary Ann Brinkley 11-13-1839
Cox, Robert H. to Tabitha L. Watkins 10-19-1866 (10-21-1866)
Cox, William H. to Eudora Whitesides 10-23-1866
Cox, William to Elizabeth J. Glidewell 8-3-1846
Cozart, Gilbert to Mary Kirby 1-1-1845 (1-7-1845)
Cozart, Hubbard to Lucy Robbins 7-23-1866 (7-24-1866)
Cozart, James B. to Irene Brown 9-5-1871
Cozart, Joshua M. to Julia Frances Marlow 2-13-1858 (2-17-1858)
Cozort, Madison to Emelina Marlow 12-29-1847 (12-30-1847)
Craig, Francis Marion to Parnina H. Norvell 12-6-1859
Craig, Saml. to Ophelia Stone 4-3-1871
Craig, Samuel to Martha Smith 9-20-1862 (9-21-1862)
Crawford, Elisha J. to Sarah Elizabeth White 8-7-1866
Crawford, John F. to Clotilda Jones 6-21-1838
Crawford, John W. W. to Virginia F. Bateman 8-29-1857 (8-1?-1857)
Creps (Cress?), James M. to Mary E. Springfield 11-14-1871
Crews, John L. to Catherine Lathrick 2-4-1856
Crews, Thomas A. to Julia Watson 3-14-1855 (3-15-1855)
Crittendon, Harvey S. to Mary A. Cobb 1-26-1853
Cromm, Joseph to Julia A. E. Stewart 10-13-1856 (10-15-1856)
Crook, Jonathan W. to Sally B. Haughton 10-2-1855 (10-3-1855)
Croom, Benjamin F. to Susan Davis 12-12-1862 (12-13-1862)
Croom, Isaac N. to Mary F. Mays 5-19-1856
Croom, Isaac to Elizabeth Stier 7-22-1840 (8-13-1840)
Croom, James to Mary Southall 10-19-1850
Croom, John to Narcissa Downing 8-27-1842 (8-28-1842)
Croom, Richard R. to Mary F. Meadows 4-21-1857 (4-29-1857)
Croom, William H. to Virginia A. Anderson 2-26-1856 (2-27-1856)
Croom, William to Caroline Carrington 6-24-1840 (7-8-1840)
Crosby, William to Mary Elizabeth Parkinson 4-15-1839
Cross, John H. to Mary C. Hutchings 11-30-1848
Crow, Hiram (of Illinois) to Harriet Davis 9-19-1862
Crowel, Peter F. to Senna A. (Mrs.) Deaton 7-1-1867
Crowell, Alfred to Harriett Slocum 6-14-1849
Crowell, Norman to Margaret Adams 9-14-1853 (9-15-1853)
Crowell, Samuel to Elizabeth Pearce 5-13-1852 (5-18-1852)
Cunningham, Jas. B. to Mary W. Wilie 9-7-1869 (9-9-1869)
Cunningham, Wm. R. to Elizabeth F. (Mrs.) Deberry 6-30-1859
Cup, Elijah to Caroline C. Alexander 12-29-1846

Cupples, Thomas J. to Nancy C. Sanders 6-19-1868 (7-5-1868)
Cupples, Thomas to Elizabeth Sipes 2-?-1848 (3-1-1848)
Curlin, William H. to Curlin Miles 7-27-1842
Currie, Jesse to Jane R. Gladney 10-29-1860
Currie, Washington to Mary S. Taylor 9-6-1853 (9-13-1853)
Curtiss, Horace H. to Mary L. Sypert 8-31-1853
Dado, Giovanni to Guiseppa A. Fransioli 7-6-1870
Daily, Thomas to Hannah Hays 10-24-1861
Dalton, Joseph M. to Mary Jane Whittington 10-13-1842
Daniel, Granberry to Nancy Ann Pool 8-16-1842
Daniel, James W. to Helen Ross 8-5-1850 (8-8-1850)
Daniel, Ralph W. to America T. Anderson 11-25-1854 (12-10-1854)
Darnall, Jesse A. to Mattie E. Askew 12-15-1868
Darr, Henry to Miriam Nicks 5-28-1840 (5-31-1840)
Darr, John to Angie C. Ervin 7-25-1839
Dashiell, Richard R. to Eliza Jane Taylor 1-10-1850 (1-15-1850)
Dashill, W. Bond to Mary Anna Jones 9-28-1871
Daughby, Reuben to Elizabeth Williams 9-9-1839
Davenport, James H. to Susan Jane Baker 9-11-1860 (9-13-1860)
Davenport, _____ to Margarett Mitchell 12-15-1838 (12-17-1838)
Davidson, Andrew M. to Mahulda Fisher 11-13-1844
Davidson, J. F. to Elizabeth J. Cash 1-3-1871 (1-5-1871)
Davie, Edward to Sarah A. Vincent 1-14-1869 (1-21-1869)
Davie, James A. L. to Addie H. Burrow 12-15-1860 (12-16-1860)
Davie, James B. to Cornelia J. Davie 7-21-1853
Davie, Nelson to Rebecca (Mrs.) Medlin 1-8-1862 (1-9-1862)
Davie, William A. W. to Mildred A. Woolfolk 4-5-1869 (4-7-1869)
Davie, William A. to Jane B. Davis 11-8-1841
Davis, Albert A. to Anne? Ragan Olds 2-26-1842
Davis, Berry A. to Eliza J. Black 6-18-1853 (7-19-1853)
Davis, David P. to Lizzie Calloway 5-8-1867
Davis, Dorsey to Nancy Nowell 3-21-1843
Davis, Edward to Mary Ann Ellington 12-21-1838 (12-25-1838)
Davis, F. M. to Mary Glenn 12-1-1856 (12-2-1856)
Davis, Henry C. to Lucy C. Nuttall 6-30-1858 (7-1-1858)
Davis, Henry W. to Martha M. Holmes 12-25-1844
Davis, James E. to Nancy Elizabeth Russell 12-12-1859
Davis, James H. to Amanda Simmons 9-1-1870 (9-24-1870)
Davis, James H. to Perlina Chipman 4-9-1853
Davis, James L. to Lucy Davis 6-26-1848 (6-29-1848)
Davis, James M. to Margaret E. Fulbright 2-9-1858
Davis, John E. to Eliza Pettigrew 3-14-1868 (3-15-1868)
Davis, John J. to Elizabeth Barton 9-27-1847
Davis, John to Caroline (Mrs.) Jackson 4-29-1871 (4-20?-1871)
Davis, Martin to Elizabeth T. Drake 10-3-1853
Davis, Pleasant R. to Sarah J. Manley 9-18-1861 (9-19-1861)
Davis, R. H. to Amanda F. Croom 12-17-1863 (11?-17-1862?)
Davis, Richard M. to Sarah Vantrice 12-20-1842 (12-29-1842)
Davis, Samuel Clark to Mary Daniel Davis 10-7-1850
Davis, Sherwood R. to Mary Jane Smith 4-2-1870 (4-3-1870)
Davis, Snowden H. to Mary E. Joyce 10-21-1850
Davis, William H. to Delila Chipman 12-7-1840
Davis, William J. to Elizabeth Terrell 3-20-1841
Davis, William J. to Sarah Ann E. Terrell 9-1-1841 (9-2-1841)
Davis, William P. to Leander Jane Murrell 3-12-1853 (3-15-1853)
Daws, William to Mariah Todd 12-16-1840 (12-17-1840)
Dawson, Jackson to Nancy E. Quinley 10-30-1841 (11-3-1841)
Dawson, James to Lydia Lawrence 1-30-1856
Dawson, James to Martha Lawrence 4-12-1854
Dawson, L. G. to Mary E. Baker 5-24-1871 (5-25-1871)
Dawson, Richard to Martha Smith 9-15-1842 (9-16-1842)
Dawson, William to Elizabeth J. Quinley 2-12-1849
Day, George W. to Elizabeth C. Weatherly 10-28-1856 (10-30-1856)
Day, George W. to Mary E. Jones 10-12-1848 (10-15-1848)
Day, John H., jr. to Margaret A. Coleman 8-29-1850
Day, John P. to Leonora Johnson 1-17-1870 (1-19-1870)
Day, Lemuel to Mary Gowen 7-21-1849 (7-26-1849)
Day, Thomas D. to Lucinda R. Sturdevant 3-4-1868
Day, William Parker to Susanna Hopper 4-8-1845
Deadrick, William Pitt to Rachel J. Hays 5-9-1855
Dean, Hardy to Jane Young 2-11-1843 (2-14-1843)
Dean, Henry H. to Laura Hudson 1-23-1854 (1-26-1854)
Dean, John A. to Mary Parker 2-25-1848 (3-2-1848)
Dearmore, John C. to Berneta R. Golden 7-19-1848 (7-20-1848)
Dearmore, John C. to Susan P. Hart 12-14-1846 (12-15-1846)

Dearmore, William J. to Vicey Ann Gaskins 2-20-1850 (2-21-1850)
Dearmore, Wm. J. to Sarah Ann Johnson 10-4-1871 (10-5-1871)
Deaton, Sampson to L. A. Dickinson 2-22-1854 (2-23-1854)
Deberry, Drury to Rebecca Baker 11-20-1858 (11-23-1858)
Deberry, John H. to Edith E. Rogers 11-27-1867 (11-28-1867)
Deberry, John H. to Louisa R. Fulgham 11-25-1856
Deberry, Matthias to Ann Ingram 11-3-1847
Deberry, Milton L. to M. J. Boon 1-25-1867 (1-31-1867)
Deberry, William W. to Eliza I. Hudson 1-4-1839
Delaney, William to Maria Fitzmorris 2-18-1871
Delass, Hugh to Mollie H. Moore 7-6-1868 (7-7-1868)
Deloach, Arthur to Elizabeth Jane Davis 11-3-1846
Deloach, John to Katie E. Dickie 3-14-1871
Deloach, Silas to Jane M. Hicks 1-14-1857 (1-15-1857)
Deloach, William T. to Eliza Perry 9-9-1850
Delph, Philip to Matilda Barnwell 8-4-1856
Denton, James R. to Emily J. McCaig 12-6-1862
Derryberry, Andrew to Cynthia Gilliam 4-8-1853
Derryberry, William J. to Narcissa Weathers 7-19-1869
Devore, James T. to Eliza F. Mason 9-7-1866 (9-9-1866)
Dew, Warren W. to Elizabeth Baker 2-18-1867 (3-12-1867)
Dew, William W. to Mary Ann Anderson 1-5-1859
Dewberry, Andrew to Rhosha McFarlan 5-3-1859
Dickens, Edmund to Catherine Burton 12-25-1838
Dickerson, William to Rhoda Vantreese 11-19-1864 (11-20-1864)
Dickey, Daniel P. to Ruena Smith 8-29-1843
Dickie, Isaac E. to Saluda J. Haynes 9-25-1848
Dickie, John to Lucy Davis 11-1-1851 (11-2-1851)
Dickinson, Benjamin F. to Amanda E. Hudson 3-26-1857
Dickinson, Robert M. to Martha W. Hobbs 12-4-1844 (12-5-1844)
Dickinson, Rufus W. to Charlotte Edmonson 1-20-1845
Dickinson, William to Caroline Moore 3-11-1858 (3-12-1858)
Dickinson, William to Mary Ann Beaty 12-25-1852 (12-26-1852)
Dickinson, Willie B. to Wilnoth C. (Mrs.) Tarver 8-2-1871 (8-3-1871)
Dickson, B. to Charity Coker 4-10-1838
Dickson, Jacob to Louisa Whiley 3-13-1868 (3-15-1868)
Dickson, Joseph M. to Emelina C. Jones 1-5-1849 (1-8-1849)
Dickson, Noah to Nancy Wilson 12-16-1847
Diggs, Dudley to Tamey Richerson 1-13-1857
Dismukes, John W. to Frances E. Bray 11-24-1866 (11-27-1866)
Dismukes, Wm. A. to Maggie Davis 8-20-1870 (8-21-1870)
Dixon, Nicholson G. to Sarah C. Ross 8-5-1858
Dixon, Wesley to Nancy E. McGlothlin 10-12-1853
Doble, Michael to Elenora L. Winfield 1-29-1870
Dodd, Boland to Levina Redding 10-28-1841
Dodd, James A. to Margaret A. Davis 1-7-1853 (1-11-1853)
Dodd, John R. to Roena J. Currie 2-12-1867
Dodd, John to Frances Gholson 8-16-1853 (8-?-1853)
Dodd, John to Mollie Rutherford 11-9-1871
Dodds, James A. to E. S. Kendrick 12-15-1839 (12-18-1839)
Dodson, William to Bettie West 10-10-1871 (10-11-1871)
Dollar, John H. to Eliza Duffy 1-?-1847 (1-14-1847)
Dollar, Lewis to Lucy J. Duffy 4-18-1854 (4-20-1854)
Dollar, William W. to Auzal Inza Moore 12-15-1858 (12-16-1858)
Dolson, Nashville to Martha McElever 5-26-1843
Donelson, John to Delia C. Waters 1-13-1849 (2-13-1849)
Donlin, Phillip A. to Susan G. Freeling 8-3-1842 (8-4-1842)
Donnell, John J. to Mary H. Jones 9-18-1866 (9-19-1866)
Dorsey, John to P. A. Matcik 11-28-1870
Douglas, Archy Y. to Martha J. Morrow 3-31-1845 (4-1-1845)
Dowling, David to Martha Cooper 5-7-1853 (5-19-1853)
Doyle, Hickerson L. to Rachael Summers 8-13-1841 (8-18-1841)
Drake, Bennet to Labertha Madders 1-5-1858 (1-6-1858)
Drake, John to Sophronia Hardin 10-16-1848 (3-10-1850)
Drake, Thomas H. to Louise Miller 11-12-1867
Drake, William J. (Dr.) to Mary Jane Walker 5-3-1859
Drake, Wm. B. to Lydia R. Thomas 7-1-1871 (7-2-1871)
Driggers, Wm. J. to Eliza C. Ross 11-23-1854
Ducker, Churchwell B. to Mary Roberson 11-7-1860 (11-8-1860)
Dudley, Alexander to Evelina Tanner 2-28-1854 (3-1-1854)
Duffey, John S. to Margaret King 2-12-1852
Duffey, Joseph W. to Emma Vail 7-?-1871 (7-28-1871)
Duffey, Patrick M. to Patsey Duffey 10-27-1862 (10-28-1862)
Duffey, Samuel to Eady King 10-22-1862 (10-23-1862)
Duffey, Samuel to Mary C. Dollar 7-4-1854

Duffie, William A. to Keady King 12-17-1846 (12-20-1846)
Duffy, Patrick M. to Sirena Owen 9-19-1844
Duffy, Simeon to Arcena Owens 7-31-1845
Duffy, Simeon to Letitia Owens 12-12-1866
Duffy, Wm. F. to Mary E. Herndon 10-14-1871 (10-18-1871)
Dunaway, William H. to Frances E. Raines 9-1-1866 (9-6-1866)
Duncan, George W. to Mary E. Pearson 11-22-1852 (11-25-1852)
Duncan, Jesse to Sophronia Reid 2-2-1850 (2-13-1850)
Duncan, John to Lucenda Reeves 4-3-1839 (4-4-1839)
Duncan, Joseph to Mary Andonon 11-7-1839
Duncan, Lewis to Jane Brown 1-4-1853
Duncan, Peter S. to Susan E. Harrison 9-30-1847
Duncan, Wm. A. to Mary B. Adams 9-27-1867 (10-1-1867)
Dunlap, Henry to Elizabeth Taylor 12-17-1866 (12-20-1866)
Dunlap, James M. to Elizabeth Carter 12-11-1848 (12-14-1848)
Dunlap, William to Harriet Taylor 10-20-1856
Dunn, James to Della Pierce 7-26-1871 (7-28-1871)
Dunnaway, John A. to Rachael Bryant 7-30-1846
Dunnway, Robert P. to Mahilda G. York 12-28-1847 (12-30-1847)
Dupriest, Protestant P. to Narcissa Bridges 8-9-1850 (8-11-1850)
Durham, Wm. W. to Bettie Henderson 12-21-1869
Durrett, Wm. R. to Nancy A. McCord 8-16-1870
Dusmuke, James A. to Octavia A. Vick 11-16-1854
Dyer, Stephen to L. Melinda Watson 10-5-1848
Dysart, John Young to Mollie M. Robinson 11-15-1869 (11-16-1869)
Eagan, Andrew M. to Martha Ann Maroney 9-2-1856
Eason, James to Lucinda Pendergrast 6-11-1856
Eason, Thomas to Ann Eliza Falden 8-31-1853
Eddington, Edmund J. to Catherine Denmark 8-24-1852 (8-25-1852)
Eddins, Washington to Caroline Given 1-24-1857 (1-28-1857)
Edington, C. D. to Rebecca Medlin 12-8-1840
Edmonson, Edmond A. to Sarah A. Murrell 3-20-1866
Edwards, Anderson to Elizabeth Wilson 4-22-1841
Edwards, James J. to Barbara Nanny 9-27-1845
Edwards, James J. to Mary C. Anderson 10-17-1844
Edwards, Jesse to Catherine Glidwell 10-25-1856
Edwards, John to Sarah Tims 7-8-1839 (7-10-1839)
Edwards, Joseph to Martha E. Norvell 11-29-1843
Edwards, Julius to Mary A. E. Dungan 11-6-1852 (11-11-1852)
Edwards, L. M. to Martha A. Bretton 6-9-1870 (6-12-1870)
Edwards, Leander D. to Harriet Hill 12-8-1866 (12-9-1866)
Edwards, R. A. to Mary A. Hale 12-11-1855 (12-12-1855)
Edwards, Samuel H. to Alice W. Cook 12-3-1867
Edwards, Silas W. to Sarah E. Thomas 12-3-1857
Edwards, Vinson to Amanda A. Harris 12-4-1866 (12-5-1866)
Edwards, William B. to Alice G. Tucker 1-28-1867
Edwards, William H. to Catherine Barrier 7-3-1866
Edwards, William H. to Lucinda Wilson 11-28-1846
Edwards, William H. to Mary Ann Epperson 3-22-1854 (3-3?-1854)
Edwards, William T. to Malvina Birmingham 5-9-1844
Elam, John D. to Martha Ann Sykes 12-8-1845
Elam, John to Rebecca Kirby 11-24-1866 (11-29-1866)
Elder, Benjamin F. to Louisa Davie 12-6-1858
Elkins, Louis to Rachael Davis 7-1-1840 (7-2-1840)
Ellenton, William H. to Nancy B. Lane 9-22-1855 (10-4-1855)
Ellington, Chasteen to Mary M. Mathis 9-17-1845 (9-18-1845)
Ellington, Dempney to Sarah E. Davis 5-28-1861 (5-30-1861)
Ellington, John to Elizabeth Williams 5-17-1838 (5-18-1838)
Ellington, Newton to Mary Richards 10-9-1866 (10-11-1866)
Ellington, Winston to Emily Johnson 8-22-1868 (8-25-1868)
Ellington, Winston to Mary Jane Young 6-6-1859 (6-8-1859)
Ellington, Wm. R. to Rowena Williams 9-21-1869 (9-29-1869)
Elliot, Thomas W. to Elizabeth Andrews 4-5-1871
Elliott, Henry J. to Mary F. Webb 2-5-1868
Elrod, James to Caroline D. Long 3-15-1855
Elsten, Milton to Margaret Miller 2-15-1858
Emerson, Marian to Mary Stone 7-4-1867 (7-7-1867)
Emison, Benjamin to Mary H. Permator 11-20-1854 (11-22-1854)
Emison, William to Bedy Richard 12-27-1850 (1-2-1851)
Epperson, Benj. F. to Martha W. Dumanet 11-13-1861 (11-17-1861)
Epperson, Samuel to Elizabeth H. Hill 11-18-1844
Eppinger, Louis to Margaretha Wittman 4-25-1861
Epps, Spencer to Nancy Marsh 1-4-1848 (1-5-1848)
Estes, Albert M. to Arabella Cates 10-19-1869
Estes, Bedford M. to Sarah Jane Johnston 4-24-1854 (5-4-1854)

Estes, Nimrod to Charlotte Walker 6-1-1841 (1-3-1842)
Evans, J. H. D. to Annie C. A. (Mrs.) Peirce 9-24-1870 (9-25-1870)
Evans, Joel T. to Lou T. McDonal 12-9-1867 (12-10-1867)
Evans, John J. to Nancy F. Jackson 12-31-1867
Evans, John to Mariah G. Swink 7-16-1839
Evans, Robert to Mary Elizabeth Johnston 9-28-1867
Evans, Willis W. to Elizabeth Medlin 3-19-1845 (3-23-1845)
Ewell, Joseph D. to Mattie J. Flemming 1-8-1868
Ewell, Thomas W. to Lundy Andrews 10-12-1853 (10-18-1853)
Ewell, Wm. B. to Margaret M. Brown 4-2-1855
Ewing, William M. to Elizabeth Caroline Currie 4-29-1857
Ewing, Zebina C. to Maria Tittleton 3-18-1850 (3-?-1850)
Exum, Joseph W. to Julia A. Wilson 9-18-1867 (9-19-1867)
Exum, Washington T. to Margaret C. Watson 12-11-1854 (12-13-1854)
Ezell, James H. to Rebecca Elizabeth Key 12-28-1858
Fairless, Norfleet to Mary A. Rooks 11-26-1840
Fanville, Jno. F. to M. Callie Wilson 2-22-1869
Faris, Ezekiel to Martha Moore 10-18-1841
Farmer, Samuel to Susan Watt 9-14-1846
Fasmyre, Augustus C. to Margaret J. Shaw 12-19-1848
Faucett, James A. to Eliza J. Stewart 6-2-1858 (6-6-1858)
Faucett, William R. to Martha J. Burrus 5-7-1870 (5-8-1870)
Faulkland, Johnson to Mary Nany Mahon 2-14-1838
Faulkner, John to Amanda C. Marlow 9-25-1850 (9-26-1850)
Fennell, John to Minerva Townsend 5-21-1870 (5-22-1870)
Fenner, John M. to Eunice B. Hugh 7-25-1844
Fenner, John s. to I. Virginia Day 2-27-1867
Fenner, Richard H. to Fanny E. Rogers 8-29-1853 (8-30-1853)
Fenner, Richard J. to Marianna Johnson 3-23-1841 (3-24-1841)
Fenner, Thomas B. to Hannah Jane Pettus 7-22-1853 (7-26-1853)
Ferguson, Charles W. to Jane C. Dunn 12-2-1869
Ferguson, Robert to Argenta Rebecca Stephens 8-2-1848
Ferrell, Harbert to Judy Daniel 2-22-1841 (3-2-1841)
Ferrell, James B. to Catherine Ross 12-23-1850 (12-26-1850)
Fesmire, Thomas to Lenora (Mrs.) Winslow 10-6-1869 (10-14-1869)
Field, Silas F. to Jane M. Talbot 4-24-1854 (4-25-1854)
Fifer, Parmenias to Sarah N. London 1-3-1860
Finch, Irvin to Susan M. Jordon 12-2-1843 (12-3-1843)
Finger, Andrew L. to Mary S. Haynes 12-15-1843 (12-20-1843)
Fisher, Eldridge L. to Sarah E. Hicox 9-21-1857
Fisher, Richd. W. to Mattie A. Gattis 12-8-1866 (12-11-1866)
Fitz (Fith?), James A. to Mariah L. Edwards 9-4-1843 (9-6-1843)
Fitz, Clement P. to Caroline E. Williamson 9-3-1849 (10-3-1849)
Fitzhugh, Ezekiel to Martha J. Ford 1-20-1852 (1-21-1852)
Fitzhugh, Jno. W. to Bettie H. Glenn 1-2-1869
Flaherty, James to Caroline Tomlinson 8-31-1846 (9-1-1846)
Fleming, Cecil to Emma Williams 1-29-1870 (1-31-1870)
Fleming, William to Nancy Bedwell 5-25-1859 (5-29-1859)
Fletcher, John T. to Caroline Compton 1-7-1840 (1-16-1840)
Fletcher, Wm. D. to Elizabeth E. Montgomery 12-12-1870
Flin, John C. to Susan F. McGuire 8-12-1856 (8-13-1856)
Flippin, E. E. to Emma Conger 7-1-1871 (7-3-1871)
Fly, Benjamin F. to Mary J. E. Mooring 1-17-1846 (1-21-1846)
Fly, Christopher C. to Amanda M. Doak 3-6-1841 (3-7-1841)
Fly, Flavius to Luvina M. Day 11-9-1852 (11-12-1852)
Fly, John L. to Sarah A. Davie 12-19-1853 (12-21-1853)
Fogarty, Wm. H. to Minerva C. Dawson 9-10-1866 (9-11-1866)
Fogg, Francis A. to Archebia Ann Swan 12-17-1839 (12-20-1839)
Fogg, Joseph A. to Eliz. R. Dickinson 10-9-1860
Follis, Francis A. to Lucinda P. Jones 10-23-1860 (10-25-1860)
Follis, Thomas H. to Elizabeth A. Jones 12-21-1859 (12-22-1859)
Fondille, W. G. to M. A. Coggins 12-14-1867
Forbis, Arthur to Martha A. L. Dollar 7-19-1847 (7-20-1847)
Ford, Peter to Elizabeth Williams 1-3-1852 (1-7-1852)
Ford, Robert P. to Martha A. Day 1-23-1850 (1-25-1850)
Ford, Solomon D. to Nancy (Mrs.) Wilkins 11-30-1860
Foreman, John to Pamina Higginbottom 11-23-1842
Forrest, Samuel B. to Mary C. McDonald 1-17-1852
Forrester, William F. to Martha J. Rocheld 10-23-1844 (10-24-1844)
Forsyth, Benj. Franklin to Mary Paralee Shivers 8-22-1871 (8-23-1871)
Fortner, Joseph E. to Lucy E. McKnight 12-17-1850
Forwell, Oscar O. to Sarah Ann Coker 7-30-1859
Fossett, Burkie A. to Jane D. Hays 8-23-1867 (8-25-1867)
Foster, Robert to Milly Ann Lynch 10-6-1866
Foster, Wildon to Barbery B. Barber 9-11-1838

Fouth, John F. to Rebecca L. Seahorn 3-30-1867
Fowler, Jno. T. to Eliza Young 2-28-1871
Fox, William L. to Mary J. Hamilton 4-21-1852 (4-27-1852)
Francis, General M. to Margaret D. Harris 6-23-1866 (6-24-1866)
Francis, Nathan to Catherine Drake 1-29-1859
Francis, Nathan to Cynthia McVey 5-1-1848
Franklin, Henry D. to Anna B. Sherwood 12-8-1869 (12-9-1869)
Franklin, James F. to Eliza A. Anderson 4-26-1858 (4-27-1858)
Franklin, John N. to Nancy Hardy 2-8-1852
Freeman, Gaston G. B. to Mary Ann Smithwick 7-6-1843 (7-7-1843)
Freeman, George W. to Samantha L. Graves 1-17-1859
Freeman, Jose. B. to Virginia Caruthers 10-25-1849
Freeman, William R. to Louisa (Mrs.) Belton 10-12-1861 (10-13-1861)
French, Robt. H. to Mary E. Taylor 12-16-1867 (12-17-1867)
Friemmer, Andrew to Martha A. Taylor 4-21-1866 (4-26-1866)
Fry, Samuel M. to Lucy Ann Ward 12-23-1848 (12-26-1848)
Fry, Thomas to Jennie McAlexander 1-31-1871
Fulbright, Alpha to Nancy Caruthers 12-31-1840
Fulbright, David L. to Missouri Harrison 11-12-1866 (11-14-1866)
Fulcher, Joseph to Sarah E. Browning 3-18-1867 (3-19-1867)
Fuller, Turner J. to Susan Tate 7-1-1841
Fullerton, James M. to Sophronia Price 9-8-1870
Fullerton, John to Martha Cooper 7-10-1866 (7-12-1866)
Funderbunk, W. J. to Martha E. Smart 4-13-1869 (4-15-1869)
Furgerson, John W. to Rebecca C. Stanly 8-19-1856 (8-20-1856)
Fussell, Jasen W. to Sarah Cook 3-5-1867 (3-7-1867)
Fussell, William N. to Martha Jane King 9-11-1866 (9-13-1866)
Fussell, Wyatt to Mary Elizabeth Maddox 4-20-1842 (4-21-1842)
Futrell, James G. to Martha Ann Lewis 9-3-1866 (9-5-1866)
Gallaway, Joseph to Emily Hopkins 1-24-1855
Gamewell, Francis to Martha J. Jackson 5-17-1849
Ganaway, Samuel G. to Margarett Gholson 10-12-1843
Gardner, Calvin to Elizabeth A. Delph 2-26-1856 (2-27-1856)
Gardner, James W. to Caroline M. Clay 3-31-1862 (4-1-1862)
Gardner, John R. to Sarah E. Alexander 3-30-1861
Gardner, Neil M. to Lavinia B. Hardgrove 6-18-1857 (6-23-1857)
Gardner, William F. to Jane Elizabeth Haltom 6-4-1855
Garland, John C. M. to Ann Eliza F. O. Perry 9-5-1854
Garland, William W. to Eliza A. Exum 1-13-1841 (1-15-1841)
Garland, William W. to Mary E. McKnight 12-18-1854 (12-19-1854)
Garrett, Alfred D. to Tennessee Freeling 1-23-1849 (1-24-1849)
Garrett, Arvell to Susan Alexander 4-4-1838 (4-5-1838)
Garrett, James P. G. to Martha Ann Sanderson 1-3-1867
Garrett, James to Sarah Nolan 1-27-1843
Garrett, Samuel I. to Eliza Rickman 2-7-1842 (2-8-1842)
Garrett, Thomas H. to Martha Jane Brown 10-29-1856
Garrett, Thomas H. to Susan B. Henderson 11-30-1859 (12-1-1859)
Garrett, Vincent to Mary Fonner 2-6-1841
Garrett, William C. to Lina Reynolds 4-3-1844 (5-17-1844)
Gaskins, Enoch to Perlina W. Dearmore 9-17-1849
Gaskins, Enoch to Susan Scott 12-10-1867 (12-24-1867)
Gaskins, Thomas G. to Matilda Raines 7-16-1858 (7-18-1858)
Gaston, Daniel M. to Minerva Grant 12-22-1866 (12-23-1866)
Gaston, Z. T. to Martha Rogers 10-29-1866 (10-30-1866)
Gately, James M. to Lumisa Howell 9-22-1857 (10-1-1857)
Gately, James M. to Mary Jane Lovill 11-9-1852 (12-22-1852)
Gates, Benjamin F. to Narcissa M. (Mrs.) Stone 5-4-1859
Gates, Robert to Callie J. Jester 10-29-1867
Gatlin, Stephen to Chelly Branch 12-16-1840 (12-17-1840)
Gattas, George to Sarah Ann Boswell 4-27-1843
Gattis, George Carson to Amanda Harris Davis 6-11-1853
Gattis, William L. to Mary A. Davis 12-21-1847 (12-22-1847)
Gentry, Napoleon to Narcissa H. Butler 7-1-1868 (7-2-1868)
George, Martin S. to Martha E. Revely 11-30-1857 (12-3-1857)
German, Kingsberry to Liley Denny 4-1-1856 (4-11-1856)
Germon, William H. to Tennessee M. Rosenbum 12-12-1853
Gibbs, Charles N. to Matilda E. Vaulx 6-5-1850
Gibbs, Felix G. to Martha Kendrick 1-10-1845
Gilbert, Wilson R. to Mary Jane Griffin 11-10-1871 (11-12-1871)
Giles, John William to Susan Connell 10-27-1866 (10-28-1866)
Gill, David to Rebeccah Fly 10-12-1840
Gill, James T. to Prudence T. Hopper 1-8-1850 (1-19-1850)
Gill, Robert to Elizabeth Frances Allen 1-21-1867 (1-22-1867)
Gillaspie, Leroy C. to Tempy S. Johnson 10-29-1852 (10-30-1852)
Gilliam, John E. to Martha Ann Gilliam 11-19-1866 (11-20-1866)

Gilliam, Mason to Olive Hopkins 2-27-1854 (2-28-1854)
Gilliam, Sandford W. to Mary M. Barnett 2-15-1861 (5-15-1861)
Gillikin, James to Amacivil Duncan 2-17-1844
Gillikins, James to Lotty L. Duncan 5-27-1850
Gilliland, Joseph to Margaret M. Robinson 2-7-1848
Gillispie, Leroy C. to Mary J. Tyson 10-28-1845 (11-1-1845)
Gillispie, Robert N. to Mary E. Fry 11-12-1845
Givens, John A. to Sallie I. Murchison 11-4-1871 (11-6-1871)
Givens, Robert H. to Rachel (Mrs.) Dodd 12-13-1867
Gladney, John A. to Catherine Davis 3-27-1869 (4-1-1869)
Glass, John E. to Susan A. Norvell 11-2-1859 (11-3-1859)
Glass, William A. to Margarett E. Faucett 10-29-1845 (10-30-1845)
Glenn, Christopher to Cynthia C. Kilpatrick 12-4-1848
Glenn, James R. to Elizabeth M. Hunter 4-3-1854 (4-5-1854)
Glenn, Jas. G. to Lucy Eugenie Hunt 10-5-1868 (10-6-1868)
Glenn, Lawson to Jane Baker 12-27-1847 (12-30-1847)
Glenn, Richard to Permelia Bates 7-19-1853
Glenn, Solomon to Nancy Anderson 4-19-1852 (4-25-1852)
Glenn, William A. to Hannah J. Kilpatrick 1-21-1867
Glidewell, Jerry T. to Annie Starkey 12-24-1867 (12-25-1867)
Glidewell, Matthew to Ann Edwards 4-6-1857 (4-8-1857)
Glidewell, Nash to Susan Tims 8-22-1838 (8-23-1838)
Glidewell, William to Sarah Tims 12-17-1840
Glidwell, Jesse to Jane Sims 8-7-1841 (8-8-1841)
Glidwell, Nineviah to Matilda Cox 7-21-1847 (7-22-1847)
Glidwell, Thomas to Jane Sims 11-4-1840
Glover, John O. to Susan A. Piercy 3-7-1850 (3-8-1850)
Glover, John to Elizabeth W. Kirby 1-5-1845 (1-8-1846)
Glover, John to Sylvia Allen 8-22-1848
Glover, Samuel to Miram S. Anderson 9-8-1858 (9-9-1858)
Goad, Henry to Mary M. Sewall 12-23-1841
Goad, John to Lucinda Piercy 8-17-1838
Goad, Malden Y. to Elizabeth Pierce 2-22-1841 (3-14-1841)
Godfrey, Solomon to Dicey (Mrs.) Davis 12-18-1860
Goforth, Calvin to Celia Dickson 2-4-1854 (2-5-1854)
Goforth, William to Mary Jane Dickson 1-28-1854 (1-31-1854)
Golden, John to Jane Stewart 12-27-1845
Golden, William to Lucinda Fisher 8-14-1845
Gooch, Alfred B. to Eleanor Watson 5-19-1841
Gooch, Allen G. to Mary E. Smith 4-27-1852 (4-28-1852)
Gooch, James C. to Delia White 2-22-1869 (2-28-1869)
Goodell, Austin to Mary Ann Newsom 6-15-1855 (6-21-1855)
Goodell, Lorenza to Laura C. Clark 8-24-1847
Goodin, Augustus B. to Martha J. Ward 10-3-1848 (10-5-1848)
Goodlett, Job H. to Mildred C. Rogers 10-28-1856 (10-29-1856)
Goodlow, Andrew J. to Margarett Ann Jones 8-17-1843
Goodrich, Edward H. to Nancy R. Rollins 6-2-1866 (6-3-1866)
Goodrich, G. P. to Martha A. Barnett 7-28-1854 (8-?-1854)
Goodrich, John C. to Eliza Harris 3-27-1844 (3-28-1844)
Goodrich, Malcolm H. to Emily B. Roane 2-11-1852 (2-12-1852)
Goodrich, Stephen B. to Caroline Luckey 7-24-1858 (7-29-1858)
Goodridge, Matthew M. to Rebecca Mason 2-12-1848 (2-17-1848)
Goodwin, Marion to Louisa Evans 12-7-1853
Gordin, Samuel to Mary Ann Graves 11-6-1838 (12-3-1838)
Gordon, Jesse B. to Josephine C. Hays 1-9-1871
Gordon, John H. to Joanna A. Preston 12-19-1861
Gordon, Robert W. to Sarah Lowell 1-7-1848 (1-20-1848)
Gordon, William J. to Harriet Tennessee Roach 11-2-1860
    (11-5-1860)
Gowan, Pleasant A. to Mary A. E. Harris 7-30-1849
Grafford, George W. to Minerva M. Mosly 11-26-1840
Graham, Anthony to Mary C. Smith 2-2-1870 (2-3-1870)
Granger, John G. to Sarha L. (Mrs.) Vault 10-14-1867 (10-15-1867)
Grant, James F. to Eliza Jane Bailey 12-25-1870 (12-28-1870)
Grant, John W. to Elizabeth J. Day 9-25-1850
Graus, Calvin to Mary L. Lea 2-11-1859
Graves, Hudson C. to Adaline S. Turner 2-22-1844 (2-26-1844)
Graves, James H. to M. Jennie Park 7-20-1868 (7-21-1868)
Graves, James R. to Louisa J. Snider 7-31-1856
Graves, James to Ann Boon 9-21-1857 (9-22-1857)
Graves, John H. to Sarah J. Thompson 11-8-1867 (11-10-1867)
Graves, Patterson to Misoura Ann Hardin 12-17-1853
Graves, Tarlton H. to Frances M. Fly 1-27-1844 (1-30-1844)
Graves, Tarlton H. to Virginia M. Oliver 8-3-1858 (9-7-1858)
Graves, Thomas M. to Emily _____ 1-29-1844 (2-1-1844)

Graves, William A. to Nancy M. Barnett 9-7-1867 (9-12-1867)
Graves, William L. to Mary Jane Turner 12-27-1854 (12-28-1854)
Graves, William M. to Jane Watson 12-3-1838
Gravette, William D. to Minerva Fitz 12-30-1847 (12-31-1847)
Gravitt, Obidiah to Sarah F. Edwards 12-22-1845
Gray, Jesse to Caroline Mooring 12-25-1847
Gray, Sidney to Nancy Ann Cozart 2-10-1842
Gray, William to Susan Boyd 10-6-1860 (10-7-1860)
Grayson, Lamuel F. to Willie Miller 12-30-1868 (12-31-1868)
Greathouse, John F. to Charlotte Crawford 1-28-1868 (1-30-1868)
Green, Alonzo O. to Mary (Mrs.) Mitchell 3-15-1867 (3-17-1867)
Green, Goodwin to Malinda C. Russell 7-16-1846 (7-28-1846)
Green, Joseph M. to Martha Humphrey 10-11-1852
Green, Robert H. to Victoria G. Taliaferro 4-23-1866
Greener, Nicholas to Martha Whitaker 2-22-1862 (2-23-1862)
Greer, James N. to Henrietta Askew 9-13-1858
Greer, John A. to Louisa Ingram 5-21-1859 (5-22-1859)
Greer, Thos. M to Mary Reid 1-1-1846
Greer, William H. to Sarah Ann Wise 7-2-1850
Gregory, John H. to Eliza Brooks 11-3-1846 (11-6-1846)
Gregory, Lewis to Neoma Duncan 9-18-1841
Gregory, William L. to Mary Jane Duncan 3-18-1852
Grey, Ephraine L. to Artelia Y. Acres 3-29-1854 (3-30-1854)
Griffin, Edward J. to Gertie Jacobs 4-18-1868 (4-20-1868)
Griffin, James to Sarah Nipper 7-13-1843
Griffin, William T. to Mary Ann Rollins 12-21-1866 (12-23-1866)
Griffin, William to Delila Baley 9-12-1838
Grimes, William to Martha J. Jones 2-6-1846
Groves, William R. to Nicey McCarver 11-17-1858
Grubbs, Thomas to Mary Gallop 1-13-1845 (1-23-1845)
Guinn, James F. to Mary Davis 6-21-1862 (6-22-1862)
Guion, Henry L. to Mary Ann McMillan 12-18-1838
Guthrie, Andrew to Mary Ann Taylor 4-12-1843
Guthrie, William H. to Permelia J. Lackey 10-6-1853
Guy, Nathaniel to Jane Nabors 11-4-1871 (11-5-1871)
Guy, Nathaniel to Mary Ann Nabors 4-10-1869 (4-15-1869)
Haas, Z. to Lizzie Dalton 4-8-1869
Haddon, James to Elizabeth Kollinsworth 1-25-1867
Haddoway, James F. to Isabela Murchison 4-23-1842 (4-24-1842)
Hadson, E. to Susanna Golden 8-16-1842 (8-18-1842)
Hafley, James M. to Mary C. Burrough 2-1-1870
Hailey, C. H. to Caroline Penny 5-18-1870
Haley, John W. to Eliza Jane Mooring 4-1-1850 (4-4-1850)
Hall, Andrew J. to Sue M. Taylor 5-16-1866
Hall, Claudius B. to Mary Eliza Flowers 4-11-1859 (4-13-1859)
Hall, Felix Josiah to Sarah Ann Elizabeth Williams 12-13-1856 (12-14-1856)
Hall, Hiriam to Sarah M. Holderfield 7-26-1843 (7-27-1843)
Hall, James N. to Ellen Morgan 4-4-1860
Hall, Lewis W. to Mattie W. Cochrane 3-5-1868
Hall, William to Sarah E. Fly 12-31-1838
Halliburton, Tinsly W. to Mary K. Davis 2-23-1843
Haltom, Benjamin F. to Nancy Blair 10-30-1850 (10-31-1850)
Haltom, Edmund to Sarah Francis Davis 12-17-1856 (12-18-1856)
Haltom, Ezekiel to Rebecca Moore 12-10-1855 (12-18-1855)
Haltom, John S. to Susan E. Young 9-24-1853 (10-6-1853)
Haltom, William B. to Catherine Johnson 3-3-1853
Haltom, William G. to Mary Ann Wrenn 2-19-1839
Hamilton, Frank B. to Dinebia Walsh 11-18-1869
Hamilton, Peyton S. to Jennett McCullock 1-13-1849 (1-23-1849)
Hamilton, William P. to Sarah J. Stewart 11-1-1858 (11-3-1858)
Hamlett, Christopher to Louisianna Mooney 1-2-1867 (1-6-1867)
Hamlett, Joseph S. to Margaret E. McNeill 9-11-1854 (9-12-1854)
Hammers, Raleigh to Mary Ann White 7-4-1859 (7-5-1859)
Hammon, William to Phalba M. Harris 2-28-1867
Hammond, Miles M. to Margaret A. Simonton 5-9-1853
Hammond, William to Elsey Hearn 9-13-1845 (9-14-1845)
Hammonds, William W. to Sarah C. Thompson 1-2-1850 (1-3-1850)
Hammons, James M. to Kittura Foxwell 12-16-1847
Hamner, Constantine S. to Martha J. Cockrill 8-18-1857 (8-19-1857)
Hampton, David M. to Mattie J. Perry 12-19-1866 (12-20-1866)
Handly, John to Visy Ham 11-29-1842
Hankins, Henry H. to Frances A. Sherman 9-23-1843 (9-28-1843)
Hapgood, Thomas to Mary F. Saxton 4-20-1867
Harber, John H. to Rachel L. Dickison 9-26-1859

Harbert, James H. to Harriet J. Gregory 1-24-1859 (1-27-1859)
Harbert, Stephen to Nancy Vincent 7-20-1840 (7-23-1840)
Harbour, Elisha T. to Martha Lawrence 8-22-1868 (8-26-1868)
Harbut, Thomas C. to Tempee Hutchison 5-11-1870
Hardage, Andrew J. to Jane Spencer 7-24-1839
Hardage, Joseph A. to Sarah Sanford 2-10-1846
Hardee, George to Elizabeth (Mrs.) Walker 5-23-1868 (5-24-1868)
Harden, Moses to _____ Jabasford? 12-15-1842
Hardgrave, Felix R. to Susan E. Bonner 2-28-1852 (3-2-1852)
Hardin, Gabriel to Mary E. Dickson 6-5-1858 (6-6-1858)
Hardin, Moses J. to Lucinda Newsom 1-11-1858 (1-12-1858)
Hardin, Moses T. to Sarah C. Newsom 9-22-1846
Hardin, Richard to Frances Moore 4-29-1843 (4-30-1843)
Hardin, William S. to Parthenia Meadows 5-7-1853 (5-10-1853)
Harding, George L. to Lou Deloach 12-12-1866 (12-20-1866)
Harding, John A. to Susannah Clanton 2-26-1867 (2-28-1867)
Harding, Nicholas D. to Nancy M. Todd 12-18-1866 (12-20-1866)
Hardwicke, Lawriston to Mollie R. Taylor 2-1-1871 (2-2-1871)
Hardy, Benjamin T. to Missouri E. Murrell 4-17-1853 (4-21-1853)
Hardy, Mark to Sarah A. Smith 8-22-1868 (8-23-1868)
Hargis, John G. to Lucy Ann Taylor 6-24-1840 (6-25-1840)
Hargis, Richard to Louisa Whitworth 12-23-1857
Harkins, Aaron W. to Ann Frances Shelton 2-4-1856
Harkins, James C. to Lurany Ann Campbell 12-17-1845 (12-18-1845)
Harns, Willie T. to Nancy Ann Replogle 2-18-1845
Harper, Archibald H. to Martha P. Miller 11-4-1871
Harper, James T. to Elizabeth Shelton 12-7-1868 (12-10-1868)
Harper, Patrick to Sally Jackson 1-5-1841 (1-10-1841)
Harper, William D. to Martha E. Wiggs 2-13-1845 (2-27-1845)
Harpole, Abram H. to Elviva M. Reden 10-19-1860 (10-21-1860)
Harrell, Thomas to Betsy Taylor 11-19-1838
Harrell, Thomas to Luan Pipkin 5-15-1848 (5-18-1848)
Harrell, William G. L. to Elizabeth Sturdivant 1-16-1850 (1-17-1850)
Harrell, William to Tabitha Pierce 10-20-1846 (10-29-1846)
Harriman, Wm. H. to Sarah E. (Mrs.) Christenberry 7-17-1868
Harrington, Hardy to Elizabeth Strain 7-28-1840
Harrington, Mathias to Nancy Grant 4-1-1856
Harris, Archibald R. to Sarah R. Estridge 2-12-1848
Harris, Benjamin to Elizabeth Nowell 7-9-1858 (7-15-1858)
Harris, C. (Dr.) to Ellen C. Allen 12-15-1842
Harris, C. (Dr.) to Mary S. Johnson 8-23-1845 (8-25-1845)
Harris, Christopher C. to Frances Ann Whittington 2-10-1848 (2-14-1848)
Harris, Daniel to Martha Jane Atkins 10-27-1866 (10-28-1866)
Harris, Daniel to Sarah Ruff 2-5-1842
Harris, E. G. to Mariah Drake 2-13-1855 (2-14-1855)
Harris, George W. to Nancy H. Smith 10-19-1839
Harris, Henry to Elizabeth R. Barker 4-15-1848 (4-18-1848)
Harris, James E. to Mary H. Drake 11-7-1857 (11-10-1857)
Harris, James W. to Isabella M. Murchison 11-16-1858 (11-18-1858)
Harris, James to Elizabeth Cross 3-3-1855
Harris, Jeptha V. to Emma F. Cobb 12-28-1869
Harris, Jno. W. to Eliza Ann McCaig 12-16-1869
Harris, John N. to Margaret O. Kile 4-19-1870 (4-21-1870)
Harris, John W. to Emma C. Goodwin 1-4-1870 (1-5-1870)
Harris, John to Jane, jr. Goodrich 4-6-1849 (4-17-1849)
Harris, Julius C. to Martha Ann King 2-28-1859 (3-3-1859)
Harris, Julius C. to Susan C. Smith 11-18-1852
Harris, Levin Hill to Clara R. Humphreys 11-15-1871 (11-22-1871)
Harris, Newton A. to Catherine C. Copeland 1-7-1861
Harris, Paul T. to Tempie A. Yarbrough 11-12-1866 (11-15-1866)
Harris, Robert to Minerva Fussell 8-6-1846 (8-20-1846)
Harris, Rowland G. to Margaret Benson 11-23-1859 (11-24-1859)
Harris, Samuel to Dolloy Thom 8-16-1838
Harris, Thomas W. to Mary E. Turley 3-24-1842
Harris, Victor M. to C. J. Transou 7-6-1858 (7-7-1858)
Harris, Willie S. to Caroline Roberts 4-17-1841
Harris, Wm. H. to Mary E. Haskins 12-14-1870
Harris, Wm. L. to Jennie Williams 5-7-1870
Harris, Wm. P. to Tabitha Cain 11-27-1868 (12-3-1868)
Harrison, Andrew J. to Eliza J. Graves 9-9-1845 (9-11-1845)
Harrison, Francis M. to Musidora Graves 8-10-1853
Harrison, Geo. T. to E. F. Mooring 4-21-1866 (4-22-1866)
Harrison, George S. to Mary Elvina M. Bishop 4-27-1838 (5-10-1838)
Harrison, James to Fannie A. Campbell 12-21-1869 (12-23-1869)

Harrison, John T. to Nannie Givens 5-6-1867 (5-16-1867)
Harrison, Kinsey to Mary Ruth Morgan 11-1-1839 (11-7-1839)
Harrison, L. R. to Martha (Mrs.) McMahon 12-6-1854
Harrison, Richard H. to Lucy G. Bishop 7-15-1852
Harrison, William N. to Nancy C. McGee 9-16-1846
Harrison, William to Virginia L. Trezavent 8-16-1870
Harston, D. W. to N. C. Wilson 12-29-1860
Harston, Henry to Susan Brant 10-13-1846 (10-14-1846)
Harston, J. Polk to Bettie Lackie 11-28-1868
Harston, Jarrod to Susan M. Fitzhugh 10-21-1871
Harston, Marmaduke Y. to Clara A. Worley 12-30-1845 (1-1-1846)
Hart, Andrew M. to Violet J. Taylor 6-12-1843 (6-13-1843)
Hart, Calvin V. to Sadie E. Alexander 2-20-1871 (2-22-1871)
Hart, James M. to Ann King 7-28-1854 *
Hart, James N. to Martha S. Mayo 11-22-1869
Hart, John to Elizabeth Clanton 12-20-1869 (12-22-1869)
Hart, Robert D. to Ellen May 10-1-1862 (10-2-1862)
Hart, William W. to Elizabeth M. Johnson 1-5-1857 (1-6-1857)
Harton, John to Catherine B. McKnight 6-8-1843
Haskins, Crred B. to Nancy Johnson 12-26-1848 (12-27-1848)
Haskins, James V. to Margaret Meaxey 7-19-1865
Hasteto, Isaac to Martha Thom 3-3-1842
Hathaway, Kinchen to Susan Cozart 12-5-1859 (12-8-1859)
Hatton, Joshua C. to Lucinda Morgan no date
Haughton, George to Harriett Barrett 9-14-1840 (9-15-1840)
Haughton, Lemuel B. to P. E. Geyle 5-8-1860 (5-9-1860)
Haughton, Willis to Mary D. Ellington 10-23-1867 (10-24-1867)
Hawson, George H. to Mary A. White 2-11-1869
Hayley, Benjamin to Mariah T. Fleming 11-24-1846 (11-25-1846)
Hayley, George to Harriet (Mrs.) Hayley 8-15-1871 (8-17-1871)
Hayley, James T. to Nancy E. Tomlin 11-6-1856
Hayley, James to Mary E. Moxley 1-23-1869 (1-24-1869)
Hayley, John B. to Margaret C. Tomlin 6-23-1860 (6-27-1860)
Hayley, John to Laura Ann Fowler 11-9-1842
Haynes, Harbert H. to Sarah E. Roberson 9-21-1843
Haynes, John G. to Laura Croom 2-16-1870 (2-17-1870)
Hays, Benjamin to Tennessee Newson 12-22-1847
Hays, Blackmon G. to Ursula P. Raines 11-30-1859
Hays, Callin to Elizabeth York 12-25-1847 (12-28-1847)
Hays, James M. to Nannie J. Brooks 11-9-1868 (11-12-1868)
Hays, Middleton to Sallie P. Caruthers 12-16-1868
Hays, Wm. B. to Mary C. Jackson 11-9-1868 (11-12-1868)
Hazlewood, Randolph to Malinda D. Digg 8-12-1839 (8-13-1839)
Hazlewood, William to Caroline T. Gill 2-11-1856
Hearn, John W. to Jearn Hearn 12-9-1854 (12-10-1854)
Hearn, Noah G. to Minerva Hartgrave 1-15-1839
Hearn, Oren A. to Frances F. Hunter 12-9-1859 (12-11-1859)
Hearn, W. N. to Elizabeth Hudson 12-21-1846
Hearn, Whitman H. to Aurelia Harris 1-11-1847
Heas, James R. to Gabella Lankford 9-1-1841
Heasenburg, John W. to Davy Theresa Alexander 6-13-1854 (6-15-1854)
Heath, Thomas I. to Mary Cason 5-28-1838 (5-21?-1838)
Hedgepath, Arthur J. to Ann Eliza Howard 8-20-1846
Hellard, George R. to Caroline V. Brown 6-1-1857 (6-2-1857)
Henderson, Calvin to Ela Patterson 3-18-1842
Henderson, Elam D. to Martha Jane Bryant 10-27-1856 (10-29-1856)
Henderson, Gabriel A. to Nancy J. Newton 8-15-1855 (8-16-1855)
Henderson, Hugh C. to Mary S. Maddox 4-28-1852
Henderson, James to Nancy A. Vinson 8-14-1855 (8-16-1855)
Henderson, Mark C. to Mary Ann Hogsett 2-6-1867 (2-7-1867)
Henderson, Mark C. to Tenie J. Nesbitt 12-29-1870 (12-30-1870)
Henderson, Milton A. to Elizabeth C. Sewell 11-9-1854
Henderson, Nathaniel to Susan Patterson 11-1-1859 (11-2-1859)
Henderson, Robert F. to Mary J. Allison 5-2-1870 (5-4-1870)
Henderson, Robert H. to Nancy Maddox 5-3-1855
Henderson, Thomas to Ann Eliza Lancaster 7-25-1848
Henderson, Thomas to Marion Patterson 11-2-1852
Henderson, William F. to Mary P. McCorry 11-8-1847
Henderson, William J. to Margarett E. Rosemond 12-17-1850
Henderson, William T. to Donia C. Hogsett 12-2-1867
Hendricks, John M. to Mary Black 12-20-1848
Hendron, John W. C. to Susan M. Williams 2-1-1841 (2-3-1841)
Henning, John D. to Elizabeth A. Brookshire 12-12-1859
Henning, William H. to Martha Ann Davis 10-15-1839

Henry, John L. to Martha Ross 11-5-1840
Henry, William to Mary E. Rutledge 12-25-1856 (12-20?-1856)
Henry, Wm. F. to Mary F. McClanahan 12-9-1868
Hensley, John to Amelia Ann Morris 4-8-1858
Herbert, Wm. T. to Martha Ann Latham 3-11-1871 (3-15-1871)
Herndon, Jerome to Mollie Gallant 12-28-1867 (1-2-1868)
Herndon, Wm. C. to Elizabeth J. Sallie 12-28-1867 (1-1-1868)
Herridge, John W. to Rosa Graham 10-20-1866
Herron, James to Lydia Gray 1-29-1839
Herron, Levi B. to Nancy Wilmoth Hutchison 12-29-1858 (12-30-1858)
Hershaw, Daniel to Rebecca Emerson 3-4-1850 (3-7-1850)
Hess, jr., Nelson I. to Ida R. Seay 11-16-1867 (11-20-1867)
Hester, John H. to Mary E. Sykes 12-28-1869
Hewit, Hazael to Malinda Sensemon 12-22-1849 (12-25-1849)
Hicks, Benjamin M. to Mary C. McClellan 10-26-1847 (10-28-1847)
Hicks, Daniel to Harriet King 5-1-1871
Hicks, Erasmus F. to Alice Jelks 3-16-1858 (3-17-1858)
Hicks, George B. to Eliza J. McClellan 10-9-1849 (10-10-1849)
Hicks, Gideon to Ann R. Deloach 12-19-1860 (12-20-1860)
Hicks, James W. to Nancy S. Taylor 10-17-1860 (10-18-1860)
Hicks, James to Elizabeth Jenkins 10-11-1852 (10-13-1852)
Hicks, John F. to Sarah W. Harbert 12-5-1853 (12-6-1853)
Hicks, John R. to Elizabeth E. Taylor 12-19-1854 (12-21-1854)
Hicks, John R. to Fannie T. Duncan 9-18-1866 (9-19-1866)
Hicks, Kenneth G. to Cynthia A. Gill 9-28-1858 (9-29-1858)
Hicks, Ransom Burns to Lydia C. Withers 10-8-1861 (10-9-1861)
Hicks, Shephard B. to Parmelia T. Watt 8-15-1848 (8-20-1848)
Higden, William H. to Almira E. Fly 6-21-1858 (6-22-1858)
Hilderbrand, Henry K. to Mary Virginia Robinson 5-19-1869
Hill, Allen to Malinda Wilson 1-25-1840
Hill, Byrd to Levinia R. Butler 10-21-1852
Hill, Charles A. to Mary Elizabeth Nelson 5-14-1839 (5-16-1839)
Hill, George to Louisana Mitchell 12-28-1848
Hill, Green L. to Louisa F. Cock 6-19-1861 (6-27-1861)
Hill, Jacob to Laura Noel 2-24-1869 (3-2-1869)
Hill, John W. to Margaret Ellen Kyle 3-28-1867
Hill, Leonidas J. to Ann R. Eddins 2-27-1856
Hill, Robert N. to Betty A. Maxey 9-10-1856
Hines, Richard to M. A. (Mrs.) Cage 8-9-1870
Hinson, John to Martha Savage 4-16-1849
Hoad, David to R. Caroline Williams 7-2-1859 (7-3-1859)
Hobbs, Ezekiel B. W. to Feriby F. Williams 10-16-1848 (10-17-1848)
Hobbs, Ezekiel B. W. to Perlina Cock 4-14-1862 (4-17-1862)
Hobbs, John to Madelena Johnson 7-12-1843 (7-13-1843)
Hodge, David T. to Margaret J. Kelly 8-28-1848 (8-31-1848)
Hodges, Josiah to Martha Waggoner 5-2-1844
Hodges, Josiah to Mary Patton 7-10-1839
Hodges, Mark to L. Annie Fogg 2-5-1867
Hogan, Atlas M. to Sarah J. E. Stevenson 8-1-1866
Hogan, Isiah to Sarah Johnson 12-20-1849
Hogan, John H. to Nancy E. Brown 9-27-1870 (9-28-1870)
Hogan, William to Elizabeth Johnson 10-8-1866 (10-11-1866)
Hogans, Caswell to Jane Johnson 8-3-1845
Hogsett, Charles to Jamima C. Sharp 3-18-1846
Hogshead, James E. to Marietta H. Prewitt 11-3-1841
Holdsworth, William to Minnie Dean 11-21-1870
Holliday, Jasper to Paralee M. Elliott 6-16-1852
Holliday, William W. to Lavicy Lovin 12-9-1847
Holliday, Zachariah to Ann Dearmore 3-21-1846 (4-2-1846)
Hollinsworth, Jarrett to Minerva H. McAlfee 10-7-1848
Holloman, Malachi to Matilda Patterson 8-5-1857
Holloman, William to Melvina Harris 1-7-1863 (1-?-1863)
Holloway, James F. to Nancy T. Marshall 1-27-1859
Holloway, William C. to Virginia Roland 11-17-1858 (12-1-1858)
Hollowell, Wm. G. (Gibson Co.) to Marianna Fitts 8-3-1870 (8-4-1870)
Holly, Marion J. to Malinda F. Thompson 12-9-1869
Holmes, Turner P. to Cherry A. Hicks 8-30-1854
Holmes, William K. to Susan E. Thompson 11-13-1845
Holt, Harvey to Rebecca Conner 7-28-1846 (7-30-1846)
Holt, Moses to Lourana Moser 9-13-1869
Holt, Murphy G. to Jane Welsh 12-28-1843 (1-4-1844)
Holtsford, Asa P. to Jane Fry 8-23-1855
Hooten, Jesse to Jane Heidleburg 2-13-1843 (2-14-1843)

Hopkins, Cullen P. to Mollie E. Casey 6-7-1867 (6-12-1867)
Hopkins, Gilbert to Drucilla Andrews 3-9-1859 (3-10-1859)
Hopkins, Logan to Josephine Brock 11-16-1857
Hopper, Barzilla to Nancy L. Piercey 4-22-1844
Hopper, Daniel to Lucinda Burres 10-4-1838
Hopper, James E. to Catherine Tanner 1-30-1841
Hopper, James M. to Susan M. Carpenter 11-16-1855 (11-20-1855)
Hopper, Ransom E. to Fannie Sharrock 11-1-1866
Hopper, Turley to Margaret Carrothers 9-22-1852 (9-23-1852)
Hopper, William P. to Elizabeth Perry 1-4-1845
Hoppers, Thos. D. to Mariah Frances (Mrs) Hoppers 8-26-1868
    (8-27-1868)
Horn, Anderson to Sarah Horn 3-18-1846
Horne, Matthew to Martha Chamberlain 3-19-8150 (3-21-1850)
Horton, John to Mary Jane Cooper 12-18-1848
Houghton, Burkett L. to Margaret E. Askew 1-17-1853 (1-18-1853)
House, James G. to Susan F. Hudson 12-5-1866 (12-6-1866)
Houston, Chas. B. to Emma Buckner 9-22-1869
Houston, James M. to Mary Lou Tomlin 2-16-1870
Houston, Jordan A. to Amanda J. Scarborough 11-14-1859
    (11-15-1859)
Howard, Francis M. to Mary N. Birdsong 10-9-1866
Howard, Joseph T. to Isabella Gordon 3-2-1869 (3-4-1869)
Howard, William P. to Elizabeth Hammond 4-23-1856
Howard, William P. to Mary K. Hammond 4-24-1869
Howell, Alexander to Susan S. Wiggs 8-3-1854
Howell, John W. to Jennie (Mrs.) Bevill 11-30-1867 (12-1-1867)
Howell, S. U. to Sallie E. Hensler 10-4-1857
Howell, Thomas to Margaret Ray 11-22-1859 (11-25-1859)
Howerton, William to Missouri C. Barron 11-23-1866 (11-25-1866)
Howlett, Green C. to Virginia Harp 9-15-1842 (9-13?-1842)
Howlett, William P. to Lucinda Patterson 10-1-1866 (10-2-1866)
Howlett, William R. to Ann Eliza Dickson 10-7-1843 (10-12-1843)
Huddleston, David to Margaret Hammon 5-4-1842 (5-5-1842)
Hudson, Francis E. to Eugenia V. Lovelace 2-13-1856 (2-14-1856)
Hudson, George to Harriet Manly 1-26-1869 (1-27-1869)
Hudson, James C. to Emily J. Collier 12-9-1850
Hudson, James P. to Hesperan A. Perry 7-8-1867
Hudson, John H. to Louisa C. Wright 1-31-1848 (2-3-1848)
Hudson, Lawrence T. to Adeliza Fulbright 12-21-1846 (12-22-1846)
Hudson, William A. to Mary A. Henderson 10-5-1841
Hudson, Wm. F. to Margaret A. Hardage 11-17-1870
Hughes, George G. to Sally H. Hill 5-8-1860 (5-9-1860)
Hughes, William R. to Mary Ann Goodall 10-28-1868 (10-29-1868)
Hughes, William to Caroline Patterson 12-28-1840
Humble, William to Frances Stone 5-25-1841 (5-26-1841)
Humble, Willie to Ann Overton 6-8-1840
Humphrey, Wiliam G. to Mary Todd 2-1-1844
Humphreys, Lemual J. to Mollie J. Hart 1-10-1870 (1-12-1870)
Hundley, James to Gilla Fuller 10-23-1849 (10-25-1849)
Hundley, John H. to Elizabeth Anderson 11-26-1860 (11-27-1860)
Hunt, Absolem D. to Fannie M. Guthrie 1-1-1868 (1-2-1868)
Hunt, Avery to Maria L. Thompson 7-4-1844
Hunt, Avery to Sarah C. Dickens 12-18-1841 (12-23-1841)
Hunt, Elisha R. to Mary Ann Price 10-11-1842 (10-13-1842)
Hunt, John F. to Louisa J. Alexander 6-1-1868 (6-3-1868)
Hunt, Robert to Margaret E. Matthews 4-28-1857 (4-29-1857)
Hunt, William H. to Eugenia Lafayette Jackson 12-22-1846
Hunt, William H. to Orleana T. Eppes 4-23-1860 (4-24-1860)
Hunter, John to Ellen L. Thasee 11-9-1843
Huntsman, C. I. to Elizabeth Edward 2-10-1844
Huntsman, Samuel to Mary Horton 10-3-1840
Hurley, George W. to Mary L. W. (Mrs.) Boyd (Becton?) 11-2-1858
Hurst, Shevarts to Matilda Upton 10-31-1842 (10-4?-1842)
Hurt, John R. to Sarah E. Chappell 6-20-1860 (6-21-1860)
Hurt, Robert H. to Susan A. Deberry 6-1-1843 (6-3-1843)
Hutcherson, Saml. to Jane Baker 3-4-1850 (3-7-1850)
Hutchings, C. C. to Martha S. Boykin 8-30-1856
Hutchings, Horace H. to Susan A. (Mrs.) Vann 6-22-1858
Hyde, Jerome B. to Sally A. Raines 4-24-1860 (4-26-1860)
Iffland, Edward to Matilda Wittman 6-29-1869 (7-1-1869)
Ince, James P. to Mary A. Nance 10-22-1855 (10-23-1855)
Ing, Jacob to Martha Perry 2-17-1844
Ingram, Jno. J. W. to Lida McClelland 10-26-1868 (10-27-1868)
Ingram, Thomas to Mary E. Dyson 8-16-1847

Ingram, Thomas, jr. to Mattie Spivey 5-29-1871 (5-31-1871)
Ingram, William G. to Polly Mills 7-2-1848
Inman, Jesse to Sarah A. McAfee 8-16-1869
Innsford, Burtis to Mary Ann Morgan 9-23-1869 (9-24-1870?)
Irven, Jas. M. to Mary Ann Thomas 1-31-1850
Irvey, Samuel to Elizabeth Jackson 5-23-1857
Irvin, John M. to Laviney Jones 10-20-1853
Irvin, Stephen B. to Martha E. Newsom 8-18-1860 (8-19-1860)
Iver, Joseph to A. Bostick 11-1-1842
Jackson, Alexander to Eunice B. Fenner 10-21-1850 (10-22-1850)
Jackson, Alexander to Susan A. Frances 1-24-1843 (1-28-1843)
Jackson, Alfred to Mary Jane Alexander 6-14-1854 (3-23-1854?)
Jackson, Andrew to Rebecca Rasberry 7-22-1841 (7-29-1841)
Jackson, Arthur A. to Hanna H. Tarbutton 3-31-1845 (4-1-1845)
Jackson, Baseley to Lydia Thompson 8-27-1849 (8-28-1849)
Jackson, Charles M. to Lucinda B. Harris 2-15-1859
Jackson, Christopher to Sarah A. Tinsley 2-20-1867 (2-21-1867)
Jackson, Cullen W. to Elizabeth Richards 1-30-1856 (1-31-1856)
Jackson, Dickson to Tobitha Rasberry 5-13-1843 (5-14-1843)
Jackson, Elisha to Ciddy Ann Williams 11-30-1859 (12-8-1859)
Jackson, Elisha to Louisa Williams 1-20-1846 (1-28-1846)
Jackson, Henry J. to Mary Jane Lcy 6-15-1861 (6-16-1861)
Jackson, Henry to Lydia F. Redding 7-16-1856 (7-17-1856)
Jackson, Isaac M. to Sarah Eliza Miller 5-25-1858 (5-26-1858)
Jackson, James M. to Martha Jane Jackson 10-10-1868 (10-14-1868)
Jackson, James W. to Anne Baker 9-23-1850 (9-25-1850)
Jackson, James to Sarah A. McElwee 11-19-1850
Jackson, Jessee to Catharine Benthall 8-2-1854 (8-3-1854)
Jackson, John to Ann M. Robinson 1-29-1842 (2-3-1842)
Jackson, John to Anna Jackson 12-13-1838 (12-20-1838)
Jackson, Meekins N. to Missouri E. Medlin 8-2-1869 (8-8-1869)
Jackson, Noel to Mary Graves 9-11-1841 (9-15-1841)
Jackson, Samuel to Mary Davis 5-22-1839 (5-25-1839)
Jackson, Thomas D. to Angeline Birmingham 12-4-1845 (12-5-1845)
Jackson, Thomas to Nancy Grant 1-15-1845 (1-16-1845)
Jackson, William H. to Elmena L. Stewart 7-25-1838 (7-26-1838)
Jackson, William H. to Frances (Mrs.) Hays 1-20-1858 (1-21-1858)
Jackson, William R. to Catherine Cline 8-7-1854 (8-15-1854)
Jackson, William to Mary S. L. J. Lemond 12-10-1857 (12-31-1857)
Jacobs, James J. to Leminda Clementine March 7-10-1866 (7-12-1866)
James, Jordan D. to Sarah L. McCrory 10-31-1859 (11-2-1859)
James, William P. to Elenora H. Hampton 10-28-1868
Jamison, David W. to Ann Eliza Henderson 12-6-1856
Jane, Henry to Mary Ann Spencer 6-15-1840
Jaretsky, Morris to Caroline Rosenthal 9-16-1869
Jarrall, Boker C. to Lucy A. Lassiter 4-3-1849
Jarrett, Hudson to Elizabeth Adkins 4-11-1856
Jarrett, William to Ann Elizebeth Fitzgerald 12-21-1854 (12-23-1854)
Jarrett, William to Stachey Garrett 2-19-1842 (2-?-1842)
Jean, Elijah to Jane Little 10-8-1850 (10-10-1850)
Jean, Norflet to Susan Bryant 9-17-1856 (9-18-1856)
Jelks, Hinton J. to Azalee M. Humphreys 1-22-1845
Jelks, John R. to Mary E. Lane 1-18-1845 (1-22-1845)
Jelks, Lemuel M. to Nancy P. Laws 5-4-1850 (5-7-1850)
Jelks, W. H. to Mary F. Blaydes 3-10-1852 (3-11-1852)
Jenkins, Eli P. to Susan H. Parker 11-29-1859
Jenkins, George to Lydia M. Armour 2-7-1839 (2-14-1839)
Jenning, Robert W. to Parmelia W. Hall 2-21-1848 (2-22-1848)
Jester, James S. to Martha Ann Davis 1-20-1854 (1-26-1854)
Jett, Thomas J. to Harriet E. Fitz 3-23-1846 (4-9-1846)
Johns, Daniel C. to Margaret E. Westerbrook 11-26-1840
Johnson, Abner to Mary K. Bailey 5-23-1867 (6-3-1867)
Johnson, Albert B. S. to Nancy M. Jones 4-13-1848 (4-18-1848)
Johnson, Augustus W. to Rachel Hadaway 8-17-1866
Johnson, Charles N. to Winnie Williamson 9-24-1867 (9-26-1867)
Johnson, Christopher L., jr. to Mary Jane McAlfee 3-31-1849
Johnson, David W. to Martha C. Williams 2-14-1859 (2-15-1859)
Johnson, Drury to Mary Ann Woods 12-13-1851 (12-14-1851)
Johnson, E. to J. J. Burns 8-28-1858
Johnson, Edwin R. to Frances M Haltom 8-31-1842
Johnson, Eli C. to Sallie E. Norwood 5-24-1870 (5-25-1870)
Johnson, Ezekial R. to Virginia A. Askew 10-26-1869 (10-28-1869)
Johnson, Felix Z. to Nancy E. Bailey 5-23-1867 (6-6-1867)
Johnson, Felix to Mary Williams 6-26-1861
Johnson, Francis M. to Amanda Haltom 9-30-1847

Johnson, George W. to Jemima Gopher 3-22-1853
Johnson, Harrison to Winnefred H. Givens 9-25-1845
Johnson, Henry C. to Ann E. (Mrs.) Kirby 11-8-1869
Johnson, Henry S. to Sarah E. Bealy 4-19-1850 (4-24-1850)
Johnson, Henry T. to Sarah (Mrs.) Betty 9-6-1869 (9-7-1869)
Johnson, Hiram to Bettie C. McLeod 8-14-1855 (8-15-1855)
Johnson, Isaac T. to Mary F. Alexander 10-12-1869 (10-13-1869)
Johnson, James F. to Eliza M. Sanders 6-19-1839
Johnson, James H. to Sarah Goode 6-19-1857
Johnson, James M. to Margaret E. Johnson 10-6-1869
Johnson, James to Lydia Ingram 12-8-1858
Johnson, James to Mary Mullen 11-16-1842 (11-20-1842)
Johnson, Jesse to Cynthia Londu 8-25-1846 (8-26-1846)
Johnson, John B. to Margaret Lacy 2-1-1858 (2-2-1858)
Johnson, John F. to Paralee Wagoner 5-13-1862 (5-14-1862)
Johnson, John H. to Drusilla T. Marsh 12-17-1853 (12-20-1853)
Johnson, John M. to Amanda Givens 6-14-1848 (6-15-1848)
Johnson, L. H. to Altimira Randolph 8-17-1838 (8-19-1838)
Johnson, Lea H. to Susan P. Dearmore 1-24-1853 (1-30-1853)
Johnson, Madison to Elizabeth Barrett 2-13-1849
Johnson, Martha A. to Reuben Sewell 9-29-1841
Johnson, Nathan to Ann Mason 1-10-1857 (1-13-1856?)
Johnson, Nathan to Nancy Goodrich 9-7-1847 (9-14-1847)
Johnson, Nathan to Rachel Thomas 7-29-1850 (7-30-1850)
Johnson, Noel K. to Rosanna Tanner 2-14-1848
Johnson, Obediah to Caroline Crowder 1-31-1870 (2-1-1870)
Johnson, Reuben to Sarah May 1-20-1846 (1-21-1846)
Johnson, Richard to Martha ____ 1-30-1847
Johnson, Richard to Mary Drake 2-27-1845
Johnson, Saml. S. to Sarah E. Hamilton 3-24-1857
Johnson, Samuel S. to Sarah L. Parker 7-3-1854
Johnson, Samuel to Mary E. Temple 3-15-1855
Johnson, Solomon to Mary A. Stewart 1-12-1847 (1-13-1847)
Johnson, Stephen M. to Susan V. Lovelace 1-6-1859
Johnson, William B. to Susan M. Ursery 8-2-1855 (8-9-1855)
Johnson, William C. to Amanda Sanders 12-9-1842
Johnson, William R. to Martha A. Crowder 3-15-1870
Johnson, William T. to Jane Thomas 1-8-1852
Johnson, William to Laurany Branch 2-26-1848 (2-29-1848)
Johnson, William to Sarah Usery 1-13-1848
Johnston, Jep. to Helen Haltom 4-7-1840 (4-30-1840)
Jones, Alexander M. to Martha K. Montgomery 1-26-1848
Jones, Alfred Britton to Sophronia Cathy Jones 7-13-1867 (7-14-1867)
Jones, Alfred H. to Phoebe Jane Clark 2-25-1846 (2-26-1846)
Jones, Allen K. to May T. Phelps 12-23-1854 (12-26-1854)
Jones, Amos W. to Amanda C. Bigelow 4-1-1857 (4-2-1857)
Jones, Andrew J. to Sarah Marcella Fortune 10-5-1868 (10-6-1868)
Jones, Atlas H. to Amanda O'Neil 12-14-1858 (12-16-1858)
Jones, Atlas H. to Martha Jane Stewart 10-11-1855
Jones, Benj. J. to Josephine Cannady 1-11-1867 (1-13-1867)
Jones, Burrell to Sarah Piercy 12-26-1853
Jones, David A. to Fannie E. Allen 3-26-1868
Jones, David A. to Mary A. Harris 11-10-1868 (11-11-1868)
Jones, David H. to Elizabeth Ann Weathers 1-15-1867
Jones, Elijah, jr. to Eveline Gatlin 4-11-1850
Jones, Geo. L. to Sarah C. Jones 1-16-1869 (1-17-1869)
Jones, George F. to Catherine I. Lofte 10-14-1840 (10-15-1840)
Jones, George to Elizabeth Young 4-11-1840
Jones, Guilford to Laura S. Cole 8-28-1850 (9-2-1850)
Jones, Hardin to Emely Wiggins 7-18-1838
Jones, Hardin to Mary Carruthers 1-9-1845 (1-10-1845)
Jones, Henry Bennet to Melissa Elizabeth Pounds 6-8-1866
Jones, Henry C. to Lucinda A. Brown 10-27-1869 (10-28-1869)
Jones, J. Frank to Martha J. Gill 12-14-1870 (12-15-1870)
Jones, James Pinckney to Martha Ann Kirksey 7-13-1858
Jones, John H. (Dr.) to Mattie E. Beaty 10-7-1867
Jones, John J. to Elizabeth Chipman 8-8-1846 (8-11-1846)
Jones, John W. to Becky Ann Bray 10-17-1870 (10-19-1870)
Jones, John to Matilda Jones 2-5-1844 (2-8-1844)
Jones, Joseph B. to Sarah A. Dismuke 8-4-1849
Jones, Manoah F. to M. Mary Goad 7-23-1853 (7-24-1853)
Jones, Nathaniel L. to Saluda Anderson 12-17-1850 (12-19-1850)
Jones, Robert to Mary M. Wilson 11-20-1852 (11-25-1852)
Jones, Sidney P. to Agnes J. Barrier 9-16-1859 (9-18-1859)
Jones, Simeon M. to Eliza Mills 7-2-1848

Jones, William F. to Eliza Ann Richetts 9-15-1858
Jones, William J. to Frances A. Locke 1-20-1852
Jones, Wilson C. to Mary Jane Darby 12-29-1845 (1-1-1845?)
Jones, Wm. W. to Prescilla Taylor 9-19-1870 (9-22-1870)
Jordan, Andrew J. to Mary M. O'Neal 7-31-1857 (8-2-1857)
Jordan, Nelson C. to Martha D. Steward 2-26-1859 (3-1-1859)
Jordon, Alscy to Mary Johnson 7-3-1841 (7-8-1841)
Jordon, Alsey to Jane Ursery 11-20-1845 (11-27-1845)
Jordon, Newton C. to Mary E. Bennett 3-15-1854 (3-23-1854)
Jordon, Raves E. to Fidelia Bledsoe 12-26-1838
Joyce, Harbert to Susan Wheeler 4-14-1845
Joyce, Harbird K. to Elizabeth Joyce 9-14-1853
Joyce, Patrick to Mariah Hallian 7-29-1869
Joyner, Littleton I. to Mary G. Childs 1-2-1844
Joyner, William F. to Nancy A. Dougan 10-22-1849
Justice, James B. to Mary A. Newsom 1-12-1857
Justice, Joel T. to Susan J. Dixon 8-14-1849
Justice, John M. to Martha A. Anderson 5-18-1852
Justice, Wm. H. to Louiser C. Lester 5-1-1866 (5-3-1866)
Kearney, Wm. H. H. to Emeline Turner 3-20-1866 (3-22-1866)
Keaton, James W. to Rebecca Webb 12-14-1859 (12-24-1859)
Keefe, Willington to Catherine Stricklin 3-20-1868
Keelen, Floridore A. to Margaret Ann Neely 7-15-1856 (7-16-1856)
Keelen, Floridore A. to Mary I. Williamson 4-8-1861
Keith, William to Mollie Steward 11-27-1869
Kellar, George W. to Kate Barber 12-21-1870
Kelley, Thomas to Mary O'Conner 8-22-1870 (8-23-1870)
Kelly, James F. to Susan M. Cole 2-20-1855
Kelly, James to Susan McCarver 9-16-1846
Kenaday, David J. to Eliza W. Harris 3-8-1838
Kendall, W. R. to Lydia Wheaton Harrison 12-27-1869
Kendrick, James to Elizabeth Russell 3-12-1856
Kendrick, W. A. to Aley M. Russell 12-28-1859
Kenneday, Samuel D. to Isabella Mews 1-2-1840
Kennedy, John A. to Sarah A. Hefley 10-28-1858 (10-30-1858)
Kenner, James to Nancy Chipman 4-1-1852 (4-3-1852)
Kenner, Thos. W. to Emily Bailey 3-17-1868 (3-18-1868)
Kerby, Martin W. to Mary Ann Bennet 7-2-1857
Key, John G. to R. E. Young 11-10-1868 (11-12-1868)
Key, Martin B. to Vilet Puckett 2-8-1853 (2-10-1853)
Kilpatrick, Andrew to Sarah Wilkins 8-16-1842 (8-18-1842)
Kilpatrick, George to Lucy Bickers 3-15-1856
Kimble, Alexander to Paralee Watt 2-8-1850
Kimbrell, A. H. to M. A. Cock 12-3-1867
Kincaid, THomsa L. to Charlotte Caonia Reid 9-2-1856 (9-3-1856)
Kincaid, Wm. S. to Ann Fry 5-23-1871
Kindrick, James to Julia May 5-6-1844 (5-7-1844)
King, Alfred to Mary L. King 11-27-1839 (11-28-1839)
King, Andrew J. to Sarah L. Jackson 1-27-1868 (1-30-1868)
King, Barney to Laney Whittington 9-29-1856 (10-16-1856)
King, George D. to Roena P. Conger 9-11-1860
King, George W. to Amanda F. Hammond 2-24-1869 (2-25-1869)
King, Hamner to Sarah C. Wilson 9-6-1858 (9-8-1858)
King, Hugh S. to Angelina Jackson 3-26-1850
King, James W. to Mary F. Walker 1-15-1857 (1-18-1857)
King, James to Jane Hamner 11-2-1839 (11-3-1839)
King, James to Mercina Rochella 11-15-1847
King, Jno. Frankliln to Naomie Jane Graves 5-23-1868 (5-26-1868)
King, John Vincent to Susan Jane Neville 1-31-1856 (2-7-1856)
King, Josiah W. to May L. B. Mitchell 12-12-1840
King, Porter B. to Mary Eliza Norvell 6-23-1857 (6-24-1857)
King, William I. G. to Mary Ann King 10-11-1838
King, William to Emily Jackson 7-2-1861 (7-3-1861)
King, Wm. S. to Nancy J. Hammond 1-4-1870 (1-5-1870)
Kirby, Alvis to Martha D. Bennett 12-4-1854 (12-5-1854)
Kirby, Habon to Mary Sowell 1-3-1849
Kirby, Henderson to Eliza Childress 4-26-1848 (4-27-1848)
Kirby, Herod to Elizabeth Dickinson 12-27-1853
Kirby, James A. to Rebecca Jane Hall 12-21-1853 (12-22-1853)
Kirby, Jesse to Nancy M. Bennett 2-24-1846
Kirby, Richard W. to Lydia Bevill 11-12-1870 (11-13-1870)
Kirk, James Y. to Sarah Elizabeth? 11-9-1868
Kirk, Samuel M. to Mary E. Boykin 9-5-1843
Kirkpatrick, Henry to Tranquilla Robertson 8-22-1843
Kirkpatrick, Jno. Alex to Caroline McClish 10-9-1848

Kizer, W. F. to H. (Mrs.) Jones 10-5-1870
Klenk, Frederick to Mary Spencer 1-3-1853
Kyle, Gale H. to Helen M. Perry 7-25-1843
Lackie, James A. to Sarah A. Jackson 2-29-1868
Lacy, Daniel S. to Mary A. Williams 4-14-1858 (4-15-1858)
Lacy, David to Sarah P. Hill 8-10-1842
Lacy, James to Anna Hill 12-14-1850
Lacy, Jno. S. to Sally M. Lawrence 12-1-1868 (12-2-1868)
Lacy, Josiah L. to Alsey Jane Johnson 12-5-1843
Lacy, Levey to Penelope E. Bryant 7-10-1848 (7-12-1848)
Lacy, Thos. to Eliza Ann Hill 10-25-1841 (10-28-1841)
Lacy, William P. to Elizabeth Latham 9-13-1858
Lacy, William P. to Elizabeth Smithwich 7-19-1853 (7-21-1853)
Lacy, William P. to Mary E. Brown 7-15-1867 (7-18-1867)
Lacy, William R. to Ann Eliza B. Lawrence 12-17-1867 (12-18-1867)
Lad, Edward to Mary T. Kimble 10-6-1866 (not executed)
Laman, Thomas to Mahulda A. Hathaway 12-14-1867 (12-18-1867)
Lambert, Franklin to Rachel Sewell 11-15-1855
Lambert, Grandonfield to Martha Estis 9-14-1839 (9-15-1839)
Lancaster, Edwin R. to Susan R. Connally 9-2-1850
Lancaster, John L. to Christiana E. Snider 10-30-1855 (10-31-1855)
Landers, Robt. A. to Mary E. Anderson 12-17-1869
Landers, William T. to Sarah J. Wood 12-17-1869 (12-19-1869)
Lane, Brandon to Tennie Bumpass 1-14-1871 (1-15-1871)
Lane, Cullud to Elizabeth Loving 1-6-1841 (2-16-1841)
Lane, John Jay to Alice Hubbard 2-28-1859 (3-2-1859)
Lane, John P. to Hepzhibad Watkins 12-17-1844 (12-19-1844)
Lane, Thomas C. to Christinna Turnage 3-4-1852 (3-8-1852)
Lane, Thomas F. to Allia G. Woodfolk 11-11-1871 (11-12-1871)
Laney, Calvert to Sarah Anderson 1-19-1846
Laney, John A. to Laura E. Cox 9-12-1871 (9-14-1871)
Langford, Abram B. to Rebecca V. Carter 5-16-1860 (5-17-1860)
Langford, Andrew B. to Cora C. Conger 8-14-1866 (8-15-1866)
Langford, Elias to Nancy C. Piercy 3-6-1850 (3-8-1850)
Langford, Joseph E. to Judia H. Butts 1-2-1860 (1-4-1860)
Langford, Littleberry to Adeline Nichol 2-1-1855 (2-4-1855)
Langford, W. B. to Bettie Ewell 7-26-1870
Langford, Willis to Elizabeth Herrington 9-24-1850 (9-25-1850)
Langston, Calvin to Martha Dawkins 2-2-1839
Langston, John C. to Sarah McGraw 11-8-1841
Langston, Major to Susan Croom 1-10-1843
Lanier, John C. to Eliza A. Robinson 10-6-1853
Lanier, Porter to Mary F. Powell 12-17-1867
Lassiter, Jesse W. to Emily E. Douglass 2-6-1871 (2-7-1871)
Lassiter, Silas to Caroline Webb 9-8-1860 (9-9-1860)
Lassiter, Silas to Emily Kerksey 1-1-1857 (1-2-1857)
Lassiter, Silas to Minerva Copeland 1-12-1855 (1-16-1855)
Lassiter, William to Elizabeth Duffey 4-3-1852 (4-7-1852)
Latham, William H. to Malinda Moore 10-31-1871
Latham, William H. to Mollie L. Haynes 11-24-1870 (12-1-1870)
Latham, William to Sarah F. Davis 7-21-1856 (7-24-1856)
Latta, Matthew F. to Margaret A. Ozier 9-8-1852
Lawrence, Elias to Sarah Davis 12-3-1840 (12-8-1840)
Lawrence, Elisha to Jane Piercy 12-26-1848
Lawrence, James H. to Frizzy A. Todd 12-8-1846 (12-9-1846)
Lawrence, Sawnee B. to Zilpha L. Taylor 10-22-1868
Lawry, James to Abagail Faulkner 6-27-1859 (6-28-1859)
Laws, George W. to Angelina Baker 9-13-1850
Layn, William W. to Mary Jane Wadley 3-10-1856 (3-16-1856)
Lea, E. W. to Elizabeth Haynes 3-4-1850 (3-7-1850)
Lea, John F. to Mary A. McClish 5-14-1855 (5-16-1855)
Lea, John G. to Nancy J. Fulbright 5-17-1854 (5-?-1854)
Lea, Lorenzo (Rev.) to Fannie (Mrs.) Cobb 3-29-1858 (3-30-1858)
Leake, Lemuel to Eveline London 3-30-1849 (4-1-1849)
Leake, Thos. H. to Martha Ann Hicks 7-14-1846
Leathers, William to Amanda Robinson 6-21-1844
Ledbetter, James R. to Martha Weaver 11-3-1841
Ledbetter, John C. to Mary E. Johnson 11-27-1852 (11-28-1852)
Lee, Ephraim J. to Mary C. E. York 6-1-1858
Lee, Joshua C. to H. V. Shumate 12-1-1853
Lee, Thomas H. to Elizabeth A. Webb 9-16-1853
Leeper, Guy to Lizzie J. Hurt 1-6-1869
Leggett, Francis M. to Nancy Ann Emerson 8-7-1867 (8-11-1867)
Leonard, Jno. W. to Martha E. Inman 2-6-1871
Lester, John M. to Elizabeth Anderson 7-2-1838 (7-19-1838)

Levy, Enoch W. to Elizabeth Edwards 10-11-1842 (10-13-1842)
Lewellen, Robert J. to Frances Moore 9-4-1850
Lewellen, W. B. to Mary Anderson 1-30-1871 (2-1-1871)
Lewis, Andrew Jackson to Lavica Parker Morrow 2-25-1859 (3-1-1859)
Lewis, Benjamin E. to Sophronia A. Fulghum 8-23-1854 (8-25-1854)
Lewis, Benjamin to Mary Nelson 11-2-1856
Lewis, James M. to Jemima J. Gately 10-25-1853
Lewis, Jesse H. to Mary E. Hardy 12-30-1848
Lewis, John T. to Olivia J. Rogers 7-27-1857 (7-29-1857)
Lewis, William A. to Elizabeth (Mrs.) Fortner 3-19-1870 (3-24-1870)
Lewis, William R. to Sarah A. Warmoth 3-17-1852 (3-18-1852)
Liggett, Hampton to Emeline Harris 11-21-1838 (11-25-1838)
Lile, John W. to Mary Jane Doak 5-27-1843
Lindsey, Robert S. to Ella Tomlin 10-24-1866
Lintchicum, John H. to Margarett L. Goodrich 8-19-1841
Little, Allen to Louisa Reese 7-6-1847
Little, William H. to Mary Temple 7-12-1847
Littlepage, Powhattan B. to Mary Jane Dearmore 4-20-1841
Lloyd, Joseph J. to Elizabeth Raines 10-20-1845
Lockard, William W. to Sarah E. Anderson 11-7-1853 (11-10-1853)
Locke, George to Leah F. Rhodes 6-10-1868 (6-11-1868)
Locke, Rollin J. to Mary McIntosh 11-30-1848
Loftin, William to Sarah Johnson 12-8-1852
Long, Benj. C. to Margaret Ann King 5-28-1868
Long, Green Berry to Minerva Millen 7-24-1843 (11-27-1843)
Long, James H. to Addie V. Brooks 1-22-1867
Long, John B. to Eliza J. Hardage 12-7-1847 (12-?-1847)
Long, William to Celia Kerr 6-16-1845
Long, Wm. H. to Bettie Fossett 12-25-1869 (12-20?-1869)
Longhorn, James L. to Margarett M. Gladney 11-22-1842
Longmire, Wm. Martin to Martha Ann Walters no date
Lovallette, Albert Talmedge to Sallie Cornelia Day 10-6-1855 (10-9-1855)
Love, Alonzo F. to Emma Haughton 4-25-1871 *
Love, John B. to Sarah Ann Bruton 6-13-1848 (6-14-1848)
Love, John M. to Elizabeth Acree 10-12-1869 (10-14-1869)
Love, William K. to Emily B. Jones 3-14-1840 (3-17-1840)
Lovelace, Wm. O. to Lureny Sanford 12-26-1853 (1-11-1854)
Lowden, John to Margarett Jester 3-1-1841
Lowdermilk, James W. to Lucinda C. Faucett 5-7-1870 (5-8-1870)
Lowe, Granville C. to Sarah M. Bevill 12-22-1859
Lowry, Robert O. to Nancy B. (Mrs.) Hardgraves 1-19-1867 (1-20-1867)
Luckey, Joseph to Susan Baker 12-24-1845 (12-27-1845)
Luckey, Samuel to Holland P. Dillard 10-15-1838 (10-16-1838)
Lumpkins, George W. to Margarett Goad 8-2-1848 (8-3-1848)
Lunnon, Hinson to Elizabeth Mitchell 11-27-1843
Lunsford, Alfred L. to Frances L. Jones 12-20-1843 (12-21-1843)
Lunsford, Burtis to Mary Ann Young 5-27-1843 (6-8-1843)
Lunsford, George A. to Susan Wilson 2-19-1861
Luron, Daniel to Susan Andrews 3-18-1840 (3-19-1840)
Lusk, James M. to Malvina Joiner 1-12-1871
Lynch, Samuel C. to Mary Jane Swan 1-7-1846
Lyon, Thomas to Adeline Sewell 6-20-1870 (7-3-1870)
Lyon, Wade W. to Mary Reid 11-2-1869
Lyon, William J. to Niecy Carroll 4-17-1861
Lyon, William T. to Rebecca King 1-1-1842 (1-3-1842)
Lytle, Gardner to Mary Elizabeth Lewis 11-12-1867 (11-13-1867)
Maddox, William J. to Mary Jane Altman 10-27-1856 (10-19?-1856)
Mahaffy, James G. to Mary Ann Taylor 3-26-1838
Mahon, George T. to Mary H. Kirkpatrick 2-7-1848 (2-?-1848)
Mainor, Nathan I. to Fannie H. May 2-10-1868 (2-12-1868)
Mallory, Wm. M. to Victoria Laney 10-26-1870 (10-28-1870)
Manley, William B. to Eliza J. Johnson 10-21-1850
Manley, William W. to Lydia A. Johnson 6-15-1860 (6-17-1860)
Manly, William to Milly Ann Morphis 11-6-1841 (11-14-1841)
Mann, John G. to Harriet Ann Long 6-27-1860 (6-28-1860)
Mann, Jos. T. to Sarah E. Tomlin 4-22-1850
Mann, Robert to Susan Walker 7-29-1844 (7-31-1844)
Mann, Willis to Sarah Taylor 9-10-1842 (9-11-1842)
Maphey, Stephen to Eliza Grant 6-6-1838
March, Daniel O. to Emeline Hopper 4-6-1852
Mark, Jesse to Kate (Mrs.) Williams 6-25-1870 (6-26-1870)
Marks, James A. to Margarett C. Russell 6-19-1845

Marley, Joseph to Mary E. Edwards 9-20-1853 (9-22-1853)
Marley, Young F. to Lizzie C. Verser 5-19-1857 (5-20-1857)
Marlow, William H. to Mahulda Cozart 12-25-1852 (12-26-1852)
Maroney, James T. to Hannah Halton 8-24-1854
Marsh, James W. to Mary C. Richardson 7-30-1847 (8-1-1847)
Marsh, John M. to Harriott Isom 6-27-1839
Marsh, Joshua B. to Sarah Butler 4-3-1848
Marsh, Thomas P. to Mary A. V. Toone 12-26-1842 (12-29-1842)
Marshall, William C. to Bettie Anderson 5-3-1870
Martin, Edward J. to Dora Crisp 1-14-1869 (1-19-1869) *
Martin, John S. to Mary F. Black 3-8-1870
Martin, W. James to Mary Funderburk 3-4-1868 (3-8-1868)
Mask, Jesse to Adeline Hammond 5-16-1855
Mason, Abner W. to Catherine Piercy 1-9-1850
Mason, David G. to Cynthia Dockins 7-3-1849
Mason, Isaac H. to Mary A. E. Cox 9-21-1846 (9-24-1846)
Mason, James A. to Ann E. Person 5-15-1871 (5-16-1871)
Mason, Joseph D. to Eliza Bigelow 9-17-1844 (9-18-1844)
Mason, Levi W. to Louisa C. Baker 1-1-1858 (1-5-1858)
Mason, Robert W. to Martha C. Herron 3-30-1859 (3-31-1859)
Mason, Rufus M. to Eunica A. Doake 10-5-1850
Mason, William B. to Aquilla Ann Brown 8-4-1841
Mason, Wm. H. to Laura Hudgens 6-19-1871 (6-22-1871)
Massey, Allen N. to Nancy A. N. Shaw 1-23-1867
Massey, Andrew to Susan Boyett 12-3-1844 (12-4-1844)
Massey, Richard to Rebecca Boyd 2-13-1841
Massey, William Henry to Mary Elizabeth Adams 2-16-1859 (2-17-1859)
Massey, Wm. H. to Mary E. Copeland 1-13-1855 (1-16-1855)
Mathews, George to Martha Hart 8-26-1867 (8-29-1867)
Mathews, Granville to Mary Marsh 12-17-1840 (12-19-1840)
Mathews, Robert S. to Nancy L. Hart 10-29-1866 (10-30-1866)
Mathis, Cyrus E. to Wilmouth J. Wat 10-30-1844
Mathis, James W. to Sarah Jane Roach 6-19-1869
Mathis, Lorenzo D. to Jane Simpson 7-18-1868 (7-19-1868)
Mathis, Robt. N. to Susan H. Combs 2-18-1867 (2-20-1867)
Matlock, Henry to Charlotte E. Wilkins 12-31-1855 (1-1-1855?)
Matthews, Edward to Mattie A. Smith 4-13-1859 (4-14-1859)
Matthews, James to A. M. Parrish 7-14-1840 (7-16-1840)
Matthews, John H. to Bettie Robinson 12-29-1869 *
Matthews, John J. to Mary A. Bostick 9-2-1847
Matthews, Samuel J. to Martha E. Richarson 12-7-1868 (12-8-1868)
Maxwell, W. L. to M. A. Garrett 5-10-1848
May, Christopher C. to Martha Ann Neill 4-22-1852 (4-28-1852)
May, Elias W. to Lucy A. Golden 12-2-1846 (12-3-1846)
May, Elias W. to Seleta West 7-24-1838
May, Newett N. to Sarah A. Lanier 11-3-1858
May, Reuben M. to Sarah E. Pullum 2-15-1854
May, Reuben M. to Sarah E. Russell 3-14-1855 (3-15-1855)
May, Robert M. to Mary C. Wilson 3-31-1866
May, Thomas G. to Sarah A. Ursery 10-31-1855 (11-1-1855)
Mayfield, G. W. to B. H. Morrow 9-12-1853 (9-13-1853)
Mayfield, George A. to Mollie McDurmit 3-22-1869 (3-24-1869)
Maynard, John M. to P. M. Thomas 4-28-1855 (5-1-1855)
Mayo, Council B. to Caroline Johnson 11-8-1843
Mayo, Council B. to Sarah A. Walsh 2-1-1870
Mayo, Fredrick to Catherine Bunton 3-5-1843
Mayo, Hardy to Sarah Givens 3-31-1853
Mayo, Joel to Cornelia A. Campbell 12-13-1855
Mayo, Jonas to Susan Fussel 3-8-1848 (3-9-1848)
Mayo, Remon to Ann E. Boon 1-10-1839
Mays, Alfred H. to Ann E. McCoy 11-7-1859 (11-8-1859)
Mays, James G. to Cyrena Jane Weaver 6-24-1859 (6-28-1859)
Mays, John W. to Paralee Simmons 1-23-1869 (1-25-1869)
McAdams, Edwin J. to Mary E. Dickson 1-21-1870 (1-30-1870)
McAdoo, E. L. to Marian Ozier 2-10-1846 (2-15-1846)
McAdoo, Ephraim L. to Frances Crowder 1-8-1859 (1-11-1859)
McAdoo, William H. to Nannie J. Duvall 12-20-1858 (12-21-1858)
McAdoo, William H. to Susan A. Haynes 3-18-1856
McAfee, Asa to Margaret Jackson 12-6-1866
McAfee, William J. to Jane C. Barnett 3-16-1858 (3-25-1858)
McAlelley, George P. to Mary Ann Goodrich 12-12-1850
McAlexander, James to Martha Smith 2-23-1852 (2-24-1852)
McAllister, Geo. D. to Julia C. C. Cole 7-8-1862
McBride, James to Mary Norton 12-15-1845 (12-18-1845)

McCafflin, Laurence to Susan L. Wigg 5-5-1870
McCain, Jacob to Mary Shoemaker 12-14-1844
McCall, Henry to Rebecca f. Bolin 12-29-1845 (12-30-1845)
McCarlin, William C. to Elizabeth Robinson 2-10-1862
McCarrus, John to Mary Ann Greeds 10-22-1838
McCarver, Isaac to Martha Glidewell 8-6-1849
McCasburn, John C. to Elizabeth W. Cole 3-24-1846
McCaslin, John M. to Sallie Barnett 5-10-1870
McClamrock, Harrison to Caroline E. Angus 12-16-1844 (12-17-1844)
McClanahan, A. S. to Laura E. Caruthers 12-18-1860
McClanahan, Samuel to Laura V. Fortune 12-28-1858 (12-29-1858)
McClellan, Robert N. to Elizabeth Ann Williams 11-20-1842 (12-1-1842)
McClellan, Robert N. to Henrietta Briggance 5-25-1860 (5-27-1860)
McClish, Andrew J. to Martha Jnae Johnson 12-27-1856 (12-28-1856)
McClohm, Joseph W. to Ann Gladney 5-10-1842 (5-12-1842)
McClure, James to Nancy N. Watt 9-22-1846
McCollum, Peter to Roxannah Estes 1-28-1854
McCook, Wm. H. to Dorothy Ann (Mrs.) Baker 3-18-1871 (3-19-1871)
McCorkle, Blythe to Sarah M. Jones 12-13-1855
McCorkle, Eli to Adaline Roberts 12-27-1847 (12-28-1847)
McCorry, Henry W. to Corriana A. Henderson 12-11-1838
McCoy, Charles to Elizabeth Morphis 12-26-1838 (12-29-1838)
McCoy, Ezekiel T. to Eady Mozelle Boon 10-22-1845 (10-23-1845)
McCoy, John to Martha A. Taylor 5-5-1870 (5-8-1870)
McCoy, Newton A. to Martha E. Hunter 11-7-1855 (11-?-1855)
McCracken, Robert L. to Caroline Fitz 2-2-1858
McCree, Davie to Lavenia J. McAdoo 1-20-1858
McCutchen, J. Thomas to Anna Adamson 11-4-1867 (11-5-1867)
McDade, Bennett W. to Susan J. Davidson 2-13-1858 (2-17-1858)
McDaniel, William to Eliza Jane Hart 11-7-1857 (11-11-1857)
McDonald, James M. to Sarah C. Maddind 11-27-1844 (11-28-1844)
McDonald, John to Mary E. Pettus 11-10-1857
McDonald, Joseph E. to Emma C. Warlick 10-3-1859 (10-6-1859)
McDonald, Saml. D. to Emma C. (Mrs.) McDonald 11-3-1869
McDummitt, WilliamD. to Asinith Bledsoe 12-24-1839
McDurmit, Thomas J. to Emeline Bowling 1-17-1857 (1-18-1857)
McDurmit, Wm. H. C. to Mary Abagail Jones 4-27-1859
McElwee, John W. to Cynthia J. Kirkpatrick 8-28-1847
McElwee, John W. to Cynthia J. Prendergrast 8-31-1847
McElwee, Saml. S. to Hannah Walker 1-27-1855
McEwin, John to Nancy H. Olahan 2-15-1838
McFadden, James to Catherine Clark 2-4-1869 (2-9-1869)
McFarland, William J. to Paralee F. King 10-29-1850
McFarland, William J. to Parthenia A. E. Dungan 2-23-1856 (12-25-1856)
McFarlen, John to Mmary Smithwick 11-25-1843
McFarlin, Dennis to Hepsy Ann Robinson 8-5-1852
McFarlin, Henry to Angelina Belton 7-27-1850 (7-28-1850)
McFarlin, James V. to America C. Poindexter 7-5-1859 (7-7-1859)
McFarlin, Joseph to Susan King 4-15-1861 (4-16-1861)
McFarlin, Washington to Armitty Brogden 1-8-1858 (6-23-1858)
McGee, Jno. H. to Rachel Estes 11-11-1868
McGevany, John to Susan McClabahan 10-30-1838 (11-1-1838)
McGhee, Benjamin to Lively Rushing 8-22-1846
McGhee, John Wesley to Cara Nipper 9-23-1856
McGill, Thomas to Caroline H. Connelly 2-2-1862 *
McGill, Wm. A. to Sallie K. McKnight 3-9-1867
McGowan, J. G. to Ann E. Ferri 9-26-1866 (9-27-1866)
McGowan, Richard to Malvina H. Childress 8-7-1841 (8-8-1841)
McGowan, Richard to Mary McFarland 11-21-1842
McGuire, George W. to Martha Jane Eddins 11-11-1856
McIlwain, Ephraim to Maggie J. Cozart 12-4-1866 (12-5-1866)
McIntosh, John to Hannah E. Hart 3-6-1839 (3-7-1839)
McIver, Daniel to Virginia B. Harrison 1-10-1843 (1-11-1843)
McJones, Ira M. to Sarah M. Garland 8-22-1839
McKee, Wm. H. to Lemisa R. Birdsong 9-12-1871 (9-13-1871)
McKenna, William J. to Rosa Ann Williams 10-11-1848 (10-12-1848)
McKey, James W. to Sarah Jane Moore 9-28-1857 (10-1-1857)
McKimon, Loftin to Elizabeth Sherman 3-4-1850
McKinney, William J. to Elizabeth T. (Mrs.) Davis 8-9-1858 (8-10-1858)
McKnight, Hamilton J. to Margaret K. Black 11-2-1847
McKnight, James M. to Mary Robley 1-18-1845

McKnight, Richard T. to Catherine Reeves 12-31-1844 (1-2-1845)
McKnight, Robert F. to Mary Jane Bradford 4-7-1859
McKnight, Robert M. to Louisanna E. Reeves 4-13-1839
McKnight, Samuel W. to Mary Louisa Sweeny 4-10-1856
McKnight, William F. to Mary E. Lester 4-15-1856
McKoy, John C. to Irena McDonald 9-7-1852 (9-9-1852)
McLemore, Robert N. to Mary Ann Eliza Boykin 9-1-1855 (9-5-1855)
McMahan, Andrew to Lucenda Ruff 5-4-1840
McMahan, J. G. to F. J. Harrell 9-26-1855 (9-27-1855)
McMaster, Saml. T. to Nancy Elizabeth Black 10-4-1858
McMaster, Thos. J. to Lidy E. Spencer 1-12-1869
McMellon, Duncan to Rebecca Ewing 11-21-1840
McMillan, Archibald to Julia A. F. Young 10-23-1856 (10-26-1856)
McMillan, James to Mary Jane Marlow 2-26-1850
McMillan, John H. to Mary Ann Speh 10-9-1871 (10-10-1871)
McMillan, Joshua to Nancy M. McMillan 8-1-1839 (8-7-1839)
McMillan, Valentine to Elizabeth Downing 1-25-1843 (1-27-1843)
McMillin, Wm. to Clementine C. Williamson 2-2-1869
McMullins, Albert T. to Joannah Boles 6-6-1859 (6-9-1859)
McNail, Thomas A. to Emily Jane Herron 11-5-1855 (11-7-1855)
McNeal, John H. to Elizabeth Rogers 9-21-1850
McNeely, James B. to Sarah S. Bradberry 3-19-1586 (3-20-1856)
McNeely, Louis to Mary A. Holmes 1-31-1854 (2-1-1854)
McRoe, James to Olivia Day 10-10-1842
McVey, Reuben to Jane Pemberton 6-6-1844 (6-11-1844)
McWilliams, Robert R. to Mary Moore 2-29-1839
Meals, Daniel J. to Sarah H. Morrow 12-6-1843 (12-7-1843)
Meals, John M. to Elizabeth E. Morrow 12-3-1846 (12-24-1846)
Meals, John M. to Margaret E. (Mrs.) Caruthers 1-19-1867 (1-22-1867)
Medlin, Bradley to Susan Rains 10-14-1840
Medlin, George C. to Jane Knight 1-20-1852 (1-21-1852)
Medlin, James H. to Rebecca M. McWilliams 10-9-1847 (10-13-1847)
Medlin, James L. to Susan A. Holyfield 4-16-1850
Medlin, James M. to Catherine Burrow 12-18-1850
Medlin, Jno. T. to Nancy A. Jones 4-12-1871 (4-13-1871)
Medlin, Moses to Dilly William 8-14-1867 (3-10-1870)
Medlin, Petser to Mary R. Perkins 11-3-1853 *
Medlin, Wiley to Emily Jones 9-9-1868 (9-10-1868)
Medling, Joseph L. to Elizabeth R. Bradberry 5-11-1838 (5-17-1838)
Mercer, Thomas B. to Catherine Chism 12-4-1838
Meriwether, James G. to Lizzie Deberry 1-24-1871 (1-25-1871)
Meriwether, Matt D. to Lydia A. Johnson 11-14-1860 (11-15-1860)
Meriwether, Thomas M. to Elvira Edmonston 7-16-1845
Meriwether, William H. to Rebecca F. Deberry 12-15-1838
Merriwether, David J. to Elizabeth Tarver 10-31-1849
Merriwether, Wm. P. to Judie A. Henning 12-20-1859 (12-21-1860)
Metcalf, John A. to Fannie Williamson 3-3-1858 (3-7-1858)
Mickens, Nat to Mary (Mrs.) McCain 5-23-1861 (5-28-1861)
Mickum, John to Mariah Williamson 9-18-1847
Midgett, Ashley to Mary E. Knight 5-6-1850 (5-8-1850)
Midyett, Nicholas L. to Louisa A. McIver 11-1-1856 (11-2-1856)
Milan, Claudius L. to Mary E. Attkisson 6-24-1868 (6-25-1868)
Miller, Andrew J. to Elizabeth Ellen Duncan 6-20-1866
Miller, George W. to Eliza Glidewell 8-4-1846 (8-5-1846)
Miller, Isaac to Sarah Farris 6-11-1853
Miller, John to Sally Kelly 2-18-1846
Miller, Nathaniel to Evalina L. Glidwell 8-27-1856
Miller, Nowes to Louisa Heidleburg 10-11-1842 (10-12-1842)
Miller, Rolin to Martha Rider 10-14-1846 (10-15-1846)
Miller, Stephen to Harriett Garland 2-27-1838
Miller, Stephen to Louisa Jane Gladney 9-28-1849 (10-2-1849)
Miller, Vann to Nancy Thurman 4-20-1854
Milligan, Harvey N. to Addie C. Hutcherson 11-16-1870
Milling, John to Lucinda E. Kincaide 5-11-1869
Mills, Andrew to Miranda A. Harris 12-17-1853
Mills, Benj. F. to Jane D. Vevely 8-8-1866 (8-16-1866)
Mills, John to Lucy Butler 12-4-1852 (12-9-1852)
Mills, Marion to Ellen Harris 5-25-1868 (5-26-1868)
Mitchell, L. B. to Louissanna Hardgrave 6-24-1839 (6-26-1839)
Mitchell, Luther N. to Darcas Bruison 8-5-1848
Mitchell, Mark to Margaret Lattimer 9-13-1853
Moize, Alfred to Bettie Moore 12-16-1867 (12-19-1867)
Moize, Lafayette to May Ann King 7-4-1850 (7-10-1850)
Monroe, Frank to Ella Fenner 11-24-1869

Montgomery, Hugh A. to Tabitha E. Hopper 2-21-1848 (2-23-1848)
Montgomery, Hugh to Mariah Williams 12-6-1843 (12-7-1843)
Montgomery, James G. to Rebecca Robinson 9-16-1841
Montgomery, William to Jane H. Boyd 3-12-1852 (3-16-1852)
Moody, David T. to Eleanor Midgett 12-19-1848 (12-20-1848)
Moon, Vicent to Sarah P. Haston 7-3-1839 (7-9-1839)
Moon, Wilson to Ann Covington 9-19-1842
Moore, Alfred P. to Eliza Jane Ferrill 10-19-1870 (10-20-1870)
Moore, Alphus P. to Temperance Brooks 12-24-1841 (12-30-1841)
Moore, George B. to Mary Jackson 1-30-1839
Moore, George W. to Sallie R. Jones 3-19-1868
Moore, Gillam J. to Mollie H. Perry 11-15-1871
Moore, Green B. to Lydia Holyfield 1-26-1847
Moore, Green to Mary Kind 1-17-1855
Moore, James M. to Letitia F. Hearn 10-5-1860 (10-9-1860)
Moore, John T. to Arabella Pope 12-28-1867
Moore, Moses to Ann F. Carrington 1-25-1840 (1-29-1840)
Moore, Nathan to Elizabeth C. Brown 9-4-1848
Moore, Raleigh to Sarah J. Nelson 9-22-1852
Moore, Robert C. to Malisa Sanders 10-31-1848
Moore, S. P. to Rebecca A. Small 11-14-1866 (11-15-1866)
Moore, Stephen to Sarah Diffy 3-6-1840
Moore, Sydney to Martha Jane Oniel 12-14-1853 (12-15-1853)
Moore, William A. to Epsey Ann Bradbury 1-15-1846
Moore, William R. to Maria Stewart 12-22-1847 (12-23-1847)
Moore, Wilson to Rebecca Quinley 1-22-1849 (2-3-1849)
Mooring, H. L. to A. B. Butler 2-27-1854 (3-2-1854)
Mooring, Henry L. to Catherine Hastings 1-4-1858
Mooring, John A. to Charlotte Mary Connell 12-20-1860 (12-21-1860)
Mooring, John C. to Eliza Jane Christian 3-9-1850 (3-12-1850)
Mooring, John W. to Sophia P. Jones 1-15-1858 (1-18-1858)
Morgan, Allen W. to Jane P. Hearn 3-18-1859
Morgan, Emmet T. to Sarah A. Wilson 7-27-1858 (8-10-1858)
Morgan, Thomas Jefferson to Sarah A. Barnes 12-15-1855 (12-18-1855)
Morgan, Thomas P. to Amanda M. Jones 11-2-1850 (11-3-1850)
Morphis, George to Elizabeth Mauldin 1-10-1842 (1-11-1842)
Morphis, George to Mary Roberts 1-6-1849
Morphis, Solomon to Mary Sanders 11-21-1846
Morrill, John M. to Georgiana H. Lea 4-23-1855
Morris, John B. to Parthenia Stewart 5-4-1854
Morris, Robert D. to Mary M. Glover 12-3-1850 (12-5-1850)
Morris, William H. to Louisa Jackson 1-25-1859
Morrow, Samuel J. to S. J. (Mrs.) Edwards 2-6-1868
Morrow, Samuel J. to Sarah F. McKnight 1-27-1852
Morse, John to Louisa Brooks 11-17-1852
Morse, Thos. to Sarah Meacham 2-11-1841
Morton, Wm. T. to Mollie E. Fancher 5-8-1871 (5-9-1871)
Mosley, Thomas F. to Mary Harrison 5-29-1871
Mosley, Thos. F. to Sarah King 1-4-1870
Moss, James H. to Emma T. Gordan 1-18-1869 (1-20-1869)
Mote, James C. to Mary Ann Taylor 9-12-1845
Moxey, Geo. A. to S. P. Winfrey 9-18-1866 (9-19-1866)
Moxley, Joseph W. to Sophia A. Rogers 11-10-1868 (11-11-1868)
Mulherin, Samuel H. to Rebecca? J. Skillern 8-2-1860
Mullins, Alexander to Rebecca Nelson 11-21-1870 (11-22-1870)
Mullins, Edward A. to Eliza A. Summers 12-10-1849
Mullins, Harvey to Sarah C. Barnett 9-11-1866 (9-12-1866)
Mullins, Thomas G. to Hannah T. Wiggins 9-10-1862 (9-11-1862)
Munn, John to May Ann Langford 5-20-1841
Munn, William to Sarah Lovitt 11-13-1839
Murchison, John R. to Susan (Mrs.) Trice 10-4-1869 (10-5-1869)
Murchison, Murdoch M. to Rhoda Vance 11-7-1852
Murchison, W. A. to U. C. Cason 11-16-1847
Murphy, John C. to Sarah E. Freeman 9-30-1868
Murrell, Alexander C. to Lavinia Swink 9-9-1871 (9-13-1871)
Murrill, John to Alithia Campbell 1-5-1850
Murry, Fountain to Jennie Bingham 8-10-1867 (8-13-1867)
Murtaugh, Thomas to Susan Reeves 2-9-1869 (2-11-1869)
Muse, James M. to Eugenia A. Brooks 11-13-1868
Muse, Thomas C. to Elizabeth C. Collier 9-5-1855 (9-12-1855)
Nanney, Addison to Mourning Norton 1-29-1852
Nanny, Hugh to Elizabeth R. Hart 11-26-1853 (11-29-1853)
Nanny, James W. to Margaret Nail 6-21-1840 (6-22-1840)
Nash, John to Martha E. Dent 10-31-1847 (11-1-1847)

Neal, Benjamin to Susan Wood 11-21-1846 (11-23-1846)
Neal, D. C. to Anna Marks 6-26-1867
Neal, Dempsey C. to Mary Ann Reavis 11-13-1856
Neal, John M. to Lucinda A. Hudson 11-23-1841 (11-25-1841)
Neal, Newton to Mary Brown 10-4-1858
Neely, Johns R. to Margarett A. L. Wells 10-29-1845 (10-31-1845)
Neely, Moses S. to Julia E. Newbern 10-25-1859 (10-30-1859)
Neely, Robert C. to Nancy (sen.) Williamson 9-14-1858
Neely, Robert M. to Martha E. McClish 10-12-1859
Neely, Samuel to Archelius Ann (Mrs.) Fogg 6-29-1858 (7-1-1858)
Neely, Thomas I. to Charity Springfield 1-29-1840
Neely, Thomas I. to Susan M. Teagart 7-31-1838 (8-4-1838)
Neely, William C. to Caroline Meacham 4-2-1852 (2-5-1852?)
Neff, Wm. D. to Mary Ann Inman 12-27-1869 (12-29-1869)
Neill, Gilbreth to Hibernia A. Person 12-8-1869
Neilson, Joseph D. to Pattie Hurt 4-30-1867 (5-1-1867)
Nelson, Charles H. to Louisa Walls 10-14-1856
Nelson, Charles to Emily B. Rooks 9-9-1869
Nelson, James H. to Christina Thompson 10-31-1859 (11-1-1859)
Nelson, James H. to Sideous I. Johnson 11-1-1842 (11-3-1842)
Nelson, Jarrett to Rebecca Thompson 12-21-1846
Nelson, John P. S. to Mary Ann Barnett 5-24-1870 (5-26-1870)
Nelson, John to Mary Jane Nelson 8-20-1859 (8-21-1859)
Nelson, John to Mary McFarlin 2-14-1846
Nelson, Noah to Ann Elizabeth Johnson 9-24-1850 (9-25-1850)
Nelson, W. T. to Anna M. Deberry 12-20-1870 (12-21-1870)
Nelson, William H. to Alice Matthews 12-5-1867 (12-8-1867)
Nelson, William H. to Elizabeth S. McAfee 11-22-1856 (12-1-1856)
Nelson, William H. to Nancy Buffalo 3-19-1846 (not executed)
Nelson, jr., John to Ruth C. McAfee 12-22-1845
Nesbitt, Thomas J. to Sophia E. Swink 4-20-1870 (4-21-1870)
Nevill, David W. to Sarah F. Thedford 10-20-1871 (10-22-1871)
Nevill, James D. to Nancy A. Davidson 12-22-1866 (12-23-1866)
Newbern, Darius D. to Elizabeth A. Hill 3-25-1850
Newbern, George W. to Louisa C. Hill 8-10-1852
Newbern, William Y. to Sarah B. Jeffrys 7-2-1840 (7-7-1840)
Newby, Oswill to Orabella Strayhorn 12-18-1841 (12-22-1841)
Newman, Dawson D. to Isabella Clemintine King 12-15-1843 (12-21-1843)
Newman, Wallace to Eliza White 10-30-1844
Newman, William W. to Margaret E. Raines 12-8-1857 (12-10-1857)
Newsom, James A. to Nancy M. Kittrell 9-14-1854 (9-19-1854)
Newsom, James E. to Mary Q. McKnight 8-29-1854
Newsom, Jenkins to Eliza A. Bond 4-17-1850
Newsom, John F. to Susan Epperson 5-4-1853
Newsom, John W. to Elizabeth Ann Meadows 3-6-1855 (3-7-1855)
Newsom, Lemuel to Nancy E. Harris 1-4-1856
Newsom, Robert N. to Nancy (Mrs.) Ross 2-16-1867 (2-17-1867)
Newsom, Robert to Narcissus Harris 10-15-1850
Newson, John to Martha Mathis 2-10-1845
Newton, Henry to Elizabeth W. Shelton 5-22-1852
Newton, Lytle to Martha Exum 3-20-1871
Newton, Lytle to Martha Wright 1-7-1858
Newton, Robt. E. to Sarah Margaret Hanes 12-10-1867
Newton, William H. to Caroline Lovelace 1-10-1871
Nichols, Joshua W. to Minerva Ann Barton 10-6-1841 (10-7-1841)
Nichols, Robt. H. to Rhoda Long 2-19-1870 (2-20-1870)
Nichols, William W. to Milly Allison 5-16-1849 (5-17-1849)
Nichols, William W. to Susan A. Shuford 10-16-1862 (10-22-1862)
Nicholson, Archibald M. to Esther Hobb 2-25-1856 (2-26-1856)
Nicholson, David S. to Senia A. Harbert 2-1-1859
Niel, Benjamin to Weltha Medling 5-11-1838 (5-17-1838)
Nivell, Nicholas to Mary M. Watt 2-2-1842 (2-3-1842)
Nobles, William A. to Elizabeth P. Mann 12-11-1847 (12-14-1847)
Nobles, William H. to Annis Johnson 4-4-1844
Nolen, David to _____ 1-30-1847
Nolen, James A. to Leeana Timms 12-17-1853 (12-18-1853)
Nolin, James M. to Sophronia Hatton 8-16-1842
Nooner, Wm. L. to L. J. (Mrs.) Taylor 11-18-1869 (11-21-1869)
Norman, Henry to Rebecca (Mrs.) Caldwell 7-17-1858 (7-18-1858)
Norrow, Benjamin to Margaret Norrow 12-5-1842 (12-7-1842)
Northern, Philip to Mary Vinson 12-4-1841
Norton, Benjamin L. to Jane Prewitt 10-6-1841 (10-7-1841)
Norton, George J. to Mary A. Elizabeth Branch 11-11-1857 (11-12-1857)

Norton, Jacob A. to Rachael March 6-28-1845 (7-1-1845)
Norton, James H. to Malvina Mills 12-8-1856 (12-9-1856)
Norton, James H. to Martha Smith 6-21-1866 (6-22-1866)
Norton, John W. to Louisa Carrington 7-23-1849
Norton, Thomas M. to Minerva Mills 9-15-1860 (9-17-1860)
Norvell, Milton D. to Nancy J. Hickman 7-10-1849
Norvell, William R. to Esther E. Anderson 10-17-1844
Norwood, John H. to Eveline V. Fredericks 6-5-1860 (6-7-1860)
Norwood, Samuel L. to Eliza Robinson 3-27-1867
Nowell, Dempsey to Elizabeth Barnett 10-29-1866 (10-30-1866)
Oakes, William J. to Margaret E. Lyons 4-11-1859
Oakley, James K. P. to Mary J. H. Barron 6-27-1860
Oates, John T. to Mary Eliza Elrod 5-7-1856 (5-8-1856)
Oates, Wyatt to Caroline Edwards 11-24-1858 (11-25-1858)
Obenchain, J. T. to Ella J. Hicks 6-8-1868
Odam, Caleb to Elizabeth C. Butler 8-30-1853 (8-31-1853)
Ohanlon, John to Kate Lynch 11-4-1869
Ohara, John E. to Henrietta Williams 12-3-1861 (12-5-1861)
Oliver, Allen F. to Mary C. Crittenton 1-2-1856 (1-3-1856)
Oliver, James G. to Mattie Hays 5-7-1868
Oliver, John C. to Sarah A. T. Berrycroft 6-2-1855
Oliver, John J. to Harriett R. Day 6-2-1853 (6-3-1853)
Oliver, John to Elizabeth Wood 9-24-1838
Oliver, John to Rebecca F. Connally 9-17-1850 (9-18-1850)
Oliver, William J. to Rebecca M. Follis 3-12-1853 (3-17-1853)
Oliver, William to Sarah Todd 4-4-1846 (4-5-1846)
Oneal, Francis M. to Anna Clark 2-28-1871 (3-1-1871)
Oneal, Harvey D. to Menerva Rone 12-9-1868 (12-13-1868)
Oneal, James H. to Rachel McCorkle 5-16-1859
Oneal, With T. to M. E. Parker 1-7-1868
Orgain, Edmond J. to Sarah J. Kimball 2-5-1850 (2-7-1850)
Osben, Daniel to Mary C. Sipes 12-26-1853 (12-27-1853)
Osburn, T. G. to Adriadna Irvin 1-10-1870 (1-11-1870)
Osgen, William to Mary Ann Vanzandt 12-26-1842 (12-27-1842)
Outerbridge, Stephen to Marina Patterson 8-19-1845
Outland, Edmond to Elenora Montgomery 10-10-1866 (10-11-1866)
Overton, Francis M. to Nancy Jane Baker 8-13-1846
Overton, Thomas to Permelia Patterson 10-5-1869
Overton, Willis to Mary I. Clark 11-28-1842
Owen, David B. to Rhoeba S. Shaw 1-6-1868 (1-7-1868)
Owen, Edward to Betsy Jane Hightower 3-4-1871 (3-5-1871)
Owens, Leonard to Amanda Barnes 9-23-1854 (10-10-1854)
Owens, William C. to Elizabeth Jane Blythe 4-21-1860 (4-22-1860)
Ozier, M. D. to Sarah O. Tucker 10-2-1855 (10-4-1855)
Ozier, Saml. M. to Annie Cook 9-26-1866
Pailey, John C. to Sarah B. Shelton 3-24-1866 (3-26-1866)
Paisley, John R. to Margaret Weatherly 9-17-1857 (9-29-1857)
Paisley, M. J. to Wm. A. Wilson 2-2-1854
Pandry, John R. to Phoeba Beddo 9-23-1869
Pardue, Joseph J. to Elizabeth C. (Mrs.) Moore 5-6-1861 (5-7-1861)
Parham, Jesse T. to Mary Jane Adderton 1-17-1857 (1-19-1857)
Parker, David H. to Mariah T. D. Reeves 5-24-1853
Parker, Dempsey to L. Baley 12-16-1839
Parker, Frnaklin J. to Eliza Dis? 6-17-1871 (6-18-1871)
Parker, Henry F. to Margaret Jane McKnight 9-10-1859 (9-11-1859)
Parker, Isaac D. to Sarah L. Huntsman 12-27-1845 (12-28-1845)
Parker, Jacob to Elizabeth H. Glover 9-22-1850
Parker, Thompson A. to Manirva A. Crause 11-28-1848 (11-30-1848)
Parker, William H. to Juliam Boone 1-5-1840 (1-7-1840)
Parkin, Washington to Harriet Boet 9-15-1842 (9-16-1842)
Parks, Richard to Amy Henry 10-28-1867 B
Parlow, Isaac to Nancy J. Day 2-8-1868 (2-13-1868)
Parlow, Nathan to Arlesia Yarbrough 8-15-1870 (8-18-1870)
Parmer, Francis to Mariah Herron 1-16-1844
Parmer, John to Elizabeth May 1-7-1841
Parrish, James N. to Lucy V. Lanier 12-9-1868 (12-16-1868)
Parrish, John A. S. to Mildred M. Childress 2-8-1841 (2-11-1841)
Parrot, Ethan H. to Mary H. Grant 12-3-1855 (12-24-1855)
Parrot, Norflet F. to Ellen Copeland 5-12-1856
Parrot, Washington to Mary Spurlock 12-17-1846
Parrot, William H. to Louisa Duncan 12-22-1841 (12-23-1841)
Pasmose, William to Fanny Kendrick 1-10-1843 (1-12-1843)
Passmore, James H. to Lucy E. Massey 1-2-1855
Passmore, Moody to Ann Eliza Searcy 11-2-1854
Patiller, Hartwell to Arabella Presley 1-27-1868

Patrick, Andrew J. to Susan B. Harpool 11-2-1846
Patrick, Andrew to Frances H. Weaver 12-29-1862 (12-30-1862)
Patrick, George W. to Irabella C. Cherry 3-19-1849
Patterson, Alexander to Martha Craig 7-28-1858
Patterson, Asa to Matilda Herse 5-3-1852
Patterson, Colen M. to Laura L. Williams 11-26-1868
Patterson, David to Nancy Amanda Kincaid 9-30-1857 (10-1-1857)
Patterson, Freeman to Martha Raines 11-30-1850 (12-3-1850)
Patterson, Freeman to Susan Ellen Margrave 9-22-1855 (9-23-1855)
Patterson, George to Charity Lane 11-27-1852
Patterson, Joseph to Mary Jane Morphis 12-13-1845
Patterson, Samuel J. to Lucinda Haislip 11-1-1852 (11-2-1852)
Pay, William R. to Alfred Sarah Smitoe 9-16-1839
Peach, Henderson to Elizabeth Chapman 1-2-1844 (1-4-1844)
Pearce, Martin to Eliza Pickens 8-14-1869 (8-15-1869)
Pearce, Thomas to Mary Jones 9-9-1871 (9-10-1871)
Pearce, William T. to Susan Catherine Hayley 3-9-1857 (3-10-1857)
Pearcy, James B. to Martha E. Hicks 12-4-1849
Pearcy, John J. to Nancy May 11-25-1857 (2-5-1857?)
Pearson, Henry J. to Martha (Mrs.) Hamilton 8-8-1867
Pearson, John E. to Mary D. Wilkes 11-7-1852 (11-10-1852)
Pearson, Thomas J. to Nannie Temple 2-20-1869 (2-24-1869)
Peeples, Nathan to Selina Seaborn 9-13-1867 (9-15-1867)
Pegues, Asbury to Mary E. Hewitt 1-27-1843 (2-1-1843)
Pemberton, John A. to Sarah C. Harrison 6-17-1846
Pendergrast, Edward (Capt.) to Mary Wardlow 7-25-1862
Pendergrast, Samuel R. N. to Synthia Jane Kirkpatrick 12-6-1843
Pendergrast, Vincent L. to Nancy Williams 11-13-1866 (11-14-1866)
Penn, William C. to Texie C. Boyce 10-21-1862
Pennington, John to Martha Hammond 8-16-1842 (8-18-1842)
Pentecost, William to Sarah Kilpatrick 12-29-1846
Perciful, James T. to Allie Bickers 12-24-1868 (1-4-1869)
Perciful, John to Mary Thompson 11-11-1856
Perciful, William to Elizabeth Glenn 3-16-1854
Percifull, Andrew to Virginia Mallory 9-25-1855
Percival, Thomas to Sarah Glidwell 11-27-1840
Perkins, George G. to Adeline Reeves 10-8-1845 (10-9-1845)
Perkins, Josephus to Eleathia J. McKnight 1-24-1852
Permenter, Ruffin to Mary Blurton 9-24-1866 (9-25-1866)
Perron, Benjamin R. to Emery Guin 1-2-1844 (1-9-1844)
Perry, Barham to Rowena Eliza Williams 8-27-1869 (9-1-1869)
Perry, Benjamin W. to Elizabeth Dick 12-22-1854
Perry, Foster to Sarah Ann Griffith 12-9-1857 (12-10-1857)
Perry, Herbert to Mary M. Howlett 11-27-1848 (11-30-1848)
Perry, James G. to Mary S. Kyle 11-20-1851
Perry, James Turner to Lou Morgan 12-17-1866 (12-20-1866)
Perry, James W. to Mary Hunter 12-22-1838
Perry, Laburn to Martha (Mrs.) Collinsworth 11-10-1869 (11-11-1869)
Perry, Merlin to Elizabeth Boon 9-12-1843 (9-21-1843)
Perry, Merlin to Sarah Ann Stone 12-5-1854
Perry, Nathaniel to Fidelia E. Williams 12-31-1868
Perry, Nicholas to Nancy Miller 9-18-1849 (9-20-1849)
Perry, Robert H. to Sarah A. Haynes 12-24-1849 (12-25-1849)
Perry, Turner to Julion Blackard 8-7-1848
Perry, Wiley to Priscilla N. Carroll 5-7-1860 (5-9-1860)
Perry, William to Mary Edwards 2-19-1870
Perryman, John to Mary Allen 1-20-1846
Person, B. Alexr. to Elenore Epperson 5-9-1866
Person, Benjamin B. to Susan E. Green 10-20-1842
Person, Thos. I. to L. M. Donald 9-20-1842 (9-29-1842)
Peters, Charles H. to Sarah J. Carrington 9-24-1866 (9-25-1866)
Peterson, John to Aurora Harrison 6-26-1866
Peterson, William D. to Martha Stewart 12-20-1842 (12-22-1842)
Pettigrew, Wm. R. to Sarah Elizabeth Ellington 9-18-1867 (9-20-1867)
Pettus, Benj. R. to Ann M. Farmer 4-6-1866 (3?-7-1866)
Pfyfer, Melchior to Barbara Truob 5-30-1868 (6-5-1869?)
Phelps, William to Lucy Medlin 3-9-1871
Phillips, Atlas to Caroline Bishop 8-15-1848
Phillips, Charles to Emily A. Freeman 11-13-1848
Phillips, David T. to Malvina Duffey 4-17-1869 (4-25-1869)
Phillips, David T. to Malvina Duffey 5-7-1866 (not executed)
Phillips, Jesse R. to Nannie J. Watkins 12-2-1869 (12-7-1869)
Phillips, John M. to Jane L. Harris 6-7-1855
Phillips, Joseph T. to Octavia H.? Jones 12-18-1860 (12-19-1860)
Phillips, William A. to Amanda F. Newsom 1-26-1858 (1-27-1858)

Phillips, William to Huldy Brinkley 4-16-1842 (4-17-1842)
Pickens, Owen to Elizabeth (Mrs.) Howell 4-26-1871
Pierce, Clement to Mary Brogden 12-30-1852
Pierce, Thomas to Martha S. Medlin 1-4-1856 (1-6-1856)
Pierce, Thomas to Rebecca Richards 12-27-1853 (12-29-1853)
Piercy, Cader to Jane Lawrence 7-19-1845 (7-20-1845)
Piercy, Everett G. to Axelina Whiteside 7-28-1847 (7-29-1847)
Piercy, George W. to Becky Jane Baker 5-26-1856
Piercy, Miles Wilson to Susan Jane Boals 8-2-1869
Piercy, William H. to Margaret Mason 3-7-1849 (3-8-1849)
Piffin, Henry A. to Margaret A. Kilpatrick 9-18-1866
Pipkin, Burton (Dr.) to Mary Chitmun 5-16-1855
Pipkins, Chesley P. to Margaret Chipman 5-18-1854
Pipkins, Hughs to Mary E. Steadman 9-25-1855 (10-10-1855)
Pittman, Jacob to Martha J. Shelly 10-30-1845
Pittman, James B. to Helen S. Cozart 3-24-1869 (3-25-1869) *
Pitts, Richard S. to Drucinda E. Young 12-18-1855
Poindexter, David to Dionca Ann Garner 4-4-1842 (4-7-1842)
Polk, Enzkial W. to Martha Jane Clay 6-22-1840 (6-23-1840)
Pollard, Edward T. to Moody F. Raggin 10-3-1871 (10-4-1871)
Pool, Alfred to Mary A. Benson 3-15-1855
Pool, Alfred to Mary Karr 9-15-1843 (9-17-1843)
Pool, Armstead P. to Martha E. Langford 8-17-1848
Pool, William to Mary E. Lea 8-21-1849 (8-23-1849)
Pope, Joseph to Sophronia Estes 5-17-1859 (5-18-1859)
Pope, Thadeus to Mary Elizabeth Stribling 12-13-1853
Pope, William to Ann Strayhorn 8-20-1838 (8-25-1838)
Pope, William to Elizabeth Dickey 2-8-1841
Pope, William to Elvira M. (Mrs.) Byrd 12-12-1859
Porter, David B. to Lucinda Golden 8-7-1848 (8-?-1848)
Poteete, Wm. Andrew to Mary Susan Gowan 5-28-1870 (5-29-1870)
Potts, Ellison T. to Judy F. Roberts 9-19-1857 (9-20-1857)
Pounds, Andrew J. to Rebecca Haislip 12-7-1860
Pounds, John T. to Mary J. Mason 7-5-1859 (7-7-1859)
Powell, Alfred P. to Trangnella A. McGee 4-1-1859
Powell, Benjamin J. to Elizabeth B. Davis 2-2-1848
Powell, John to Elizabeth Pruden 10-4-1847 (10-5-1847)
Powell, Naum to Harriet Cobb 5-18-1857 (5-19-1857)
Powell, Stephen M. to Mildred E. Shelton 11-7-1859 (11-8-1859)
Pratt, Moses E. to Mary Jane Oliver 9-9-1871 (9-10-1871)
Pratt, Moses E. to Mary M. McCabe 12-23-1867 (12-24-1867)
Presley, Denning to Emily (Mrs.) Pole 2-8-1868
Preston, Walter E. to Fannie Middleton Hays 3-9-1858 (3-10-1858)
Prewett, John M. to Elizabeth H. Russell 11-30-1859
Prewett, Robt. E. to Dicy Ann Robinson 10-31-1868 (11-3-1868)
Price, Campbell to Sophronia Hicks 2-9-1867 (2-10-1867)
Price, Elijah (Memphis TN) to Mary S. Swink 4-17-1853
Price, Geo. W. to Margaret L. Hopper 12-24-1869
Price, James H. to Helen P. Potts 12-15-1868 (12-16-1868)
Price, John F. to Euphania Wadlington 1-19-1870
Price, John to Rebecca Ann Taylor 3-30-1854
Price, Joshua to Eloner Leadbetter 12-3-1838
Price, Nathaniel M. to Harrell McKnight 10-2-1843 (10-5-1843)
Price, Richard M. to Susan Ann Duffer 11-13-1869 (11-14-1869)
Price, William W. to Nancy C. Robison 12-8-1841 (12-9-1841)
Price, William to Bettie Christman 10-15-1868
Priddy, George L. to Jane Conner 3-1-1870 (3-3-1870)
Priest, Thomas to Harriet Priest 7-9-1860 (7-10-1860)
Privett, William F. to Martha M. Laxton 8-31-1843
Pryor, John P. to Eliza P. Long 9-19-1845
Puckett, Peter P. to Margaret T. Delf 10-8-1849 (10-9-1849)
Pugh, Jesse to Zelpha Dickson 5-26-1842 (5-27-1842)
Pugh, Willoughby to Martha Kerr 10-8-1840
Pybas, J. C. to A. M. Clark 5-2-1870 (5-3-1870)
Pyles, Francis M. to Cynthia Thompson 9-7-1854
Quinley, David M. to Exalina Lawrence 2-12-1850
Quinley, Richard B. to Jane A. Biggers 12-23-1848 (12-25-1848)
Quinly, David M. to Sylvia L. Moore 6-29-1846
Quinly, Wm. C. to Martha J. Dawson 9-3-1842 (9-4-1842)
Ragan, Alexander to Anna R. McCrory 9-3-1861
Ragsdale, Alexander to Valery Miller 10-12-1843
Ragsdale, William J. to Susan Davis 8-14-1847 (8-17-1847)
Rainey, Peter to Mary Garrett 6-10-1846
Rainey, Thos. C. to Mary A. Beaty 12-20-1869
Rainey, William D. to Mary J. Hefley 7-18-1859 (7-20-1859)

Rains, Albert A. to Susan P. Graves 12-22-1859
Rains, Elisha to Elizabeth F. Hathaway 10-10-1862 (10-23-1862)
Rains, Stephen to Elda McGee 11-2-1839
Ramsey, George to Mary Alston 6-10-1867 (6-11-1867)
Ramsey, Green H. to Lavenia (Mrs.) Arnold 11-1-1869
Rando, Carmelo to Carmela Gabriele 1-10-1856
Randolph, James F. to Parmelia Williams 10-8-1859
Raney, Robert G. to Terry Butler 11-18-1843
Rankin, B. B. to Sophronia Williams 12-31-1860
Rankin, Joseph T. to Kitty Dobbs 11-10-1854 (11-12-1854)
Rawlings, Thomas to Jane M. Jones 1-29-1855 (2-1-1855)
Ray, Eli to Eliza Newsom 12-15-1866 (12-16-1866)
Ray, James C. to Addie Smith 12-21-1870 (12-22-1870)
Read, Benjamin to Martha Anderson 9-6-1842 (9-8-1842)
Reams, Joshua M. to Artela F. Davis 12-2-1868 (12-4-1868)
Reaves, John H. to Susan Baker 5-26-1856
Reavis, James M. to Margaret A. Brown 2-13-1862
Rector, Alex P. to Clarkey Ann Williams 5-21-1870 (5-22-1870)
Reddin, Harmon to Elizabeth Witherlington 12-28-1839
Reed, John R. to Mary C. McIver 3-18-1841 (3-19-1841)
Reed, William C. to Elizabeth Carruth 7-12-1841
Reeves, Charles W. to Mary Elizabeth Nelson 12-7-1869
Reeves, George W. to Mary Ann Carter 9-15-1856 (9-23-1856)
Reeves, Jacob J. R. to Mary Ann McCollough 12-7-1855
Reeves, Joel W. to America Ann Crenshaw 1-14-1850 (1-15-1850)
Reeves, Robert S. to Luroney B. Parker 1-18-1847 (1-21-1847)
Reeves, William to Mary Ann Shelly 9-18-1843
Reid, Augustus C. to Laura Taylor 3-1-1869 (3-3-1869)
Reid, David to Sarah F. Williamson 10-3-1849 (10-10-1849)
Reid, James G. to Mattie Wharton 11-6-1866 (11-8-1866)
Reid, John to Lide A. Greer 10-1-1867 (10-2-1867)
Reid, Thomas A. to Laura Hutchison 11-16-1869 (11-18-1869)
Rene, jr., James to Sarah Crosby 6-7-1845 (6-9-1845)
Reneow, I.L.. to Margaret A. (Mrs.) Howell 9-9-1870
Renshaw, John to Easter Anderson 5-21-1842 (5-24-1842)
Replogle, Benjamin to Sally Ann Duncan 9-19-1854 (9-21-1854)
Rice, Rufus W. to Adelia E. Harbert 4-5-1853
Richards, James B. to Holtan Moore 9-18-1866 (9-20-1866)
Richards, Redmond to Manerva Pierce 10-9-1850 (10-10-1850)
Richardson, Elam to Bazilla Jane Davis 1-11-1853
Richardson, Geo. W. to Mary Carr 6-8-1871 (6-11-1871)
Richardson, Geo. W. to Sarah F. Hattom 12-10-1866
Richardson, Goodman to Rebecca Cupples 7-14-1849
Richardson, Samuel to Lucretia Paralee Latham 11-19-1855
Richardson, W. B. to Martha Ione Williams 10-1-1842 (10-6-1842)
Richars, William to Nancy Williams 8-15-1842
Rickman, Marcus to Nancy E. Wilkinson 8-21-1841 (8-23-1841)
Riden, Thomas to Sarah Patrick 7-2-1839
Rider, Louis to Emsey Hollyfield 7-12-1839 (7-2?-1839)
Ripley, William P. to Biddy (Mrs.) Bond 11-28-1860
Ripley, William P. to M. D. Dickinson 9-18-1849 (9-20-1849)
Ritchy, James G. to James? Smithdorch 1-15-1841
Rives, John F. to Mary E. Bailey 5-14-1846
Roach, Admiral G. to Mary A. C. Tedford 10-21-1868 (10-22-1868)
Roach, John A. to Eliza J. Starkey 8-13-1867 (8-16-1867)
Roark, Aulsey D. to Jane McWilliams 12-29-1845 (1-1-1846)
Robards, E. C. to Sarah M. Walker 4-16-1867
Robb, James to Patience Bradley 8-16-1848
Roberson, John D. to Elizabeth J. Barron 9-22-1843 (9-28-1843)
Roberson, John M. to Elizabeth Brigham 1-2-1850
Roberts, Charles N. to Flora Oliver 9-11-1857 (9-10?-1857)
Roberts, David E. to Margaret Andrews 8-15-1861
Roberts, Harvey A. to Isabella Roberts 4-3-1855
Robertson, Alexander C. to Mary Eliza Vaulx 11-11-1852
Robertson, James to Minerva Rushing 10-27-1841 (10-28-1841)
Robertson, Josiah S. to Pernetta E. Williams 9-28-1867 (9-29-1867)
Robertson, S. S. to M. E. Sledge 8-15-1855
Robertson, William P. to Louanna Harris 9-3-1867 (9-4-1867)
Robinson, Elijah to Frances E. McAdoo 12-8-1858 (12-12-1858)
Robinson, Elipha Z. to Nancy Jane Dodson 4-21-1857 (4-26-1857)
Robinson, F. M. to Susan E. Luster 12-29-1853 (12-29-1853)
Robinson, Hugh B. to Arabella Herndon 8-8-1868 (9-3-1868)
Robinson, Hugh B. to Sarah M. Tigrett 12-19-1838
Robinson, James L. to Catherine E. Brooks 3-4-1859
Robinson, James P. to Anna Bell Sutton 12-30-1868 (1-19-1869)

Robinson, John E. to Caroline Roe 10-11-1869 (10-14-1869)
Robinson, John W. to Martha Burrus 11-22-1842 (11-23-1842)
Robinson, John to Jane Vail 1-22-1848 (1-23-1848)
Robinson, William J. to Mary E. Williamson 4-30-1850 (5-1-1850)
Robinson, William S. to Josephine Wagster 10-8-1867 (10-10-1867)
Robinson, Wm. C. to _____ 6-26-1867
Robison, John L. to Catherine Burson 11-29-1862
Robley, Charles B. to Nancy (Mrs.) Staton 3-31-1870
Robley, John R. to Ellen B. Black 12-25-1852 (12-28-1852)
Rochell, John S. to Agnes A. Stone 11-29-1854
Rocksey, Gidion to Rebecca Rogers 7-22-1841
Rodenhizer, John to Emilina Davis 8-21-1858 (8-22-1858)
Rodgers, John T. to Adeline McMillan 4-30-1866 (5-4-1866)
Rodick, Gray to Candis Wright 1-20-1840 (1-22-1840)
Roe, N. to Drucilla Gastings 1-7-1840 (2-2-1840)
Rogers, Archibald S. to Margaret E. Fry 7-15-1856 (7-17-1856)
Rogers, Archibald S. to Nancy G. Weaver 2-20-1849 (2-22-1849)
Rogers, George C. to Ann Caroline Derrah 12-17-1840
Rogers, H. H. to M. K. Hughes 2-1-1870 (2-2-1870)
Rogers, John C. to Mary Ann Butler 4-12-1847
Rogers, Jubelee P. to Mary H. Burrow 4-15-1847
Rogers, Robert L. to Sarah Jane Haynie 1-17-1843
Rollins, Augustin to Elizabeth Harns 3-29-1843
Rollins, Elbert to Sarah Ann Caurdel 4-27-1857
Rollins, Enoch to Mary Brown 12-12-1838 (12-13-1838)
Rollins, Gastin to Mary E. Harris 5-27-1846 (6-4-1846)
Rollins, James to Elizabeth K. Blackmon 2-21-1855 (2-25-1855)
Rone, John T. to Jonnie L. Blackmon 1-3-1867 (1-6-1867)
Rooker, Edward T. to Mary M. Adams 4-3-1858 (4-4-1858)
Rooker, George W. to Ann Eliza Holt 9-15-1856 (9-17-1856)
Rooker, William J. to Susan Jane Phillips 1-3-1860 (1-5-1860)
Rooks, Bailey G. to Lucy May 9-24-1840
Rooks, Fullington to Martha Fearless 1-30-1847
Rooks, James D. to Mary Elizah Estes 11-24-1870
Rooks, William R. to Mary F. Maynard 9-19-1863 (9-20-1862?)
Rosamon, George M. to Mary L. Reddin 10-22-1866 (10-24-1866)
Rose, James M. to Lucinda M. Taylor 8-1-1871 (8-2-1871)
Rose, William J. to Isabella Brooks 12-16-1867
Ross, J. Coleman to Fannie (Mrs.) Adams 1-24-1867 (1-27-1867)
Ross, Stephen D. to Sarah W. Jones 2-16-1838 (2-23-1838)
Rosser, Henry to Rebecca C. Williamson 8-15-1870
Rosser, William to Tempence A. Anderson 9-7-1854
Rowlett, John R. to Eliza Garland 11-11-1841
Rowsey, John W. to Catherine E. Fry 11-12-1861 (11-14-1861)
Rozell, B. L. to Lizzie C. Lyon 2-26-1855 (2-27-1855)
Ruddle, Cornelius to Sarah Emeline Graves 7-23-1849 (7-12?-1849)
Ruff, James E. to Rebecca M. Hale 10-26-1847 (10-28-1847)
Ruffin, John B. to Mary T. Anderson 3-12-1856 (3-13-1856)
Ruffin, Robert J. to Melissa A. Williamson 4-24-1856
Rush, Wm. H. to Sarah A. Kershaw 6-14-1871 (6-15-1871)
Rushing, Joel to Sarah S. (Mrs.) Vick 2-2-1858 (2-3-1858)
Rushing, Simeon B. to Callie A. Sykes 12-28-1870 (12-29-1870)
Rushing, Stanly to Elizabeth McCallister 1-9-1847
Russell, C. B. to Mary F. Gattis 11-8-1859 (11-9-1859)
Russell, Christinberry to Jane Macon 11-14-1849
Russell, John S. to Mariah Flowers 8-4-1846 (8-6-1846)
Russell, jr., Jesse to Sarah E. Teague 4-22-1868
Rust, Daniel to Sarah Haslip 1-21-1841
Rutherford, Robt. M. to Eliza Gordon 12-13-1866
Rutherford, Wm. L. to Sarah A. Perry 11-28-1866 (11-29-1866)
Salter, Thomas C. to Nannie B. Hubbard 8-7-1866 (8-8-1866)
Sanderlin, Lemuel to Mary Moody 12-24-1850
Sanders, John M. to Mary Ann Waddell 9-11-1856
Sanders, Joshua J. to Rachael Mason 12-22-1840 (12-23-1840)
Sanders, Thomas to Margaret Birdsong 8-27-1859 (8-28-1859)
Sanders, William H. to Martha Jane Waddle 12-12-1840 (12-14-1840)
Sandrey, John to Susan Betts 1-22-1844
Sanford, Edward L. to Mary F. Simmons 12-23-1857
Sanford, Patrick H. to Mary C. Ball 1-5-1859 (1-6-1859)
Sanford, Robert B. to Catherine Ann Chambers 12-23-1839 (12-24-1839)
Sanford, William A. to Sarah J. Ball 1-29-1855
Sauls, Calvin to Winney Johnson 10-4-1847
Sauls, Patrick to Elizabeth Waddleton 1-30-1843 (2-2-1843)
Sawyer, Calier F. to Mary F. Beaty 2-8-1870

Scarborough, George A. to Sarah A. Mainord 5-2-1870 (5-5-1870)
Scarborough, John B. to Sarah E. Swink 7-30-1856
Scarborough, William to Malinda Herron 4-14-1841
Scarbrough, James to Sarah (Mrs.) McBryde 4-13-1869 (4-14-1869)
Scharmahoran, J. W. C. to Laura C. Taylor 1-1-1859 (1-7-1859)
Scott, George R. to Euginia J. Hudson 10-27-1866 (10-30-1866)
Scott, George R. to Hester Ann Halton 2-7-1839 (2-14-1839)
Scott, James F. to Lizzie Puckett 12-10-1868
Scott, Joseph to Eliza S. McElver 2-18-1840
Scott, Preston B. to Jane E. Campbell 11-12-1861 (11-13-1861)
Scott, William to Eliza I. Green 10-20-1843
Screws, Edmund D. to Charity Castles 3-26-1846 (4-2-1846)
Scruggs, Phineas T. to Malinda C. Hewett 5-22-1861 (5-23-1861)
Seat, L. G. B to Virginia Ann Fly 1-5-1854
Seat, William H. to Sarah Jane Butler 8-25-1856 (8-26-1856)
Seehorn, William J. to Martha A. Rone 4-28-1860 (4-29-1860)
Seeley, Freeman H. to Martha J. Graham 5-19-1866 (5-20-1866)
Sellars, Andrew Jackson to Sarah Amanda Alexander 1-18-1871 (1-19-1871)
Sellers, James to Margaret McChord 9-17-1855
Selph, Anderson P. to Sallie A Jackson 12-24-1867 (12-29-1867)
Selph, D. H. to Lavinia E. Stewart 12-21-1852
Senter, Thomas J. to Sarah J. Fly 11-1-1848 (11-2-1848)
Settle, Alexander to Eliza Jane Pollock 7-30-1870 (8-5-1870)
Seuberth, Conrad to Amelia Jane Hight 11-22-1855
Sevier, Adam to Nancy Cook 12-5-1838
Sewell, Dempsey N. to Amanda Henderson 2-1-1849
Sewell, Joseph H. to Marianna Hampton 5-8-1871 (5-9-1871)
Sewell, Martin to Rachel Howell 2-8-1867 (2-10-1867)
Sewell, Reuben to Martha A. Johnson 9-29-1841
Sexton, Henry M. to Lucy Jane Walston 7-4-1866 (7-5-1866)
Sexton, Lincefield to Hellen Jones 7-16-1844 (7-4?-1844)
Sexton, William W. to Emily Hewett 8-16-1867 (8-18-1867)
Shackleford, Richmond N. to Martha Ann Moses 11-9-1854
Shane, Alexander C. to Malinda Mays 6-26-1861
Shane, John to Clara Day 9-4-1866
Shapard, Lewis B. to Catherine G. Vaulx 7-24-1860
Sharp, Columbus C. to Louisa Estes 12-22-1857
Sharp, Cyrum to Mary C. Baxter 1-16-1849
Sharp, George A. to Martha E. Hawse 12-14-1852 (12-15-1852)
Sharp, James M. to France R. (Mrs.) Boon 10-27-1868
Sharp, Joseph C. to Margarett Ann Action 6-19-1839
Sharp, Joseph C. to Sarah E. Hill 2-16-1857 (2-17-1857)
Sharp, Joseph G. to Martha Mizell 11-16-1843
Sharp, Robt. M. to Virginia A. Pyles 10-24-1866 (10-25-1866)
Sharpe, Saml. to Idotha Fulghum 6-19-1866
Shaw, James A. to Mary H. Boswell 4-28-1849 (4-29-1849)
Shaw, James M. to Martha A. Nix 1-27-1852
Shaw, James M. to Parthenia J. Carwell 8-21-1869 (8-22-1869)
Shaw, Martin to Ann Z. Williams 8-3-1846
Shaw, Martin to Mariah I. Boyd 1-14-1839 (1-15-1839)
Sheahan, James A. to Adeline Able 10-20-1858 (10-21-1858)
Sheldon, Oney to Caroline Chamberlain 12-28-1848
Shelly, Thomas C. to Maria Redwine 6-14-1856
Shelton, George T. to Sarah E. Wiggs 10-20-1859
Shelton, Henry W. to Malinda Robinson 1-5-1858
Shelton, John L. to Mary Dugan 9-12-1870
Shelton, John W. to Artimissa Powell 11-2-1852
Shelton, Judithan C. to Lydia Powell 12-21-1859 (12-22-1859)
Shelton, Stephen L. to Ann Cornelia Montgomery 8-16-1869 (8-19-1869)
Shelton, William C. to Mattie J. Parrish 12-17-1867 (12-19-1867)
Shelton, William M. to Margaret E. Campbell 2-17-1849
Shelton, Wm. M. to Sallie J. Duncan 10-4-1870
Shelton, Wynn to Julia Ann Tyner 11-7-1850
Sherman, Boyce E. to Martha E. Revely 10-15-1857 (10-18-1857)
Sherman, M. B. to Caroline Jackson 9-22-1856
Sherrill, John F. to Susan M. Temple 10-12-1850
Sherrod, Felix G. to Lou Jane Davis 5-4-1868 (5-18-1868)
Sherrod, Richard to Sarah Jane Taylor 6-9-1856
Shew, Jacob to Fannie C. Thompson 7-27-1870 (7-28-1870)
Shipes, Edwin P. to Sinay McCombs 9-4-1854 (9-5-1854)
Shipps, Cyrus C. to Pauline A. Newbern 12-13-1858 (12-14-1858)
Shirley, Benjamin J. to Martha Boman 11-29-1855
Shivers, James to Mary Malina Garrison 3-27-1843

Shivers, P. to Elizabeth I. Watkins 2-3-1840 (2-6-1840)
Shoemaker, William to Earry? Basford 10-30-1839
Short, Howell to Catharine Miller 10-24-1842
Short, James H. to Elizabeth Hollyman 12-14-1847 (12-25-1847)
Shuffield, Washington D. to Ruth A. Duncan 7-31-1850 (8-1-1850)
Simmons, Almarine to Fannie E. Franklin 11-12-1867 (11-14-1867)
Simmons, Augustus B. to Elizabeth Temple Allen 3-13-1866 (3-18-1866)
Simmons, E. N. to Elizabeth A. Nail 1-6-1840
Simmons, Harrison to Mary Francis Rainey 1-15-1868
Simmons, John C. to Rebecca L. Garland 10-21-1867 (10-22-1867)
Simmons, John P. to Martha E. Lock 9-30-1848
Simmons, Lemuel D. to Amy Bacon 9-17-1842
Simmons, Peter to Ann Elizabeth Chester 9-7-1857 (9-10-1857)
Simmons, S. A. to Fannie E. Tally 7-21-1870 (7-24-1870)
Simmons, Thomas A. to Margaret J. Hart 12-21-1848
Simmons, William to Martha Ann Smith 12-10-1839
Simpson, Henry N. to Nancy Jane Holderfield 7-28-1868
Simpson, John Madison to Martha Combs 11-22-1853 (11-24-1853)
Sims, Josephus to Rachel J. Hopper 12-28-1852 (12-29-1852)
Sims, Robert W. to Nancy Mitchell 8-1-1853 (8-3-1853)
Sims, Robert W. to Sarah E. King 10-10-1862 (10-23-1862)
Sinclair, John F. to Louisa C. Jelks 10-29-1849 (10-31-1849)
Singer, Samuel to Mary A. E. Smith 2-3-1859
Singler, John C. to Sarah D. Francis 12-24-1870 (12-25-1870)
Sipes, William J. to Susan E. Revely 12-24-1862 (12-25-1862)
Skillern, Anderson S. to Temperance Springfield 1-25-1847
Skillern, Anderson to Mary Ann Buckannon 12-1-1841
Skillern, James P. to Susan McGown 12-28-1841
Skillern, John Henry to Sallie J. Alston 11-19-1870 (11-23-1870)
Slack, William L. to Sarah A. Johnston 8-21-1843 (8-24-1843)
Slaton, William to Nancy Nelson 8-8-1859 (8-11-1859)
Slator, Edward C. to Ary C. Cole 11-27-1854 (11-28-1854) *
Sloan, George F. to Mary Raines 11-21-1860 (11-22-1860)
Sloan, John Bunyan to Nancy E. Matthews 6-25-1869 (6-27-1869)
Sloan, Miles F. to Fidelia E. Mathews 9-10-1866 (9-12-1866)
Sloan, Miles J. to Louisa F. Watt 11-14-1861 (11-17-1861)
Slocum, Thomas J. to Luzinda Walker 7-23-1857 (7-27-1857)
Smith, Amphias to Martha L. Jarnagin 12-16-1844 (12-19-1844)
Smith, Daniel to Sarah Byrum 7-17-1849
Smith, Edward L. M. to Martha Ann Tennessee Lewis 7-18-1860 (7-19-1860)
Smith, Eli to Jennie Lewis 11-14-1871 (11-15-1871)
Smith, Elija to Martha E. Pace 12-19-1854
Smith, Etheldred L. to Rebecca Ann Fenner 12-17-1856
Smith, Francis G. to Elizabeth M. Carrington 12-20-1852
Smith, George A. to Martha K. Gleeson 12-8-1847 (12-9-1847)
Smith, George L. to Fanny H. Webb 11-8-1853
Smith, Gideon to Sarah A. Cook 1-4-1869
Smith, H. F. to Maggie A. Bell 11-12-1867
Smith, Hansford to Elizabeth Barnes 9-13-1839 (9-19-1839)
Smith, Hasting J. to Emelina Birmingham 2-19-1840
Smith, Henry D. (of Ala.) to Lizzie V. Fenner 4-28-1869 (4-29-1869)
Smith, Jackson to Sarah Jane Mayo 2-23-1858
Smith, James S. to Lyde Wethers 1-19-1870 (1-20-1870)
Smith, James to Amanda Gossett 12-24-1860
Smith, Jno. B. to Frances H. McLary 7-27-1858
Smith, John D. to Isabella M. Dickson 12-19-1840
Smith, John L. to Margaret Conner 4-15-1869
Smith, John M. to Rutha Ann Vann 10-15-1858
Smith, John N. to Fannie M. Shaw 9-20-1854 (9-19?-1854)
Smith, John T. to Christain A. Wooley 7-19-1858 (7-21-1858)
Smith, Joseph E. to Mary E. Barnett 8-24-1840 (8-25-1840)
Smith, Lafayette to Louisanna Pettigrew 3-5-1866 (3-6-1866)
Smith, Marshall E. to Mollie A. Moore 12-6-1866
Smith, Nathan C. to Rebecca Haislip 7-31-1854 (8-1-1854)
Smith, Robert to Missouri Angeline Tims 5-2-1857 (5-1?-1857)
Smith, Solomon to Louisa E. Jackson 7-16-1856 (7-17-1856)
Smith, Thomas H. to Susan C. Newsom 9-11-1862 (9-15-1862)
Smith, Thos. G. N. to Mary Upton 12-7-1854
Smith, W. A. to Mary J. Sharp 12-10-1866 (12-12-1866)
Smith, William G. to Cynthia J. Warlick 1-18-1848
Smith, William to Susan Fussell 6-12-1860
Smithern, William H. to Elizabeth R. Neil 2-4-1843
Smithson, John S. to Eliza J. Sanford 2-24-1853

Smithwich, William G. to Rebecca Hoppers 1-5-1850 (1-9-1850)
Smithwick, Samuel S. S. to Mary Jane Hopper 1-27-1862 (1-29-1862)
Sneed, Archibald J. to Ella B. Mays 1-19-1869 (1-20-1869)
Sneed, Richard A. to Ann R. Bullock 12-15-1869
Snipes, Farrington B. to Elizabeth Bond 5-3-1854
Snipes, Farrington B. to Tempie Johnston 11-30-1868 (12-3-1868)
Snowden, Thos. P. to Mary Worl 12-24-1838
Solomon, Louis to Rachel Goldzinsky 8-17-1871
Sorrell, Thomas to Keziah Battle 9-7-1861 (9-8-1861)
Sowell, Cader to Elizabeth I. Odle 2-27-1840
Sowell, Henry F. to Frances E. White 12-30-1869
Sparks, William to Lucy Davis 4-16-1855 (4-10?-1855)
Spears, Hudson J. to Sarah Graves 6-3-1850 (6-30-1850)
Spears, James M. to Emma E. Shivers 12-31-1869 (1-2-1870)
Spears, John M. to Mariah Graves 4-28-1846 (4-29-1846)
Spears, Thomas to Queen A. Gordon 12-18-1856 (12-22-1856)
Spence, Brittan to Bettie Cox 2-24-1868 (2-26-1868)
Spencer, Benj. Marion to Sarah (Mrs.) Woollard 7-6-1869
Spencer, Duncan M. to Harriet A. Connor 12-29-1859 (1-1-1860)
Spencer, Elijah H. to Amanda Johnson 7-26-1851 (7-31-1851)
Spencer, Jno. C. to Lizzie Gordon 2-28-1871 (3-2-1871)
Spivey, Calvin to Elizabeth Preson 1-6-1842
Spivey, Calvin to Mary E. A. Mizell 1-28-1847
Spraggins, James W. to Lucinda Jane Brewer 11-24-1869 (11-25-1869)
Spragins, Noel to Eliza Jones 1-30-1844 (2-1-1844)
Spring, Berry L. to Mary J. Wilie 12-18-1860 (12-19-1860)
Springfield, Baker C. to Callie E. Totten 11-23-1869 (11-24-1869)
Spurlock, Timothy P. to Ann Huntsman 12-21-1840 (12-22-1840)
Stanfield, Oliver to Mandy Jane Conder 2-28-1871 (3-1-1871)
Stanley, Harrison L. H. to Malinda Mays 3-7-1861
Stanley, Hays to Nancy Meacham 6-2-1853 (7-2-1853)
Stanley, Omer H. to Jane M. W. Langford 12-22-1852 (12-23-1852)
Stapleton, William K. to Margaret Boyd 4-15-1841
Starkey, Jarvis to Nancy C. Butler 10-25-1858 (10-27-1858)
Steadman, Jno. A. to Annie E. Haskins 11-8-1869 (11-11-1869)
Steadman, Nathan W. to Nancy Stewart 12-19-1855
Steed, Calier A. to Ellen B. Burus 1-20-1857
Steed, James N. to Jane Ewing 1-11-1859
Steepleton, Jonathan to Polly Covington 4-2-1844
Steepleton, William K. to Delilah Lambert 11-8-1850
Stephen, Isaac C. to Mary Jane York 10-29-1839
Stephens, Andrew to Minerva Jane Griffin 8-21-1860
Stephens, John to Maring Jones 5-5-1841 (5-17-1841)
Stephens, John to Polly McCain 2-10-1848 (2-11-1848)
Stephens, Ruben K. to Minerva Williams 11-2-1870 (11-3-1870)
Stephens, Thos. N. to Elizabeth Alison 10-10-1843 (10-12-1843)
Stephens, William H. to Barbara Miller 12-31-1838 (1-2-1839)
Stephens, Wm. A. to Harriet M. Gaskins 11-19-1866 (11-21-1866)
Stephenson, James M. to Martha A. Rooks 3-16-1866 (3-18-1866)
Stephenson, Thomas N. to Alsa Ann Alison 4-25-1843
Stephenson, Thomas N. to Catherine Kendrick 3-15-1848
Sterling, Robert to Penelope P. Campbell 6-5-1856
Stevens, A. to Sophronia Adams 10-23-1862
Stevenson, James to Jane Smith 1-6-1855
Stewart, Andrew C. to Mary A. Bradberry 2-16-1846
Stewart, B. G. to Mary A. Goodrich 12-19-1839 (12-23-1839)
Stewart, C. B. to J. Lou Hamilton 6-13-1871
Stewart, Charles L. to Ann Eliza Brent 1-31-1848
Stewart, James to Mary Ann Rose 6-29-1867 (7-1-1867)
Stewart, Seaborn J. to Dicey King 1-14-1845 (1-19-1845)
Stewart, William E. to Elizabeth B. Duffy 3-8-1853 (3-8-1853)
Stewart, William E. to Mary Elizabeth Parrish 9-21-1860 (9-23-1860)
Stewart, Wilson E. to Margaret C. Bostick 10-17-1859
Stewart, Wilson E. to Mary A. Alexander 8-5-1878 (8-10-1868?)
Stobaugh, Albert to Nancy Jane Taylor 2-10-1857
Stobaugh, Ansolem to Julia R. Rooks 8-31-1870 (9-1-1870)
Stobaugh, James to Rebecca Edwards 5-24-1838
Stobaugh, Robert to Nancy Buffalo 1-4-1869 (1-6-1869)
Stoe, William N. to Elizabeth C. (Mrs.) Rowsey 12-30-1868
   (12-31-1868)
Stone, Clark L. to Margarett Yerout 2-15-1842
Stone, Hartwell M. to Sarah Eveline Delph 3-31-1856
Stone, James M. to Nancy Jane Roach 3-7-1866
Stone, John G. to Mary Nolen 3-27-1838 (3-29-1838)
Stone, Lemuel to Margarett Lacey 1-23-1849 (1-24-1849)

Stone, Medlin to Rebecca Kilpatrick 2-17-1869 (2-21-1869)
Stone, Wesly to Adeline Toone 8-30-1844
Stone, William K. to Sarah E. Emmerson 11-25-1844
Storey, James L. to Narcissa Johnson 5-15-1841 (5-19-1841)
Storey, Littleton to Margarett Johnson 3-5-1844
Story, Alexander to Elizabeth Johnson 2-10-1843
Story, Otis L. to Rebecca M. Reeves 3-5-1841 (3-1?-1841)
Stout, Lorenzo D. to Catharine (Mrs.) Green 2-18-1858 (7-15-1858)
Stovall, William C. to Martha Ann Matthews 10-30-1847 (11-4-1847)
Stover, George W. to Ann Burk 12-20-1854
Strain, Charles T. to Mary Jane McCorkle 12-26-1860 (1-2-1860?)
Strans, Parminue to Mary Jeffries 8-1-1840 (8-4-1840)
Strayhorn, John Y. to Francis T. Bryan 12-4-1854
Strayhorn, Newell T. to Lucy A. Smith 1-3-1844
Strayhorn, Robert J. to Frances N. Pope 1-26-1859 (1-27-1859)
Sturdevant, John Ingram to Lydia A. Bradford 11-24-1868
   (11-25-1868)
Sturdevant, Thomas J. to Mary Ann A. Garrett 9-14-1858
Sturdevant, William J. to Joanna Dew 1-15-1861 (1-16-1861)
Sturdivant, Benjamin to Elizabeth Templeton 1-4-1848
Sturdivant, Washington to Mary Ann Ford 7-21-1852 (7-23-1852)
Sturkie, John A. to Emily C. Moxley 4-9-1866 (4-10-1866)
Sturtivant, Jess to Elizabeth Smith 7-10-1841 (7-14-1841)
Stute, William G. to Cynthia W. Rucker 10-31-1842 (11-4-1842)
Sullivan, A. C. to S. Sullivan 11-9-1839
Sullivan, Eliazer to Martha Glidewell 9-26-1870 (9-28-1870)
Sullivan, Jerimiah to Eliza Lambert 1-17-1843
Sullivan, Preston to Mary Sprows 4-3-1841 (5-5-1841)
Suser, Wiley to Eliz. J. Chipman 5-13-1853
Sweeney, Hugh to Mahala Anderson 8-30-1862 (8-31-1862)
Sweeny, James A. to Sarah Jane Harrison 1-11-1848
Swink, Geo. W. to Ann E. Buchanan 5-14-1869
Swink, Henry H. to Sallie M. Williams 5-23-1871
Swink, James to Sarah A. Mays 11-2-1852 (12-2-1852)
Sykes, Jno. W. to Mary E. Williamson 1-10-1871 (1-11-1871)
Sykes, John W. to Sarah T. Vick 8-28-1846
Sykes, Samuel S. to Carolina A. Williams 4-10-1848
Sykes, William J. to Arabella L. Kennon 1-31-1848
Sykes, Wm. J. to Mary G. Waggoner 11-20-1866
Sypes, John F. N. to Susana Maria Johnson 11-6-1868 (11-8-1868)
Talbot, Edward to Missouri P. Wheeler 9-26-1870 (9-27-1870)
Talbot, Geo. W. to Orva Ann Jayne 6-25-1849 (6-27-1849)
Talbot, Joseph H. to Martha Freeman 8-16-1842
Talbot, Lawrence E. to Joe May Rice 2-16-1871
Talley, Benjamin to Thurza Ann Stewart 2-28-1841
Talley, D. F. to E. M. Brooks 2-8-1871
Talley, Dudley C. to Martha A. (Mrs.) Exum 1-13-1870
Tarver, Julian to Monian Yates 12-17-1867 (12-18-1867)
Tate, Jerome B. to Nancy A. Hardage 12-24-1859
Taylor, Andrew to Sue Utley 9-14-1870 (9-15-1870)
Taylor, Craven L. to Elizabeth Tull 11-7-1854
Taylor, Daniel to Nancy Read 9-10-1857
Taylor, Edmond to Parasade M. Meriweather 3-23-1843 (3-28-1843)
Taylor, James A. to Jane Caroline Meriwether 12-5-1839
Taylor, James Allen to Margaret (Mrs.) Tysen 9-14-1869 (9-16-1869)
Taylor, John J. to Dicey Ham 3-19-1850
Taylor, John J. to Lucy Mills 11-16-1857
Taylor, John J. to Mary Alexander 7-20-1846
Taylor, Lawson D. to Lacy J. Fry 11-26-1849 (11-29-1849)
Taylor, Moses to Cynthia Alexander 1-9-1843 (1-12-1843)
Taylor, Robert to Mary D. Hale 5-12-1842
Taylor, Robt. W. to Mary E. Pentecost 6-22-1866
Taylor, Sylvanus to Henretta J. Kirby 10-12-1850 *
Taylor, Thomas H. to Jane Ingram 5-1-1849
Taylor, Thomas T. to Elizabeth Hathaway 12-21-1859
Taylor, Thomas to Martha Davis 11-18-1850 (11-19-1850)
Taylor, William J. to Mahala L. Stewart 7-18-1870 (7-21-1870)
Taylor, William to Rutha McFarland 3-13-1838 (3-22-1838)
Taylor, Wyatt A. to Tennessee V. Collins 7-29-1858
Teague, Abner to Mary J. Allison 3-16-1866
Teague, William to Amanda Williams 8-27-1846
Teague, Wm. T. to Mattie C. Dean 3-9-1870 (3-10-1870)
Teahen, Wm. M. to Mattie Matthews 12-20-1870 (12-21-1870)
Teal, James C. to Penelope Fairless 3-10-1838
Teddleton, Joseph to Elizabeth Ursery 8-9-1867 (8-10-1867)

Telfair, Edward to Mary R. Davie 10-28-1850
Temple, John S. to Lavinia F. Sherrill 9-15-1856
Temple, William S. to Elizabeth Sherl 11-27-1854 (11-30-1854) *
Temple, Wm. S. to Margarett M Ballard 4-18-1843
Temples, John I. to Elizabeth S. Marsh 3-24-1869 (3-28-1869)
Terrell, Banister to Josephine Moore 12-20-1856
Terry, William H. to Sarah E. Scott 12-16-1852
Tetterton, Matthew to Martha M. Greenwell 1-31-1849 (2-1-1849)
Tettleton, Bryant to Elizabeth Parker 12-30-1846
Tettleton, Silas to Jane Langston 10-14-1841
Thacker, Levi to Martha Avery 3-23-1867 (3-24-1867)
Thedford, Walter L. to Nancy N. Cash 1-16-1869 (1-20-1869)
Thedford, William to Sophronia Edwards 10-4-1849 (1-8-1849?)
Thom, Wily to Amelia Welch 11-26-1838 (11-29-1838)
Thomas, Henry A. to Sarah Jane Vanpelt 2-7-1850 (2-8-1850)
Thomas, James H. to N. Jane Sharp 11-3-1868 (11-4-1868)
Thomas, James W. B. to Jane M. Mcclish 3-13-1844
Thomas, Jesse W. to Mary J. Somers 12-3-1845 (12-4-1845)
Thomas, Joel A. to Mary E. Emerson 1-27-1869 (1-28-1869)
Thomas, John H. to N. E. Taylor 10-26-1857 (10-27-1857)
Thomas, John H. to Nannie D. Cole 10-29-1859 (11-1-1859)
Thomas, John H. to Virgina A. (Mrs.) Sharp 1-26-1869
Thomas, John J. to Sarah Jane McIver 12-8-1845 (12-9-1845)
Thomas, Lucius J. to Rebecca J. Hays 7-27-1859
Thomas, Samuel M. to Elizabeth Reavis 11-6-1849
Thomas, Wiley W. to Margarett H. Patterson 7-16-1849 (7-17-1849)
Thomas, William J. to Louisa J. Sharp 12-21-1858
Thompson, Alexander to Mary Eliza Barnett 12-19-1866 (12-20-1866)
Thompson, Archibald to Mary Holland 3-9-1840 (3-12-1840)
Thompson, Benjamin L. to Susan Guthrie 3-15-1840 (3-25-1840)
Thompson, George G. to Mary E. Ruddle 12-14-1870
Thompson, Hugh A. to Josephine Rone 11-21-1862 (12-3-1862)
Thompson, James B. to Sarah Jane Barnett 5-2-1842
Thompson, James J. to Mary Jane McCauley 12-?-1858 (12-9-1858)
Thompson, James T. to Mary J. Worrell 2-31-1852
Thompson, Jonthan to Nancy Clampitt 3-30-1844
Thompson, Miners L. to Sarah A. Tidwell 4-29-1844 (5-7-1844)
Thompson, Neil to Sarah Jane Mullins 9-11-1866 (9-13-1866)
Thompson, Sidney I. to Martha I. Redden 3-12-1842
Thompson, Terrel to Neely A. M. Freeman 9-1-1845 (9-4-1845)
Thompson, Thomas B. to Elizabeth Hamlett 10-25-1856 (10-26-1856)
Thompson, Thomas B. to Mary A. Robinson 2-2-1853
Thompson, Thomas T. to Eliza Jane Ellington 5-13-1861 (5-17-1861)
Thompson, Thomas to Elizabeth E. Alexander 8-18-1846 (8-19-1846)
Thompson, William F. to Mosiah Bregance 2-21-1838
Thompson, Wm. D. to Fannie Senter 12-11-1866 (12-12-1866)
Thompson, Wm. J. to Maggie J. Sims 12-10-1870 (12-11-1870)
Thorn, Joseph to Martha Ann Blythe 12-18-1848 (12-21-1848)
Thorn, Martin to Halma A. Brown 11-23-1845 (11-28-1845)
Thornton, I. to Hanah Morris 12-28-1839 (12-30-1839)
Thornton, James to Lourena (Mrs.) Reeves 5-17-1867 (5-19-1867)
Thues, Henry L. to Caroline Satterfield 2-12-1859 (2-13-1859)
Thurman, David T. to Frances Pippin 1-30-1854
Thurman, David T. to Moniza Lawrence 10-28-1858
Thurman, William to Malsina Miller 6-11-1849 (6-12-1849)
Tidwell, Franklin B. to Prior A. J. Lane 11-23-1842 (11-24-1842)
Tidwell, Joseph D. to Eliza A. Harris 10-31-1866
Tidwell, William M. to Mary Person 6-17-1841
Timms, Nathaniel to Sarah Hardin 1-20-1849 (1-21-1849)
Timms, Vinson to Matilda Timms 7-23-1849
Tims, George W. to Missouri Ann Tims 2-27-1856 (2-28-1856)
Tims, John T. to Jane (Mrs.) Glidewell 9-7-1858 (9-9-1858)
Tims, Larkin to Rebecca Roberts 6-10-1843 (6-11-1843)
Tims, Valentine to Martha Horn 12-23-1846
Tims, William to Mary Glidewell 8-6-1852
Tiner, John W. to Sarah A. Williamson 11-24-1859
Todd, George H. to Amanda Ross 4-13-1852 (4-15-1852)
Todd, James L. to Roenna M. E. Walden 8-2-1848
Todd, William to Jane C. Pipkin 1-12-1858 (1-14-1858)
Tolley, Wilson to Martha Johnson 3-28-1840 (3-1?-1840)
Tomlin, George M. to Sarah M. Carpenter 11-27-1850 (11-28-1851?)
Tomlin, James W. to Martha A. McClellen 2-17-1852
Tomlin, James W. to Penelope Estes 12-14-1861 (12-15-1861)
Tomlinson, James M. to Rachel Askew 3-9-1848
Tomlinson, John A. to Frances C. Jackson 4-25-1848

Tomlinson, Thomas D. to Martha E. Person 8-27-1866 (8-28-1866)
Tomlinson, William E. to Emma G. Harris 11-19-1866 (11-21-1866)
Tomlinson, William to Louisa Jackson 10-1-1839 (10-2-1839)
Toone, Coleman to Elizabeth Marsh 7-26-1852
Toten, Archibold W. O. to Harriett C. Hurt 3-29-1843
Towell, W. R. to Lidia Waddle 12-23-1839 (1-7-1840)
Townes, James M. to Mary Jane Fortune 4-26-1870 (4-27-1870)
Towns, Robert W. to Margaret W. Temple 11-27-1854 (11-30-1854)
Trader, Doddridge to Mary C. May 8-2-1859 (8-3-1859)
Trafford, George to Martha H. Clay 6-19-1868
Transau, Edward T. to Mary T. Pearson 12-7-1855 (12-13-1854?)
Transee, Benjamin F. to Sarah Ann Wilson 10-4-1847
Trask, William l. to Lucy Delapp 6-19-1858 (6-21-1858)
Traylor, Thomas to Ramola N. Angus 1-5-1841
Treadwell, Robt. A. to Susie Long 2-9-1869
Trice, William to Sarah Edwards 12-19-1868
Trotter, George W. to Sarah Elizabeth Meriwether 4-28-1857
Trousdale, John to Elizabeth Mooney 12-26-1842 (12-27-1842)
Tubbs, Francis M. to Olive V. (Mrs.) Shelby 11-19-1870 (11-20-1870)
Tucker, Coleman H. to Julianne C. Finger 7-14-1845 (7-15-1845)
Tucker, Jesse D. to Marinda C. Haltom 12-2-1869 (12-5-1869)
Tuggle, Thos. I. to Ann Elvill 11-6-1841 (11-12-1841)
Tull, John to Jane A. Burgh 1-27-1842
Tully, A. to Sarah W. Aldridge 4-13-1843
Tupell, James V. to Louis A. Stone 10-3-1844
Turner, David W. to Emma J. Mathis 3-2-1870 (3-8-1870)
Turner, David W. to Melcenia V. Barnett 2-16-1857 (2-19-1857)
Turner, Elijah to Nancy Jane Morgan 4-8-1867 (4-9-1867)
Turner, George W. to Caroline C. Hobbs 1-18-1848 (1-19-1848)
Turner, James to Nancy Nicholson 1-12-1856 (1-13-1856)
Turner, John C. to Frances E. Cardwell 12-21-1857
Turner, John W. to Margaret B. McLemore 2-10-1855 (2-13-1855)
Turner, Luther to Georgian Thomas 4-10-1858 (4-11-1858)
Turner, Samuel G. to Mary Jane Senter 12-6-1852 (12-7-1852)
Turner, William H. to Elizabeth Cole 2-5-1844 (2-13-1844)
Tyson, Gaither to Fannie Meriwether 12-11-1866 (12-12-1866)
Tyson, John A. to Ann Jane Cartmell 2-1-1843 (2-2-1843)
Tyson, Johnson B. to Mary M. Alston 6-27-1849 (6-28-1849)
Underwood, Edmund G. to Lucy J. Boswell 1-17-1853
Upton, George W. to Martha J. Parlow 7-1-1867 (7-17-1867)
Ursery, Dempsey to Emily Johnson 3-22-1852 (3-23-1852)
Ursery, Jno. M. to Mahala A. Jordan 1-13-1869
Ursery, John Harvey to Sarah Hogan 8-22-1866
Ursery, William H. to Fannie Dixon 9-13-1867 (9-15-1867)
Ursery, William to Abigail F. Mason 8-3-1837 (8-3-1847?)
Usery, John W. to Mary E. Usery 9-24-1870 (9-27-1870)
Using, George to Lucy Eastwood 10-16-1839
Utley, Burrell W. to Mary C. Hellard 12-11-1855 (12-12-1855)
Utley, Jonathan to Lucinda D. Oliver 5-23-1846
Utley, Joseph S. to Perline Duncan 5-14-1849 (5-17-1849)
Utley, Panes T. to Susan C. Alexander 2-8-1841
Utley, Thos. B. to Ellen Woolfolk 11-3-1868 (11-4-1868)
Valentine, Janes to Mary Jane Webb 9-8-1853 (9-11-1853)
Van Pelt, William to Daruishia Belmont Jones 7-22-1868 (7-17?-1868)
Vanhook, Jacob E. to Nancy S. Whitlow 11-19-1844
Vanhook, Solomon W. to E. K. Williams 1-25-1871
Vann, Valentine S. to Susan A. Robinson 1-3-1855 (1-4-1855)
Vanpelt, William to Nancy Emily Jones 7-28-1866 (7-29-1866)
Vantreece, Benj. F. to S. C. (Mrs.) Adams 1-15-1867 (1-17-1867)
Vantrees, William to Martha A. Nanny 4-16-1850 (4-17-1850)
Vantreese, Benjamin F. to Elizabeth Weaks 9-29-1852
Vantreese, John to Nancy Hicks 10-2-1847 (10-6-1847)
Vantreese, Thomas to Jane Williams 1-31-1855 (2-1-1855)
Vantreese, William C. to Sabetha W. Lovelace 6-8-1840 (6-10-1840)
Vantreese, Wm. A. to Mary Ann Williams 12-8-1866 (12-20-1866)
Vantress, William to Mary A. Stone 4-22-1848 (4-26-1848)
Vantrice, William to Martha I. Hayley 1-10-1845 (SB 1843?)
Vaughter, Richard B. to Martha Ann Gregory 12-4-1854 (12-7-1854)
Vaulx, John W. to Eliza J. Caldwell 5-31-1869 *
Vesser, Calvin C. to Mary E. Day 9-30-1867
Vestal, James W. to Amanda Jane Barr 9-17-1867 (9-18-1867)
Vick, Allen P. to Elvira G. Sykes 10-27-1869 (10-28-1869)
Vick, Joshua S. to Susan Castles 1-22-1845
Vick, Nathan to Sarah Prewitt 1-5-1843
Vincent, John A. to Sarah A. Anderson 1-9-1850

Vincent, Thomas S. to Leonilla E. Gamewell 12-1-1869
Vincent, William to Evaline Brown 9-26-1866 (9-27-1866)
Vinson, George to Sarah Hardin 6-24-1852
Vinson, James M. to Matilda Chisolm 2-5-1842 (2-10-1842)
Volentine, John R. to Elizabeth Cobb 5-24-1869
Voss, Zelmon to Elizabeth Parker 4-29-1857
Waddell, Buren B. to Fannie L. Tarver 6-9-1857
Wade, George to Basora McClaland 11-15-1854 (11-18-1854)
Wade, Osias to Bolsoa Vann 7-30-1855
Wadkin, John S. to T. N. Hamilton 12-13-1839
Wadley, William R. to Mary Jane Brower 10-15-1862 (10-19-1862)
Wadlington, John to Sarah Jane Gravit 8-15-1859 (8-16-1859)
Waggoner, George to Margaret C. Whitworth 4-26-1861
Waggoner, John W. to Lucy Bradford 3-18-1862
Waggoner, Stephen B. to Mary G. Whitworth 12-23-1856
Waldrup, James R. to Harriet Ann Stegall 12-7-1867 (12-10-1867)
Walker, Enoch R. to Nancy Ann Sewell 11-18-1868 (11-19-1868)
Walker, Felix to Ellen Cromwell 10-4-1838 (10-4-1838)
Walker, Jasper N. to M. F. Moore 12-2-1867 (12-3-1867)
Walker, Joel to Mary E. Brimingham 10-3-1853 (10-4-1853)
Walker, John F. to Amelia Ann Brown 3-20-1855 (3-21-1855)
Walker, John N. to Martha Ann Hudson 10-26-1867 (11-7-1867)
Walker, John N. to Mary B. Lewis 5-14-1870 (5-19-1870)
Walker, Joseph Newton to Zillah Syrena Roberts 7-6-1866 (7-8-1866)
Walker, Thomas W. to Florida E. Wood 8-23-1858 (8-25-1858)
Walker, Valintine to Otey Walker 1-18-1850 (1-20-1850)
Walker, Volentine to Liuisa? Walker 11-1-1870 (11-2-1870)
Walker, William P. to Martha A. Bailey 9-23-1852 (9-24-1852)
Walker, William to Neely Ellender Walker 8-8-1846 (8-9-1846)
Wallace, Everett to Mary Jane Williams 7-28-1857 (7-30-1857)
Wallace, William B. to Mary E. Williams 3-28-1848
Waller, Jonas M. to Mary Gardner 2-26-1862 (2-27-1862)
Waller, William D. to Ann L. Rogers 2-27-1862
Wallingford, Thomas W. to Unity Jane Brigget Bell 12-17-1855
Walsh, John L. to Martha C. Garland 11-18-1856 (11-30-1856)
Walsh, John L. to Martha J. Murchison 2-16-1849
Walters, Frank M. to Lucy Ann Tooms 12-7-1857 (12-10-1867?)
Walters, Jno. W. to Mary F. King 1-1-1869 (1-3-1869)
Walton, Isaac D. to Lucy Ann Fenner 3-1-1859 (3-2-1859)
Ward, James T. to Benvilla Nichols 9-4-1839
Ward, James T. to Elvy Jane Edwards 8-16-1854 (8-18-1854)
Ward, Jesse B. to Jane C. Haynes 11-24-1866
Ward, Minus M. to Susan Green 11-8-1856 (11-11-1856)
Ward, O. D. to Jane McCoy 3-5-1849 (3-14-1849)
Ware, L. H. to Elizabeth H. Vinson 1-20-1846
Warmath, Henry H. to Frances A. Clement 6-12-1855
Warmath, Henry to Mary Jarratt 11-3-1842 (11-5-1842)
Warmoth, Chesterfield to Mary Jane Roseman 1-10-1859 (1-11-1859)
Warner, Joseph to Martha Alexander 9-24-1857
Warner, Joseph to Mary G. Whitworth 9-4-1856 (noncomeatibus)
Warrel, Cardy to Frances J. Strain 7-3-1852
Warren, James M. to Rutha L. Roseman 12-9-1862
Warren, James W. to Arella Futrell 10-6-1847 (10-6-1847)
Warren, Thomas R. to Rebecca Ann Gattis 12-15-1848 (12-20-1848)
Watkins, Benjamin F. to Sarah P. Harding 1-19-1857
Watkins, Henry C. to Malvina H. Day 11-5-1845
Watkins, John S. to Eliza S. Brown 4-7-1868
Watkins, John S. to Jane S. Todd 11-8-1843 (11-9-1843)
Watkins, Samuel S. to Louisa C. Harris 12-20-1847 (12-21-1847)
Watkins, Walton to Susie Trezevant 10-17-1871 (10-18-1871)
Watlington, Francis W. to Mollie J. Anderson 4-26-1867 (4-27-1867)
Watlington, Sterling M. to Catharine Croom 5-14-1866
Watlington, William T. to Elizabeth Ozier 8-5-1847
Watson, Anail to Mary Elizabeth White 7-1-1854 (7-2-1854)
Watson, George W. to Cassa Ann Hendricks 2-8-1854
Watson, James T. to Nancy L. Edwards 1-27-1869 (1-28-1869)
Watson, Robert Z. to Francis Ann Burras 9-8-1853 (9-7?-1853)
Watson, Thomas to Narcissa Anderson 9-20-1859
Watson, William H. to Sarah R. Tyner 2-4-1843 (2-10-1843)
Watson, William to Martha J. Campbell 2-8-1853
Watt, Samuel to Martha C. Quinly 12-18-1841 (12-19-1841)
Watt, Thomas J. to Nancy E. Lyon 9-4-1867 (9-5-1867)
Watt, Thomas J. to Sarah A. Lyon 1-4-1854 (1-12-1854)
Watt, jr., James N. to Sarah Jane Lyon 3-16-1850
Waynick, A. R. to Mollie J. Lanier 10-13-1856 (10-30-1856)

Weakes, John R. to Mary Ann Hopper 12-21-1869 (12-23-1869)
Weare, Franklin H. to Belviretta Cain 11-16-1857 (11-19-1857)
Weatherly, Andrew D. to Asenith M. Marshall 12-7-1858 (12-8-1858)
Weatherly, James to Mary J. Volentine 11-7-1860
Weatherly, Lucius L. to Virginia C. (Mrs.) Stratton 5-4-1869
   (5-6-1869)
Weatherly, Robert to Melissa Ann Wood 11-13-1866
Weatherly, Rufus A. to Rutha Jane Dickinson 12-12-1859
Weatherly, Saml. H. to Martha Ann Valentine 11-13-1866
Weatherly, William M. to Mary Ann Reevely 12-15-1856
Weatherly, William W. to Sarah F. Winston 12-15-1858 (12-5?-1858)
Weathers, Charles H. to Mary Holloman 12-11-1867 (12-12-1867)
Weaver, Alfred N. to Hawkins Mangrum 11-12-1860 (11-13-1860)
Weaver, Claibourne to Sarah A. E. Harton 7-19-1843 (7-20-1843)
Weaver, Phillip to Nancy G. Taylor 11-15-1841
Webb, Claiborne to Susan J. McCrory 2-4-1856
Webb, James K. to Celia A. Duncan 11-19-1847 (11-20-1848?)
Webb, Norman to Wethly Webb 12-7-1843
Webb, Robert T. to Harriet M. White 10-31-1860 (11-1-1860)
Webb, William A. to Mary Ann Sanders 4-9-1841 (4-13-1841)
Webb, William R. to Cynthia Ann Elliot 12-22-1866 (12-26-1866)
Webb, Wm. A. to Elizabeth Botton 12-29-1868 (12-31-1868)
Weir, Donald D. to Ann B. Weir 2-14-1842 (2-15-1842)
Weir, John P. to Elizabeth W. Rogers 5-5-1842
Welch, Jacob W. to Francis J. (Mrs.) Taylor 4-15-1862 (4-27-1862)
Welch, Willie J. to Mary A. Brown 9-27-1866
Wells, Alexander to Julia C. McWhirter 12-18-1868
Wells, John to Mary Jane Peyton 6-6-1857 (6-7-1857)
Wells, William H. to Mary Ann Latham 12-23-1850 (12-24-1850)
Welsh, Henry A. to Mary Jane Harding 9-11-1854 (9-13-1854)
West, James R. to Jerome W. Harris 9-4-1841
West, James to Ann Florence 10-25-1858 (11-7-1858)
West, John D. to Elizabeth Lett 2-10-1871 (2-11-1871)
West, John to Sarah Ann Dickinson 1-13-1853
West, Olen to Martha Ann Johnson 11-1-1841
West, Philip H. to Nancy E. Autry 12-17-1858 (not executed)
West, Wm. F. to Phebe Gateley 8-6-1850 (8-7-1850)
Whaton, James C. to Mary Jane Murchison 9-2-1841 (9-?-1841)
White, Albert C. to R. F. Hilliard 12-22-1869
White, Alonza to Jane Thomas 6-22-1848
White, Benj. F. to Emeline Bushard 12-19-1866 (12-20-1866)
White, Daniel to Margarett Dowin 8-20-1838
White, James Henry to Nancy Johnson 5-23-1866
White, James M. to Ann C. Johnston 10-2-1838
White, James N. to Sarah Jane Edwards 9-7-1868
White, James R. to Sarah R. Rider 12-22-1840 (12-24-1840)
White, James to Emily H. Davie 9-19-1855
White, John B. to Sarah J. Chandler 3-10-1868
White, John M. to Jane M. Simpson 8-4-1846
White, John W. to Josephine Wilhelm 9-8-1866 (9-9-1866)
White, Joseph B. to Elvina Taylor 8-3-1868
White, Joseph to Tabitha Baker 8-4-1852
White, Nolen S. to Maria E. Mason 9-19-1871 (9-20-1871)
Whitelaw, John F. to Maria L. Cole 11-5-1849 (11-8-1849)
Whitenton, Othneil to Christenia R. Cock 1-13-1858
Whiteside, Joseph E. to Margaret A. Alexander 11-21-1855
   (11-22-1855)
Whiteside, Robert to Nancy Ann Alexander 3-24-1855
Whitesides, Thomas to Diannah Cox 9-20-1866
Whitfield, Richard M. to Mary F. Love 1-1-1855
Whitington, James to Cottury Betts 2-5-1844
Whitlaw, Henry to Elizabeth Smith 4-28-1849 (4-29-1849)
Whitlow, Francis M. to Ann Fenner 2-2-1857 (2-5-1857)
Whitlow, Nathan H. to Mary Elizabeth Webb 11-1-1854
Whittenton, George A. to Elizabeth Bledsoe 2-5-1846
Whittenton, James M. to Mattie A. Moore 1-6-1870
Whittenton, Quintillian T. to Delilah Owen 10-11-1862
Whittington, Gibson to Elizabeth Williams 8-20-1840
Whittington, Nathan W. to Malvina Irvin 9-6-1842
Whitworth, Ezekiel T. to Catherine Collins 3-5-1856
Whitworth, Francis M. to Amanda M. Waggoner 3-16-1854
Whitworth, Robert to Isabella Hobbs 10-15-1857 (10-16-1857)
Whyte, James E. to Barthinia S. Webb 7-22-1847
Wiggins, Harris to Ellen Chisum 7-1-1851
Wiggs, Loi R. to Caroline Wiggs 10-1-1840

Wilbon, John R. to Mattie Hall 12-22-1869

Wilhelm, John D. to Annie C. White 8-28-1866 (8-30-1866)

Wilie, James M. to Jane Delapp 4-11-1853 (4-12-1853)

Wilkerson, John to Eliza Jerman 1-27-1843 (1-30-1843)

Wilkerson, Wm. D. to Mary E. (Mrs.) Freding 8-8-1870 (8-9-1870)

Wilkins, Charles Thos. to Molly Catherine Townzel 5-20-1870 (5-22-1870)

Wilkins, Feereby to Catherine Sturdivant 12-9-1850 (12-11-1850)

Wilkins, James A. to Martha Estes 9-1-1845 (9-4-1845)

Wilkinson, John R. to Sallie E. Reddick 3-7-1871

Wilks, Joseph to Rebecca J. Kirkpatrick 12-6-1847 (12-7-1847)

Willett, James T. to Mary E. Day 11-15-1862 (11-19-1862)

Willett, John to Martha Mitchell 4-4-1842 (4-7-1842)

Williams, Allen to Lucy Bledsoe 7-21-1842

Williams, Alvin R. to Mary M. Dickerson 12-14-1859 (12-15-1859)

Williams, Andrew J. to Sarah Jane Thomas 9-26-1860 (10-2-1860)

Williams, Anthony T. to Margarett L. Eddins 3-27-1850

Williams, Aron W. to Uphrasia America Fr. Browder 12-17-1855 (12-20-1855)

Williams, Arthur to Gilly Hundley 11-4-1857

Williams, Arthur to Nancy Holloman 2-16-1869 (2-17-1869)

Williams, Baxter J. to Mary C. Taylor 9-23-1841 (9-30-1841)

Williams, Benjamin to Peggy Medly 9-4-1839 (9-1?-1839)

Williams, Berry H. to Frances Ellington 12-22-1868 (12-23-1868)

Williams, Berry H. to Mary Ritty Freno 2-4-1857 (2-5-1857)

Williams, Chapman to Eliza Detherage 11-28-1838

Williams, Collin to Catherine Massey 1-10-1854 (1-11-1854)

Williams, David to Margarett L. Morrison 2-10-1849

Williams, Drury B. to Martha Taylor 8-31-1852 (9-5-1852)

Williams, Drury B. to Rebecca Jane Davis 10-20-1857 (10-22-1857)

Williams, Elijah H. to Amanda J. Davis 12-23-1867 (12-27-1867)

Williams, Isaac Volentine to Artie Caroline Smith 11-20-1855

Williams, J. L. to Artie Woolfolk 12-6-1870 (12-7-1870)

Williams, Jacob to Delilah Allison 1-12-1854

Williams, James Wesley to Margaret Hart 9-28-1868

Williams, John F. to Susan Marshall 6-13-1842 (6-16-1842)

Williams, Jones to Susan Anderson 1-25-1853

Williams, Lawrence P. to Caroline Chasum 9-9-1847 (9-10-1847)

Williams, Lorenzo D. to Dialtha Emeline Bomar 6-5-1857 (6-7-1857)

Williams, Markens to Almeda Moss 12-21-1842

Williams, Mathew to Harriett Medlin 5-16-1840 (5-17-1840)

Williams, Meekins to Penina Bogant 3-29-1866 (4-1-1866)

Williams, Nathiel W. to Paradise Huntsman 5-30-1855

Williams, Newton to Sophronia Ellington 12-15-1850 (12-17-1850)

Williams, Peter to Viola Jackson 12-14-1849 (12-19-1849)

Williams, Ralph to Mary Jane Emerson 12-15-1868 (12-17-1868)

Williams, Robert B. to Martha E. Manley 7-19-1853

Williams, Robert J. to Martha J. Johnson 12-22-1852

Williams, Rounsville to Ann Elizabeth Whitworth 12-28-1859 (12-29-1859)

Williams, Samuel to Mary Jane Hill 12-13-1842 (12-15-1842)

Williams, Sanders to Geraldine Garrison 11-21-1870 (11-23-1870)

Williams, Thomas B. to Matilda Haynes 5-21-1861

Williams, W. B. to Margaret C. Bostick 7-28-1856

Williams, W. D. to Siddy Ann M. Medlin 12-16-1859 (12-18-1859)

Williams, W. P. to Almedia L. Jackson 10-19-1870 (10-20-1870)

Williams, W. P. to Julia Ann Eliza Edwards 11-22-1860 (11-25-1860)

Williams, William A. P. to Mary Ann Billington 5-2-1854 (5-4-1854)

Williams, William H. to Aly Hall 9-12-1840 (9-25-1840)

Williams, William to Mary Morgan Adams 12-18-1848 (12-19-1848)

Williams, Williford to Mary Ann Richards 1-8-1862 (1-9-1862)

Williams, Willis W. to Mary E. (Mrs.) Morrill 2-25-1867 (2-27-1867)

Williams, Wilson to Elizabeth V. Baker 10-1-1859 (10-2-1859)

Williams, Winfield to Jane Robinson 12-11-1847 (12-22-1847)

Williamson, George S. to Emanda E. Whitlow 2-11-1871

Williamson, George to George R. Haskins 4-15-1844

Williamson, Haywood to Elizabeth Maroney 1-3-1856

Williamson, John A. to Rebecca C. Fly 6-30-1857 (7-1-1857)

Williamson, Joseph T. to Julia A. Cozart 4-8-1856 (4-9-1856)

Williamson, Mathew to Mary Jane Halton 1-22-1868 (1-26-1868)

Williford, David J. to Granada Tyler 1-5-1870 (1-6-1870)

Willis, Albert to Ann Baker 2-7-1850

Willis, William to Elizabeth Neely 6-9-1866 (6-10-1866)

Willoughby, Eugene R. to Susan A. Deloach 12-3-1866 (12-6-1866)

Willoughby, John W. to Nannie J. Watkins 6-27-1867

Wilson, Allen I. to Ellener Chandler 12-7-1843

Wilson, Allen J. to Mary M. Chandler 9-10-1855

Wilson, Calvell to Emeline Reeves 1-12-1838 (12-13-1838)

Wilson, Cyrus to Louisa Hamilton 1-21-1840

Wilson, Geor. W. to Martha Ruffin 12-15-1842

Wilson, James B. to Emeline Whitington 8-22-1843 (8-23-1843)

Wilson, James to Elizabeth Sevier 10-13-1841

Wilson, John A. to Elizabeth Caruthers 11-5-1838 (11-6-1838)

Wilson, John to Jane Darmon 9-22-1842 (9-?-1842)

Wilson, Robert L. to Nancy A. Reed 1-17-1841 (1-18-1841)

Wilson, WM. A. to M. J. Paisley 1-31-1854 (2-2-1854)

Wilson, Whitson H. to Martha F. Johnson 10-4-1858 (10-6-1858)

Wilson, William D. to Eliza Williamson 9-3-1842 (9-4-1842)

Wilson, William P. to Sarah Jane Taylor 12-27-1854

Wilson, William Robert to Lucinda Leake 1-18-1856

Winchester, Wm. D. to Mary Ann Currie 2-6-1858

Winfree, Frank B. to Nannie E. Williams 2-28-1871

Wingrove, Edwin L. to Virginia Howlett 1-8-1862 (1-9-1862)

Winn, William A. to Sarah A. Bailey 12-19-1866 (12-25-1866)

Winn, Wm. Alexr. to Elizabeth Jane Norvell 12-15-1857 (12-17-1857)

Winne, Peter C. to Lizzie M. Eaton 12-23-1869

Winslow, Alson G. to Lenora Andrews 1-28-1853 (1-3-1853?)

Winslow, Thomas H. to Melvina Harris 10-5-1866 (10-7-1866)

Winston, Arnold to Nancy (Mrs.) Denton 11-9-1857 (11-10-1857)

Winston, James H. to Martha M. Jones 1-11-1843 (1-12-1843)

Winston, John W. to Julia F. McCaig 5-28-1870 (5-31-1870)

Winston, Joseph E. to Margaret Nicholson 2-26-1848 (3-1-1848)

Winston, N. B. to Margaret C. Garland 9-13-1856 (9-17-1856)

Winston, William N. to Winney Ann Conger 9-28-1848

Wisdom, Scott to Pattie Smith 6-17-1870 (6-18-1870)

Witherspoon, H. H. to Bettie Bond 10-24-1871 (10-25-1871)

Witherspoon, jr., William to Hallie Rice 3-29-1868 (4-2-1868)

Wollard, James M. to Julia R. (Mrs.) Mylor 5-21-1868

Womack, James G. to Elizabeth Lager Theus 12-24-1844

Womble, William W. to Narcissa C. Sherman 3-9-1848

Wood, Charles L. to Ama L. Read 4-5-1856 (4-6-1856)

Wood, Ferd. to Laura Shaw 5-8-1871 (5-9-1871)

Wood, James E. to Milly Grant 11-15-1858 (11-16-1858)

Wood, Jason L. to Nannie C. Pentecost 1-4-1870

Wood, Jeromiah P. to Martha Woods 5-27-1868 (5-28-1868)

Wood, R. W. to Margaret Mason 3-14-1870 (3-15-1870)

Wood, Willis to Elizabeth Smith 6-23-1846

Woodard, Aaron W. to Zelpha Woodard 3-12-1838 (5-20-1838)

Woodard, James M. to Sarah McFarland 12-19-1840 (12-14?-1840)

Woodard, John R. to Mary E. (Mrs.) Chitman 2-25-1867 (2-26-1867)

Woodard, Wm. P. to Tennessee Roberson 12-24-1866 (12-25-1866)

Wooddell, William J. to Harriet B. Caruthers 2-21-1853 (2-22-1853)

Woodell, John to Eady Bruce 9-27-1847 (9-29-1847)

Woodelle, David C. to Louisa J. Harston 9-5-1849

Woodfolk, John R. to Almera Niel 2-23-1842 (2-24-1842)

Woods, Andrew D. to Mary A. Woods 2-14-1870 (2-15-1870)

Woods, Caleb to Ann E. Murchison 8-5-1846 (8-13-1846)

Woods, William H. to Jane Barnett 10-22-1847 (10-26-1847)

Woodson, John to Martha Rebecca Ann Lewis 8-26-1867 (8-28-1867)

Woodward, Bennet to Nancy Powel 10-25-1862 (10-26-1862)

Wooley, John W. to Sarah E. Shaw 12-6-1858

Woolfolk, John G. to Sue Pearson 11-3-1868 (11-5-1868)

Woolfolk, John R. to Julia Preston 2-18-1861 (6-18-1861)

Wooten, Memory to Elizabeth Henderson 12-31-1868

Wooten, Wm. S. to Margaret A. Outland 12-15-1870

Word, Benj. A. (of AR) to Ida Hutcherson 2-22-1870

Worrell, Henry to Mary A. L. Butts 11-26-1849

Worrell, Peter to Nancy Bell 6-2-1856

Wortham, Green to M. P. E. Mason 11-26-1860 (11-27-1860)

Wrenn, David J. to Lucinda Evans 7-5-1841 (7-6-1841)

Wright, Charles W. to Mary T. Hudgins 2-24-1869 (2-25-1869)

Wright, Francis to Elizabeth Latham 8-21-1853 (8-23-1853)

Wright, George H. to Margarett H. Doak 11-26-1839

Wright, John to Francis Dupriest 1-3-1848

Wright, Thomas D. to Mary Jane Reevely 11-13-1855

Wyatt, Charles T. to Martha E. Nanny 7-27-1869 (7-28-1869)

Wyatt, Robert C. to Elizabeth J. Matthews 3-13-1858 (3-18-1858)

Wynkoop, Henry W. to Mary C. Wilson 6-3-1862

Yancey, William to Margarett Dugan 12-23-1841

Yancy, F. W. to Susan R. Beverage 1-18-1844

Able, Adeline to James A. Sheahan 10-20-1858 (10-21-1858)
Acre, Mary Ann to John Cofer 6-29-1839 (7-2-1839)
Acree, Elizabeth to John M. Love 10-12-1869 (10-14-1869)
Acres, Artelia Y. to Ephraine L. Grey 3-29-1854 (3-30-1854)
Action, Margarett Ann to Joseph C. Sharp 6-19-1839
Action, Sarah L. to John Brooks 12-7-1848
Adams, Agasy Caroline to William Malichi Allison 11-18-1857
Adams, Fannie (Mrs.) to J. Coleman Ross 1-24-1867 (1-27-1867)
Adams, Margaret to Norman Crowell 9-14-1853 (9-15-1853)
Adams, Mary B. to Wm. A. Duncan 9-27-1867 (10-1-1867)
Adams, Mary Elizabeth to William Henry Massey 2-16-1859 (2-17-1859)
Adams, Mary M. to Edward T. Rooker 4-3-1858 (4-4-1858)
Adams, Mary Morgan to William Williams 12-18-1848 (12-19-1848)
Adams, S. C. (Mrs.) to Benj. F. Vantreece 1-15-1867 (1-17-1867)
Adams, Sophronia to A. Stevens 10-23-1862
Adamson, Anna to J. Thomas McCutchen 11-4-1867 (11-5-1867)
Adcock, Edney J. to Joseph A. Covington 8-11-1866 (8-12-1866)
Adderton, Mary Jane to Jesse T. Parham 1-17-1857 (1-19-1857)
Adkins, Elizabeth to Hudson Jarrett 4-11-1856
Aldridge, Sarah W. to A. Tully 4-15-1843
Alexander, Caroline C. to Elijah Cass 12-29-1846
Alexander, Caroline C. to Elijah Cup 12-29-1846
Alexander, Cynthia to Moses Taylor 1-9-1843 (1-12-1843)
Alexander, Davy Theresa to John W. Heasenburg 6-13-1854 (6-15-1854)
Alexander, Elizabeth E. to Thomas Thompson 8-18-1846 (8-19-1846)
Alexander, Louisa J. to John F. Hunt 6-1-1868 (6-3-1868)
Alexander, Margaret A. to Joseph E. Whiteside 11-21-1855 (11-22-1855)
Alexander, Martha to Joseph Warner 9-24-1857
Alexander, Mary A. to John Coppedge 8-29-1855 (9-4-1855)
Alexander, Mary A. to Wilson E. Stewart 8-5-1878 (8-10-1868?)
Alexander, Mary F. to Isaac T. Johnson 10-12-1869 (10-13-1869)
Alexander, Mary Jane to Alfred Jackson 6-14-1854 (3-23-1854?)
Alexander, Mary Jane to Martin D. Alexander 5-14-1853
Alexander, Mary W. to Alexr. C. Caldwell 11-7-1860
Alexander, Mary to John J. Taylor 7-20-1846
Alexander, Nancy Ann to Robert Whiteside 3-24-1855
Alexander, Sadie E. to Calvin V. Hart 2-20-1871 (2-22-1871)
Alexander, Sarah Amanda to Andrew Jackson Sellars 1-18-1871 (1-19-1871)
Alexander, Sarah E. to John R. Gardner 3-30-1861
Alexander, Sarah E. to Joseph A. Betty 2-2-1852 (2-10-1852)
Alexander, Sarah to Jasper N. Butler 2-17-1857 (2-26-1857)
Alexander, Susan C. to Panes T. Utley 2-8-1841
Alexander, Susan to Arvell Garrett 4-4-1838 (4-5-1838)
Alison, Alsa Ann to Thomas N. Stephenson 4-25-1843
Alison, Elizabeth to Thos. N. Stephens 10-10-1843 (10-12-1843)
Allen, Elizabeth Frances to Robert Gill 1-21-1867 (1-22-1867)
Allen, Elizabeth Temple to Augustus B. Simmons 3-13-1866 (3-18-1866)
Allen, Ellen C. to C. (Dr.) Harris 12-15-1842
Allen, Fannie E. to David A. Jones 3-26-1868
Allen, Louisa Malinda to Matthew B. Barnett 3-19-1870 (3-22-1870)
Allen, Mary to John Perryman 1-20-1846
Allen, Sylvia to John Glover 8-22-1848
Allison, Amanda to Thomas Black 12-2-1846 (12-3-1846)
Allison, Delilah to Jacob Williams 1-12-1854
Allison, Margaret to John B. Alexander 7-14-1866 (7-15-1866)
Allison, Mary J. to Abner Teague 3-16-1866
Allison, Mary J. to Robert F. Henderson 5-2-1870 (5-4-1870)
Allison, Milly to William W. Nichols 5-16-1849 (5-17-1849)
Alston, Mary M. to Johnson B. Tyson 6-27-1849 (6-28-1849)
Alston, Mary to George Ramsey 6-10-1867 (6-11-1867)
Alston, Sallie J. to John Henry Skillern 11-19-1870 (11-23-1870)
Altman, Mary Jane to William J. Maddox 10-27-1856 (10-19?-1856)
Anderson, America T. to Ralph W. Daniel 11-25-1854 (12-10-1854)
Anderson, Bettie to William C. Marshall 5-3-1870
Anderson, Easter to John Renshaw 5-21-1842 (5-24-1842)
Anderson, Eliza A. to James F. Franklin 4-26-1858 (4-27-1858)
Anderson, Elizabeth to John H. Hundley 11-26-1860 (11-27-1860)
Anderson, Elizabeth to John M. Lester 7-2-1838 (7-19-1838)
Anderson, Esther E. to William R. Norvell 10-17-1844
Anderson, Lucrita A. to William H. Cooper 12-14-1838

Anderson, Mahala to Hugh Sweeney 8-30-1862 (8-31-1862)
Anderson, Margaret A. to William Yearout 3-2-1840
Anderson, Martha A. to John M. Justice 5-18-1852
Anderson, Martha to Benjamin Read 9-6-1842 (9-8-1842)
Anderson, Mary A. to George W. Brown 4-23-1860 (4-25-1860)
Anderson, Mary Ann to William W. Dew 1-5-1859
Anderson, Mary C. to James J. Edwards 10-17-1844
Anderson, Mary E. to Robt. A. Landers 12-17-1869
Anderson, Mary T. to John B. Ruffin 3-12-1856 (3-13-1856)
Anderson, Mary to W. B. Lewellen 1-30-1871 (2-1-1871)
Anderson, Matilda to Edward Barnes 5-1-1849 (5-3-1849)
Anderson, Miram S. to Samuel Glover 9-8-1858 (9-9-1858)
Anderson, Miriam L. to James Blackman 1-4-1843 (1-5-1843)
Anderson, Mollie J. to Francis W. Watlington 4-26-1867 (4-27-1867)
Anderson, Nancy to Solomon Glenn 4-19-1852 (4-25-1852)
Anderson, Narcissa to Thomas Watson 9-20-1859
Anderson, Saluda to Nathaniel L. Jones 12-17-1850 (12-19-1850)
Anderson, Sarah A. to John A. Vincent 1-9-1850
Anderson, Sarah E. to William W. Lockard 11-7-1853 (11-10-1853)
Anderson, Sarah to Calvert Laney 1-19-1846
Anderson, Sophronia to Franklin Brock 7-12-1853 (7-14-1853)
Anderson, Susan to Jones Williams 1-25-1853
Anderson, Tempence A. to William Rosser 9-7-1854
Anderson, Virginia A. to William H. Croom 2-26-1856 (2-27-1856)
Andonon, Mary to Joseph Duncan 11-7-1839
Andrews, Drucilla to Gilbert Hopkins 3-9-1859 (3-10-1859)
Andrews, Elizabeth to Thomas W. Elliot 4-5-1871
Andrews, Lenora to Alson G. Winslow 1-28-1853 (1-3-1853?)
Andrews, Lundy to Thomas W. Ewell 10-12-1853 (10-18-1853)
Andrews, Margaret to David E. Roberts 8-15-1861
Andrews, Susan to Daniel Luron 3-18-1840 (3-19-1840)
Angus, Caroline E. to Harrison McClamrock 12-16-1844 (12-17-1844)
Angus, Ramola N. to Thomas Traylor 1-5-1841
Appleby, Martha to T. Walker Allen 5-20-1869 (5-23-1869)
Armour, Lydia M. to George Jenkins 2-7-1839 (2-14-1839)
Armstrong, Malvina to James Carter 12-22-1846 (12-24-1846)
Arnis, Elizabeth S. to George J. Buckingham 12-18-1866 (12-19-1866)
Arnold, Lavenia (Mrs.) to Green H. Ramsey 11-1-1869
Ashworth, Sarah to Jas. C. W. Causler 1-4-1869 (1-7-1869)
Askew, Henrietta to James N. Greer 9-13-1858
Askew, Lucim to Eli Brown 3-13-1866
Askew, Margaret E. to Burkett L. Houghton 1-17-1853 (1-18-1853)
Askew, Mattie E. to Jesse A. Darnall 12-15-1868
Askew, Rachel to James M. Tomlinson 3-9-1848
Askew, Virginia A. to Ezekial R. Johnson 10-26-1869 (10-28-1869)
Atkins, Martha Jane to Daniel Harris 10-27-1866 (10-28-1866)
Attkisson, Mary E. to Claudius L. Milan 6-24-1868 (6-25-1868)
Autry, Nancy E. to Philip H. West 12-17-1858 (not executed)
Avery, Martha to Levi Thacker 3-23-1867 (3-24-1867)
Bacon, Amy to Lemuel D. Simmons 9-17-1842
Bailey, Dizia Ann to Jeremiah Bailey 6-22-1857 (6-23-1857)
Bailey, Eliza Jane to James F. Grant 12-25-1870 (12-28-1870)
Bailey, Emily to Thos. W. Kenner 3-17-1868 (3-18-1868)
Bailey, Martha A. to William P. Walker 9-23-1852 (9-24-1852)
Bailey, Martha Ann to Elijah H. Carter 6-15-1867 (6-16-1867)
Bailey, Martha C. to Elijah Bailey 12-28-1866 (12-31-1866)
Bailey, Mary E. to John F. Rives 5-14-1846
Bailey, Mary K. to Abner Johnson 5-23-1867 (6-3-1867)
Bailey, Nancy E. to Felix Z. Johnson 5-23-1867 (6-6-1867)
Bailey, Sarah A. to William A. Winn 12-19-1866 (12-25-1866)
Bains, Hannah to Daniel Butler 10-29-1860
Baker, Angelina to George W. Laws 9-13-1850
Baker, Ann to Albert Willis 2-7-1850
Baker, Anne to James W. Jackson 9-23-1850 (9-25-1850)
Baker, Becky Jane to George W. Piercy 5-26-1856
Baker, Dorothy Ann (Mrs.) to Wm. H. McCook 3-18-1871 (3-19-1871)
Baker, Elizabeth V. to Wilson Williams 10-1-1859 (10-2-1859)
Baker, Elizabeth to Warren W. Dew 2-18-1867 (3-12-1867)
Baker, Jane to Lawson Glenn 12-27-1847 (12-30-1847)
Baker, Jane to Saml. Hutcherson 3-4-1850 (3-7-1850)
Baker, Louisa C. to Levi W. Mason 1-1-1858 (1-5-1858)
Baker, Mary E. to L. G. Dawson 5-24-1871 (5-25-1871)
Baker, Nancy Jane to Francis M. Overton 8-13-1866
Baker, Rebecca to Drury Deberry 11-20-1858 (11-23-1858)

Baker, Susan Jane to James H. Davenport 9-11-1860 (9-13-1860)
Baker, Susan to John H. Reaves 5-26-1856
Baker, Susan to Joseph Luckey 12-24-1845 (12-27-1845)
Baker, Tabitha to Joseph White 8-4-1852
Baley, Delila to William Griffin 9-12-1838
Baley, L. to Dempsey Parker 12-16-1839
Ball, Mary C. to Patrick H. Sanford 1-5-1859 (1-6-1859)
Ball, Sarah J. to William A. Sanford 1-29-1855
Ballard, Margarett M to Wm. S. Temple 4-18-1843
Barber, Barbery B. to Wildon Foster 9-11-1838
Barber, Kate to George W. Kellar 12-21-1870
Barker, Elizabeth R. to Henry Harris 4-15-1848 (4-18-1848)
Barnes, Amanda to Leonard Owens 9-23-1854 (10-10-1854)
Barnes, Elizabeth to Hansford Smith 9-13-1839 (9-19-1839)
Barnes, Sarah A. to Thomas Jefferson Morgan 12-15-1855 (12-18-1855)
Barnett, Elizabeth F. to Littleberry Arnold 12-15-1862 (12-17-1862)
Barnett, Elizabeth to Dempsey Nowell 10-29-1866 (10-30-1866)
Barnett, Jane C. to William J. McAfee 3-16-1858 (3-25-1858)
Barnett, Jane to William H. Woods 10-22-1847 (10-26-1847)
Barnett, Martha A. to G. P. Goodrich 7-28-1854 (8-?-1854)
Barnett, Mary Ann to John P. S. Nelson 5-24-1870 (5-26-1870)
Barnett, Mary E. to Joseph E. Smith 8-24-1840 (8-25-1840)
Barnett, Mary Eliza to Alexander Thompson 12-19-1866 (12-20-1866)
Barnett, Mary M. to Sandford W. Gilliam 2-15-1861 (5-15-1861)
Barnett, Melcenia V. to David W. Turner 2-16-1857 (2-19-1857)
Barnett, Nancy M. to William A. Graves 9-7-1867 (9-12-1867)
Barnett, Sallie to John M. McCaslin 5-10-1870
Barnett, Sarah C. to Harvey Mullins 9-11-1866 (9-12-1866)
Barnett, Sarah Jane to James B. Thompson 5-2-1842
Barnett, Susan J. to Peter B. Barnett 9-2-1859 (9-8-1859)
Barnwell, Matilda to Philip Delph 8-4-1856
Barr, Amanda Jane to James W. Vestal 9-17-1867 (9-18-1867)
Barr, Pattie to Chalres T. Bates 8-16-1871 (8-19-1871)
Barrett, Arabella to George W. Baker 8-15-1846 (8-17-1846)
Barrett, Elizabeth to Madison Johnson 2-13-1849
Barrett, Harriett to George Haughton 9-14-1840 (9-15-1840)
Barrier, Agnes J. to Sidney P. Jones 9-16-1859 (9-18-1859)
Barrier, Catherine to William H. Edwards 7-3-1866
Barrier, Mary to Adolphus Britton 9-27-1848 (11-27-1848)
Barron, Elizabeth J. to John D. Roberson 9-22-1843 (9-28-1843)
Barron, Mary J. H. to James K. P. Oakley 6-27-1860
Barron, Missouri C. to William Howerton 11-23-1866 (11-25-1866)
Barton, Elizabeth to John J. Davis 9-27-1847
Barton, Minerva Ann to Joshua W. Nichols 10-6-1841 (10-7-1841)
Barton, Nancy to Thomas Blair 1-1-1868 (1-2-1868)
Basford, Earry? to William Shoemaker 10-30-1839
Bass, Matilda to Richard Bennett 7-31-1839
Bateman, Virginia F. to John W. W. Crawford 8-29-1857 (8-1?-1857)
Bates, Permelia to Richard Glenn 7-19-1853
Battle, Keziah to Thomas Sorrell 9-7-1861 (9-8-1861)
Baxter, Mary C. to Cyrum Sharp 1-16-1849
Beal, Mollie to Francis O. Browning 12-9-1867
Bealy, Sarah E. to Henry S. Johnson 4-19-1850 (4-24-1850)
Beard, Margaret to Jonas Young 8-5-1847
Beaty, Mary A. to Thos. C. Rainey 12-20-1869
Beaty, Mary Ann to William Dickinson 12-25-1852 (12-26-1852)
Beaty, Mary F. to Calier F. Sawyer 2-8-1870
Beaty, Mattie E. to John H. (Dr.) Jones 10-7-1867
Becton, Mary L. W. to Milton B. Boyd 10-26-1850 (10-27-1850)
Beddo, Phoeba to John R. Pandry 9-23-1869
Bedwell, Nancy to William Fleming 5-25-1859 (5-29-1859)
Bell, Amanda J. to George W. Cain 9-9-1871 (9-10-1871)
Bell, Maggie A. to H. F. Smith 11-12-1867
Bell, Nancy to Peter Worrell 6-2-1856
Bell, Unity Jane Brigget to Thomas W. Wallingford 12-17-1855
Belton, Angelina to Henry McFarlin 7-27-1850 (7-28-1850)
Belton, Jane to William Allen 3-12-1850 (3-14-1850)
Belton, Louisa (Mrs.) to William R. Freeman 10-12-1861 (10-13-1861)
Belton, Margaret to George Brogden 12-26-1854 (12-27-1854)
Bennet, Mary Ann to Martin W. Kerby 7-2-1857
Bennett, Martha D. to Alvis Kirby 12-4-1854 (12-5-1854)
Bennett, Mary E. to Newton C. Jordon 3-15-1854 (3-23-1854)
Bennett, Nancy M. to Jesse Kirby 2-24-1846
Benson, Elizabeth R. to Thomas B. Casey 10-11-1858 (10-13-1858)

Benson, Margaret to Rowland G. Harris 11-23-1859 (11-24-1859)
Benson, Mary A. to Alfred Pool 3-15-1855
Benthall, Catharine to Jessee Jackson 8-2-1854 (8-3-1854)
Benton, Elizabeth J. A. to James N. Carruthers 1-1-1845
Berrycroft, Sarah A. T. to John C. Oliver 6-2-1855
Betts, Cottury to James Whitington 2-5-1844
Betts, Susan to John Sandrey 1-22-1844
Betty, Martha A. to John W. Allison 10-24-1859
Betty, Sarah (Mrs.) to Henry T. Johnson 9-6-1869 (9-7-1869)
Beverage, Susan R. to F. W. Yancy 1-18-1844
Bevill, America Catherine to F. S. Clements 8-26-1868 (8-27-1868)
Bevill, Jennie (Mrs.) to John W. Howell 11-30-1867 (12-1-1867)
Bevill, Lydia to Richard W. Kirby 11-12-1870 (11-13-1870)
Bevill, Sarah M. to Granville C. Lowe 12-22-1859
Bickers, Allie to James T. Perciful 12-24-1868 (1-4-1869)
Bickers, Lucy to George Kilpatrick 3-15-1856
Bigelow, Amanda C. to Amos W. Jones 4-1-1857 (4-2-1857)
Bigelow, Eliza to Joseph D. Mason 9-17-1844 (9-18-1844)
Biggers, Jane A. to Richard B. Quinley 12-23-1848 (12-25-1848)
Billington, Mary Ann to William A. P. Williams 5-2-1854 (5-4-1854)
Bingham, Amanda to Lafayette Barrier 12-4-1860
Bingham, Jennie to Fountain Murry 8-10-1867 (8-13-1867)
Birdsong, Lemisa R. to Wm. H. McKee 9-12-1871 (9-13-1871)
Birdsong, Margaret to Thomas Sanders 8-27-1859 (8-28-1859)
Birdsong, Mary N. to Francis M. Howard 10-9-1866
Birmingham, Angeline to Thomas D. Jackson 12-4-1845 (12-5-1845)
Birmingham, Emelina to Hasting J. Smith 2-19-1840
Birmingham, Malvina to William T. Edwards 5-9-1844
Bishop, Caroline to Atlas Phillips 8-15-1848
Bishop, Lucy G. to Richard H. Harrison 7-15-1852
Bishop, Mary Elvina M. to George S. Harrison 4-27-1838 (5-10-1838)
Bivens, Sallie to James A. Collins 12-6-1866
Black, Eliza J. to Berry A. Davis 6-18-1853 (7-19-1853)
Black, Ellen B. to John R. Robley 12-25-1852 (12-28-1852)
Black, Margaret K. to Hamilton J. McKnight 11-2-1847
Black, Mary F. to John S. Martin 3-8-1870
Black, Mary to John M. Hendricks 12-20-1848
Black, Nancy Elizabeth to Saml. T. McMaster 10-4-1858
Black, Nancy J. to James M. Anderson 7-13-1840
Black, Nancy to Thomas F. Barton 12-28-1847 (12-30-1847)
Blackard, Julion to Turner Perry 8-7-1848
Blackmon, E. I. to William A. Benson 9-22-1842
Blackmon, Elizabeth K. to James Rollins 2-21-1855 (2-25-1855)
Blackmon, Jonnie L. to John T. Rone 1-3-1867 (1-6-1867)
Blair, Nancy to Benjamin F. Haltom 10-30-1850 (10-31-1850)
Blan, Martha Jane to James R. Connell 1-15-1843
Blaydes, Mary F. to W. H. Jelks 3-10-1852 (3-11-1852)
Bledsoe, Amanda M. to John T. Beveridge 12-20-1854 (12-21-1854)
Bledsoe, Asinith to WilliamD. McDummitt 12-24-1839
Bledsoe, Elizabeth to George A. Whittenton 2-5-1846
Bledsoe, Fidelia to Raves E. Jordon 12-26-1838
Bledsoe, Lucy to Allen Williams 7-21-1842
Blurton, Mary to Ruffin Permenter 9-24-1866 (9-25-1866)
Blythe, Elizabeth Jane to William C. Owens 4-21-1860 (4-22-1860)
Blythe, Martha Ann to Joseph Thorn 12-18-1848 (12-21-1848)
Boals, Emeline to James Capher 8-11-1847 (8-12-1847)
Boals, Malissa to Richard T. Bolton 1-9-1849 (1-10-1849)
Boals, Susan Jane to Miles Wilson Piercy 8-2-1869
Boaz, Mary S. to Liberty W. Brimingham 10-18-1859 (10-20-1859)
Boce, Mary A. to Thos. C. Busick 10-30-1844
Boet, Harriet to Washington Parkin 9-15-1842 (9-16-1842)
Bogant, Penina to Meekins Williams 3-29-1866 (4-1-1866)
Boles, Joannah to Albert T. McMullins 6-6-1859 (6-9-1859)
Bolin, Rebecca f. to Henry McCall 12-29-1845 (12-30-1845)
Boman, Martha to Benjamin J. Shirley 11-29-1855
Bomar, Dialtha Emeline to Lorenzo D. Williams 6-5-1857 (6-7-1857)
Bond, Bettie to H. H. Witherspoon 10-24-1871 (10-25-1871)
Bond, Biddy (Mrs.) to William P. Ripley 11-28-1860
Bond, Eliza A. to Jenkins Newsom 4-17-1850
Bond, Elizabeth to Farrington B. Snipes 5-3-1854
Bond, Hannah O. to Whitmell T. Bond 5-3-1852 (5-4-1852)
Bond, Sarah J. to Chas. J. Calloway 12-13-1869 (12-14-1869)
Bone, Martha to Benj. F. Bond 2-19-1861
Boner, Julia S. (Mrs.) to William A. Anthony 3-1-1858 (3-8-1858)
Bonner, Susan E. to Felix R. Hardgrave 2-28-1852 (3-2-1852)

Bools, Lucety to Allen Carr 1-4-1859 (1-5-1859)
Boon, Ann E. to Remon Mayo 1-10-1839
Boon, Ann to James Graves 9-21-1857 (9-22-1857)
Boon, Eady Mozelle to Ezekiel T. McCoy 10-22-1845 (10-23-1845)
Boon, Elizabeth to Merlin Perry 9-12-1843 (9-21-1843)
Boon, France R. (Mrs.) to James M. Sharp 10-27-1868
Boon, Laura A. to George W. Cocke 1-15-1856
Boon, M. J. to Milton L. Deberry 1-25-1867 (1-31-1867)
Boon, Mary W. to James M. Brown 5-3-1856 (5-4-1856)
Boon, Mary to James H. Aubrey 8-23-1845 (8-25-1845)
Boone, Juliam to William H. Parker 1-5-1840 (1-7-1840)
Boone, Margaret J. to Enoch Bryan 7-29-1840
Bostick, A. to Joseph Iver 11-1-1842
Bostick, Margaret C. to W. B. Williams 7-28-1856
Bostick, Margaret C. to Wilson E. Stewart 10-17-1859
Bostick, Mary A. to John J. Matthews 9-2-1847
Bostrick, Sophronia to Bartlett F. Bird 12-18-1850
Boswell, Lucy J. to Edmund G. Underwood 1-17-1853
Boswell, Mary H. to James A. Shaw 4-28-1849 (4-29-1849)
Boswell, Sarah Ann to George Gattas 4-27-1843
Botton, Elizabeth to Wm. A. Webb 12-29-1868 (12-31-1868)
Bowling, Emeline to Thomas J. McDurmit 1-17-1857 (1-18-1857)
Bowman, Mary (Mrs.) to Joshua M. Bowman 12-14-1867 (12-15-1867)
Boyce, Texie C. to William C. Penn 10-21-1862
Boyd (Becton?), Mary L. W. (Mrs.) to George W. Hurley 11-2-1858
Boyd, Jane H. to William Montgomery 3-12-1852 (3-16-1852)
Boyd, Margaret to William K. Stapleton 4-15-1841
Boyd, Mariah I. to Martin Shaw 1-14-1839 (1-15-1839)
Boyd, Martha Jane to Henry C. Cassels 1-7-1867
Boyd, Rebecca to Richard Massey 2-13-1841
Boyd, Susan to William Gray 10-6-1860 (10-7-1860)
Boyett, Susan to Andrew Massey 12-3-1844 (12-4-1844)
Boykin, Martha S. to C. C. Hutchings 8-30-1856
Boykin, Mary Ann Eliza to Robert N. McLemore 9-1-1855 (9-5-1855)
Boykin, Mary E. to Samuel M. Kirk 9-5-1843
Bradberry, Delia to Robert Clark 10-8-1870
Bradberry, Elizabeth R. to Joseph L. Medling 5-11-1838 (5-17-1838)
Bradberry, Mary A. to Andrew C. Stewart 2-16-1846
Bradberry, Sarah S. to James B. McNeely 3-19-1586 (3-20-1856)
Bradbury, Epsey Ann to William A. Moore 1-15-1846
Bradford, Elvira to Dempsey Cox 11-14-1866 (11-15-1866)
Bradford, Lucy to John W. Waggoner 3-18-1862
Bradford, Lydia A. to John Ingram Sturdevant 11-24-1868 (11-25-1868)
Bradford, Mary Jane to Robert F. McKnight 4-7-1859
Bradley, Patience to James Robb 8-16-1848
Branch, Chelly to Stephen Gatlin 12-16-1840 (12-17-1840)
Branch, Elizabeth to Bogan Branch 9-10-1842 (9-20-1842)
Branch, Laurany to William Johnson 2-26-1848 (2-29-1848)
Branch, Mary A. Elizabeth to George J. Norton 11-11-1857 (11-12-1857)
Brandon, Sarah Jane to W. C. Cartwright 4-1-1850
Brant, Susan to Henry Harston 10-13-1846 (10-14-1846)
Brantley, Ann E. to J. B. Compton 1-31-1854 (2-2-1854)
Bray, Becky Ann to John W. Jones 10-17-1870 (10-19-1870)
Bray, Frances E. to John W. Dismukes 11-24-1866 (11-27-1866)
Bregance, Mosiah to William F. Thompson 2-21-1838
Brent, Ann Eliza to Charles L. Stewart 1-31-1848
Bretton, Martha A. to L. M. Edwards 6-9-1870 (6-12-1870)
Brewer, Lucinda Jane to James W. Spraggins 11-24-1869 (11-25-1869)
Bridges, Narcissa to Protestant P. Dupriest 8-9-1850 (8-11-1850)
Brigance, Zelphia J. to Ransom H. Bell 1-24-1870 (1-25-1870)
Briggance, Henrietta to Robert N. McClellan 5-25-1860 (5-27-1860)
Brigham, Elizabeth to John M. Roberson 1-2-1850
Brimingham, Malvina to William D. Carnetzer 12-29-1859
Brimingham, Mary E. to Joel Walker 10-3-1853 (10-4-1853)
Brinkley, Huldy to Charles Chamberlin 12-27-1841
Brinkley, Huldy to William Phillips 4-16-1842 (4-17-1842)
Brinkley, Mary Ann to P. G. Cox 11-13-1839
Briton, Frances to Thomas Britton 4-1-1850
Britton, Bertha H. to Fredrick Anderson 2-23-1846 (2-26-1846)
Britton, Nancy P. to Daniel W. Bunten 5-12-1860 (5-?-1860)
Brock, Josephine to Logan Hopkins 11-16-1857
Brogden, Armitty to Washington McFarlin 1-8-1858 (6-23-1858)
Brogden, Mary to Clement Pierce 12-30-1852

Brook, Sarah to Andrew J. Byner 9-1-1841
Brooks, Addie V. to James H. Long 1-22-1867
Brooks, Catherine E. to James L. Robinson 3-4-1859
Brooks, E. M. to D. F. Talley 2-8-1871
Brooks, Eliza to John H. Gregory 11-3-1846 (11-6-1846)
Brooks, Eugenia to James M. Muse 11-13-1868
Brooks, Fannie to William Brooks 11-13-1866
Brooks, Isabella to William J. Rose 12-16-1867
Brooks, Lizzie H. to George K. Brooks 11-13-1866
Brooks, Louisa to John Morse 11-17-1852
Brooks, Nannie J. to James M. Hays 11-9-1868 (11-12-1868)
Brooks, Sarah to Wesly Blackburn 12-29-1846 (12-31-1846)
Brooks, Temperance to Alphus P. Moore 12-24-1841 (12-30-1841)
Brookshire, Elizabeth A. to John D. Henning 12-12-1859
Browder, Uphrasia America Fr. to Aron W. Williams 12-17-1855 (12-20-1855)
Brower, Mary Jane to William R. Wadley 10-15-1862 (10-19-1862)
Brown, Amelia Ann to John F. Walker 3-20-1855 (3-21-1855)
Brown, Aquilla Ann to William B. Mason 8-4-1841
Brown, Caroline V. to George R. Hellard 6-1-1857 (6-2-1857)
Brown, Eliza S. to John S. Watkins 4-7-1868
Brown, Elizabeth C. to Nathan Moore 9-4-1848
Brown, Elizabeth N. to William S. Calloway 1-22-1840
Brown, Emily to Marcus L. Bevill 10-4-1860
Brown, Evaline to William Vincent 9-26-1866 (9-27-1866)
Brown, Halma A. to Martin Thorn 11-23-1845 (11-28-1845)
Brown, Irene to James B. Cozart 9-5-1871
Brown, Jane to Lewis Duncan 1-4-1853
Brown, Julia Ann to John Tyler Anderson 10-9-1860
Brown, Lucinda A. to Henry C. Jones 10-27-1869 (10-28-1869)
Brown, Margaret A. to James M. Reavis 2-13-1862
Brown, Margaret M. to Wm. B. Ewell 4-2-1855
Brown, Martha Jane to Thomas H. Garrett 10-29-1856
Brown, Mary A. to Willie J. Welch 9-27-1866
Brown, Mary E. to William P. Lacy 7-15-1867 (7-18-1867)
Brown, Mary to Enoch Rollins 12-12-1838 (12-13-1838)
Brown, Mary to Newton Neal 10-4-1858
Brown, Nancy E. to John H. Hogan 9-27-1870 (9-28-1870)
Brown, Sarah to John Blair 1-22-1839
Brown, Susan A. M. to Meciagah Bullock 9-29-1841
Browning, Sarah E. to Joseph Fulcher 3-18-1867 (3-19-1867)
Bruce, Eady to John Woodell 9-27-1847 (9-29-1847)
Bruison, Darcas to Luther N. Mitchell 8-5-1848
Bruton, Sarah Ann to John B. Love 6-13-1848 (6-14-1848)
Bryan, Francis T. to John Y. Strayhorn 12-4-1854
Bryant, Eveline to Henry Conner 12-16-1845 (12-18-1845)
Bryant, Martha Jane to Elam D. Henderson 10-27-1856 (10-29-1856)
Bryant, Penelope E. to Levey Lacy 7-10-1848 (7-12-1848)
Bryant, Rachael to John A. Dunnaway 7-30-1846
Bryant, Susan to Norflet Jean 9-17-1856 (9-18-1856)
Buchanan, Ann E. to Geo. W. Swink 5-14-1869
Buckannon, Mary Ann to Anderson Skillern 12-1-1841
Buckner, Emma to Chas. B. Houston 9-22-1869
Buffalo, Nancy to Robert Stobaugh 1-4-1869 (1-6-1869)
Buffalo, Nancy to William H. Nelson 3-19-1866 (not executed)
Bugg, Jane V. to Albert L. Burrow 11-28-1842 (11-22?-1842)
Bullock, Ann R. to Richard A. Sneed 12-15-1869
Bumpass, Martha Ann to Milos C. Cook 1-16-1842
Bumpass, Tennie to Brandon Lane 1-14-1871 (1-15-1871)
Bunton, Catherine to Fredrick Mayo 3-5-1843
Burgh, Jane A. to John Tull 1-27-1842
Burk, Ann to George W. Stover 12-20-1854
Burnam, Mary Ann to Alfred Bigloe 11-13-1854 (11-16-1854)
Burns, J. J. to E. Johnson 8-28-1858
Burras, Francis Ann to Robert Z. Watson 9-8-1853 (9-7?-1853)
Burres, Lucinda to Daniel Hopper 10-4-1838
Burrough, Mary C. to James M. Hafley 2-1-1870
Burrow, Addie H. to James A. L. Davie 12-15-1860 (12-16-1860)
Burrow, Catherine to James M. Medlin 12-18-1850
Burrow, Margaret Ann to James Balentine 2-19-1857
Burrow, Mary H. to Jubelee P. Rogers 4-15-1847
Burrus, Martha J. to William R. Faucett 5-7-1870 (5-8-1870)
Burrus, Martha to John W. Robinson 11-22-1842 (11-23-1842)
Burson, Catherine to John L. Robison 11-29-1862
Burton, Catherine to Edmund Dickens 12-25-1838

Burus, Ellen B. to Calier A. Steed 1-20-1857
Bushard, Emeline to Benj. F. White 12-19-1866 (12-20-1866)
Butler, A. B. to H. L. Mooring 2-27-1854 (3-2-1854)
Butler, Ann E. to John T. Brown 11-23-1859 (11-24-1859)
Butler, Elizabeth C. to Caleb Odam 8-30-1853 (8-31-1853)
Butler, Elizabeth M. to Jackson G. Butler 12-4-1852 (12-8-1852)
Butler, Frances C. to Minus O. Adams 1-10-1859 (1-11-1859)
Butler, Levinia R. to Byrd Hill 10-21-1852
Butler, Lucy to John Mills 12-4-1852 (12-9-1852)
Butler, Margaret A. to Tapley Adam 8-24-1853 (8-25-1853)
Butler, Mary Ann to John C. Rogers 4-12-1847
Butler, Nancy C. to Jarvis Starkey 10-25-1858 (10-27-1858)
Butler, Narcissa H. to Napoleon Gentry 7-1-1868 (7-2-1868)
Butler, Sarah Jane to William H. Seat 8-25-1856 (8-26-1856)
Butler, Sarah to Joshua B. Marsh 4-3-1848
Butler, Terry to Robert G. Raney 11-18-1843
Butts, Judia H. to Joseph E. Langford 1-2-1860 (1-4-1860)
Butts, Mary A. L. to Henry Worrell 11-26-1849
Butts, Mary A. to Isaac Bagnell 1-24-1849
Byrd, Elvira M. (Mrs.) to William Pope 12-12-1859
Byrn, Penelope to William H. Bryan 1-21-1843 (1-24-1843)
Byrum, Sarah to Daniel Smith 7-17-1849
Cage, M. A. (Mrs.) to Richard Hines 8-9-1870
Cain, Belviretta to Franklin H. Weare 11-16-1857 (11-19-1857)
Cain, Tabitha to Wm. P. Harris 11-27-1868 (12-3-1868)
Caldwell, Eliza J. to John W. Vaulx 5-31-1869 *
Caldwell, Rebecca (Mrs.) to Henry Norman 7-17-1858 (7-18-1858)
Calloway, Lizzie to David P. Davis 5-8-1867
Campbell, Alithia to John Murrill 11-5-1850
Campbell, Cornelia A. to Joel Mayo 12-13-1855
Campbell, Fannie A. to James Harrison 12-21-1869 (12-23-1869)
Campbell, Jane E. to Preston B. Scott 11-12-1861 (11-13-1861)
Campbell, Lurany Ann to James C. Harkins 12-17-1845 (12-18-1845)
Campbell, Margaret E. to William M. Shelton 2-17-1849
Campbell, Martha J. to William Watson 2-8-1853
Campbell, Penelope P. to Robert Sterling 6-5-1856
Cannady, Josephine to Benj. J. Jones 1-11-1867 (1-13-1867)
Cardwell, Frances E. to John C. Turner 12-21-1857
Carpenter, Sarah M. to George M. Tomlin 11-27-1850 (11-28-1851?)
Carpenter, Susan M. to James M. Hopper 11-16-1855 (11-20-1855)
Carr, Mary to Geo. W. Richardson 6-8-1871 (6-11-1871)
Carring, Caroline to Levi Bostick 10-15-1846
Carrington, Ann F. to Moses Moore 1-25-1840 (1-29-1840)
Carrington, Caroline to William Croom 6-24-1840 (7-8-1840)
Carrington, Elizabeth M. to Francis G. Smith 12-20-1852
Carrington, Louisa to John W. Norton 7-23-1849
Carrington, Mary to John Bostick 12-30-1845 (12-31-1845)
Carrington, Sarah J. to Charles H. Peters 9-24-1866 (9-25-1866)
Carroll, Niecy to William J. Lyon 4-17-1861
Carroll, Priscilla N. to Wiley Perry 5-7-1860 (5-9-1860)
Carrothers, Margaret to Turley Hopper 9-22-1852 (9-23-1852)
Carruth, Elizabeth to William C. Reed 7-12-1841
Carruthers, Mary to Hardin Jones 1-9-1845 (1-10-1845)
Carter, Elizabeth to James M. Dunlap 12-11-1848 (12-14-1848)
Carter, Mary Ann to George W. Reeves 9-15-1856 (9-23-1856)
Carter, Mary Ann to Thomas L. Carter 6-2-1869
Carter, Rebecca V. to Abram B. Langford 5-16-1860 (5-17-1860)
Cartmell, Ann Jane to John A. Tyson 2-1-1843 (2-2-1843)
Caruthers, Elizabeth to John A. Wilson 11-5-1838 (11-6-1838)
Caruthers, Harriet B. to William J. Wooddell 2-21-1853 (2-22-1853)
Caruthers, Laura A. to A. S. McClanahan 12-18-1860
Caruthers, Margaret E. (Mrs.) to John M. Meals 1-19-1867 (1-22-1867)
Caruthers, Mariah Olivia to William W. Chisum 3-11-1867
Caruthers, Nancy to Alpha Fulbright 12-31-1840
Caruthers, Sallie P. to Middleton Hays 12-16-1868
Caruthers, Virginia to Jose. B. Freeman 10-25-1849
Carwell, Parthenia J. to James M. Shaw 8-21-1869 (8-22-1869)
Casey, Mollie E. to Cullen P. Hopkins 6-7-1867 (6-12-1867)
Casey, Tennessee to James C. Casey 8-15-1870 (8-17-1870)
Cash, Elizabeth J. to J. F. Davidson 1-3-1871 (1-5-1871)
Cash, Nancy N. to Walter L. Thedford 1-16-1869 (1-20-1869)
Cash, Sarah to Thomas Askew 6-22-1857
Cason, Mary to Thomas I. Heath 5-28-1838 (5-21?-1838)
Cason, U. C. to W. A. Murchison 11-16-1847

Castles, Charity to Edmund D. Screws 3-26-1846 (4-2-1846)
Castles, Susan to Joshua S. Vick 1-22-1845
Cate, Ann D. W. to Daniel F. Birmingham 5-19-1846
Cates, Arabella to Albert M. Estes 10-19-1869
Caurdel, Sarah Ann to Elbert Rollins 4-27-1857
Chamberlain, Caroline to Oney Sheldon 12-28-1848
Chamberlain, Martha to Matthew Horne 3-19-8150 (3-21-1850)
Chamberlin, Susan to Charles W. Chamberlin 1-13-1841 (1-14-1841)
Chambers, Catherine Ann to Robert B. Sanford 12-23-1839 (12-24-1839)
Chambers, Eliza Jane to Philander D. W. Conger 12-14-1842 (12-15-1842)
Chandler, Ellener to Allen I. Wilson 12-7-1843
Chandler, Elvira to Isham Burrow 2-14-1838
Chandler, Hannah to Duncan L. Alexander 1-31-1854
Chandler, Jane to John Young 10-29-1846
Chandler, Mary M. to Allen J. Wilson 9-10-1855
Chandler, Sarah J. to John B. White 3-10-1868
Chaney, Belinda to Thomas Caffrey 12-10-1850
Chapman, Eliza to William L. Bond 12-2-1844 (12-4-1844)
Chapman, Elizabeth to Henderson Peach 1-2-1844 (1-4-1844)
Chapman, Nancy to Andrew Conner 6-21-1845 (6-24-1845)
Chappell, Sarah E. to John R. Hurt 6-20-1860 (6-21-1860)
Chasum, Caroline to Lawrence P. Williams 9-9-1847 (9-10-1847)
Cherry, Irabella C. to George W. Patrick 3-19-1849
Chester, Ann Elizabeth to Peter Simmons 9-7-1857 (9-10-1857)
Chester, Mary J. to George W. Bond 10-6-1845 (10-7-1845)
Childress, Eliza to Henderson Kirby 4-26-1848 (4-27-1848)
Childress, Malvina H. to Richard McGowan 8-7-1841 (8-8-1841)
Childress, Martha to Edwin Clark 8-17-1852
Childress, Mildred M. to John A. S. Parrish 2-8-1841 (2-11-1841)
Childs, Mary G. to Littleton I. Joyner 1-2-1844
Chipman, Delila to William H. Davis 12-7-1840
Chipman, Eliz. J. to Wiley Suser 5-13-1853
Chipman, Elizabeth to John J. Jones 8-8-1846 (8-11-1846)
Chipman, Margaret to Chesley P. Pipkins 5-18-1854
Chipman, Nancy to James Kenner 4-1-1852 (4-3-1852)
Chipman, Perlina to James H. Davis 4-9-1853
Chism, Catherine to Thomas B. Mercer 12-4-1838
Chisolm, Matilda to James M. Vinson 2-5-1842 (2-10-1842)
Chisum, Ellen to Harris Wiggins 7-1-1851
Chitman, Mary E. (Mrs.) to John R. Woodard 2-25-1867 (2-26-1867)
Chitmun, Mary to Burton (Dr.) Pipkin 5-16-1855
Christenberry, Sarah E. (Mrs.) to Wm. H. Harriman 7-17-1868
Christian, Eliza Jane to John C. Mooring 3-9-1850 (3-12-1850)
Christian, June to I. H. Barham 2-14-1840 (2-16-1840)
Christman, Bettie to William Price 10-15-1868
Clampitt, Nancy to Jonthan Thompson 3-30-1844
Clanton, Elizabeth to John Hart 12-20-1869 (12-22-1869)
Clanton, Susannah to John A. Harding 2-26-1867 (2-28-1867)
Clark, A. M. to J. C. Pybas 5-2-1870 (5-3-1870)
Clark, Anna to Francis M. Oneal 2-28-1871 (3-1-1871)
Clark, Catherine to James McFadden 2-4-1869 (2-9-1869)
Clark, Laura C. to Lorenza Goodell 8-24-1847
Clark, Mary I. to Willis Overton 11-28-1842
Clark, Phoebe Jane to Alfred H. Jones 2-25-1846 (2-26-1846)
Clay, Caroline M. to James W. Gardner 3-31-1862 (4-1-1862)
Clay, Martha H. to George Trafford 6-19-1868
Clay, Martha Jane to Enzkial W. Polk 6-22-1840 (6-23-1840)
Clement, Frances A. to Henry H. Warmath 6-12-1855
Clements, Udora J. to George D. Buffalow 2-20-1871 (2-21-1871)
Cline, Catherine to William R. Jackson 8-7-1854 (8-15-1854)
Cline, Sarah to Jacob Daniel Cline 3-30-1841
Coats, Susan E. (Mrs.) to Franklin E. Collins 6-26-1869 (6-27-1869)
Cobb, Elizabeth to John R. Volentine 5-24-1869
Cobb, Emma F. to Jeptha V. Harris 12-28-1869
Cobb, Fannie (Mrs.) to Lorenzo (Rev.) Lea 3-29-1858 (3-30-1858)
Cobb, Harriet to Naum Powell 5-18-1857 (5-19-1857)
Cobb, Mary A. to Harvey S. Crittendon 1-26-1853
Cobb, Mary Jane to James M. Alexander 11-17-1871
Cochrane, Mattie W. to Lewis W. Hall 3-5-1868
Cock, Christenia R. to Othneil Whitenton 1-13-1858
Cock, Louisa F. to Green L. Hill 6-19-1861 (6-27-1861)
Cock, M. A. to A. H. Kimbrell 12-3-1867
Cock, Perlina to Ezekiel B. W. Hobbs 4-14-1862 (4-17-1862)

Cockrill, Martha J. to Constantine S. Hamner 8-18-1857 (8-19-1857)

Coggins, M. A. to W. G. Fondille 12-14-1867

Coggins, Mary L. to Edward Buckner 8-14-1860 (8-15-1860)

Coker, Charity to B. Dickson 4-10-1838

Coker, Sarah Ann to Oscar O. Forwell 7-30-1859

Cole, Ary C. to Edward C. Slator 11-27-1854 (11-28-1854) *

Cole, Elizabeth W. to John C. McCasburn 3-24-1846

Cole, Elizabeth to William H. Turner 2-5-1844 (2-13-1844)

Cole, Julia C. C. to Geo. D. McAllister 7-8-1862

Cole, Laura S. to Guilford Jones 8-28-1850 (9-2-1850)

Cole, Maria L. to John F. Whitelaw 11-5-1849 (11-8-1849)

Cole, Nannie D. to John H. Thomas 10-29-1859 (11-1-1859)

Cole, Paralee to Wm. Thomas Chappell 4-11-1870 (4-5?-1870)

Cole, Susan M. to James F. Kelly 2-20-1855

Coleman, Margaret A. to John H., jr. Day 8-29-1850

Collier, Elizabeth C. to Thomas C. Muse 9-5-1855 (9-12-1855)

Collier, Emily J. to James C. Hudson 12-9-1850

Collins, Catherine to Ezekiel T. Whitworth 3-5-1856

Collins, Tennessee V. to Wyatt A. Taylor 7-29-1858

Collinsworth, Martha (Mrs.) to Laburn Perry 11-10-1869 (11-11-1869)

Combs, Martha to John Madison Simpson 11-22-1853 (11-24-1853)

Combs, Susan H. to Robt. N. Mathis 2-18-1867 (2-20-1867)

Compton, Caroline to John T. Fletcher 1-7-1840 (1-16-1840)

Conder, Mandy Jane to Oliver Stanfield 2-28-1871 (3-1-1871)

Conger, A. W. to Joel R. Chappell 9-23-1839 (9-24-1839)

Conger, Cora C. to Andrew B. Langford 8-14-1866 (8-15-1866)

Conger, Emma to E. E. Flippin 7-1-1871 (7-3-1871) *

Conger, Roena P. to George D. King 9-11-1860

Conger, Winney Ann to William N. Winston 9-28-1848

Connally, Rebecca F. to John Oliver 9-17-1850 (9-18-1850)

Connally, Susan R. to Edwin R. Lancaster 9-2-1850

Connell, Charlotte Mary to John A. Mooring 12-20-1860 (12-21-1860)

Connell, Susan to John William Giles 10-27-1866 (10-28-1866)

Connelly, Caroline H. to Thomas McGill 2-2-1862 *

Conner, Jane to George L. Priddy 3-1-1870 (3-3-1870)

Conner, Margaret to John L. Smith 4-15-1869

Conner, Rebecca to Harvey Holt 7-28-1846 (7-30-1846)

Connor, Harriet A. to Duncan M. Spencer 12-29-1859 (1-1-1860)

Cook, Alice W. to Samuel H. Edwards 12-3-1867

Cook, Annie to Saml. M. Ozier 9-26-1866

Cook, Elizabeth to Thomas Baker 3-4-1839 (3-5-1839)

Cook, Evelina to Alexander T. Cole 10-26-1850 (10-28-1850)

Cook, Judie B. to William Brown 7-18-1855 (7-19-1855)

Cook, Mary Jane to Allen Cannady 11-16-1870 (11-17-1870)

Cook, May Ann to Ransom H. Bryan 12-17-1838 (12-18-1838)

Cook, Nancy to Adam Sevier 12-5-1838

Cook, Sarah A. to Gideon Smith 1-4-1869

Cook, Sarah to Jasen W. Fussell 3-5-1867 (3-7-1867)

Coopender, Sarah to Hugh Blevins 1-18-1840 (1-19-1840)

Cooper, Isabella to George Bishop 3-3-1857 (3-4-1857)

Cooper, Martha to David Dowling 5-7-1853 (5-19-1853)

Cooper, Martha to John Fullerton 7-10-1866 (7-12-1866)

Cooper, Mary Jane to John Horton 12-18-1848

Copeland, Catherine C. to Newton J. Harris 1-7-1861

Copeland, Ellen to Norflet F. Parrot 5-12-1856

Copeland, Mary E. to Wm. H. Massey 1-13-1855 (1-16-1855)

Copeland, Minerva to Silas Lassiter 1-12-1855 (1-16-1855)

Copher, Susan to Michie Acre 7-1-1843 (7-2-1843)

Covington, Ann to Wilson Moon 9-19-1842

Covington, Polly to Jonathan Steepleton 4-2-1844

Cox, Bettie to Brittan Spence 2-24-1868 (2-26-1868)

Cox, Diannah to Thomas Whitesides 9-20-1866

Cox, Eliza E. to James M. Boykin 12-6-1861 (12-8-1861)

Cox, Elizabeth to Young Bradford 11-24-1846 (11-25-1846)

Cox, Frances to Wm. P. Anderson 1-15-1870 (1-16-1870)

Cox, Laura E. to John A. Laney 9-12-1871 (9-14-1871)

Cox, Mary A. E. to Isaac H. Mason 9-21-1846 (9-24-1846)

Cox, Matilda to Nineviah Glidwell 7-21-1847 (7-22-1847)

Cozart, Helen S. to James B. Pittman 3-24-1869 (3-25-1869) *

Cozart, Julia A. to Joseph T. Williamson 4-8-1856 (4-9-1856)

Cozart, Maggie J. to Ephraim McIlwain 12-4-1866 (12-5-1866)

Cozart, Mahulda to William H. Marlow 12-25-1852 (12-26-1852)

Cozart, Nancy Ann to Sidney Gray 2-10-1842

Cozart, Susan to Kinchen Hathaway 12-5-1859 (12-8-1859)

Craig, Martha to Alexander Patterson 7-28-1858

Crause, Manirva A. to Thompson A. Parker 11-28-1848 (11-30-1848)

Crawford, Charlotte to John F. Greathouse 1-28-1868 (1-30-1868)

Crenshaw, America Ann to Joel W. Reeves 1-14-1850 (1-15-1850)

Crisp, Dora to Edward J. Martin 1-14-1869 (1-19-1869) *

Crist, Mary E. K. to Wm. D. Anthony 8-7-1867 (8-8-1867)

Crittenton, Mary C. to Allen F. Oliver 1-2-1856 (1-3-1856)

Cromwell, Ellen to Felix Walker 10-4-1838 (10-4-1838)

Croom, Amanda F. to R. H. Davis 12-17-1863 (11?-17-1862?)

Croom, Catharine to Sterling M. Watlington 5-14-1866

Croom, Jane to Samuel Bobbit 12-8-1841 (12-9-1841)

Croom, Laura to John G. Haynes 2-16-1870 (2-17-1870)

Croom, Susan to Major Langston 1-10-1843

Crop, Elizabeth C. to Jefferson Burton 11-17-1840

Crosby, Sarah to James Rene, jr. 6-7-1845 (6-9-1845)

Cross, Elizabeth to James Harris 3-3-1855

Crowder, Caroline to Obediah Johnson 1-31-1870 (2-1-1870)

Crowder, Frances to Ephraim L. McAdoo 1-8-1859 (1-11-1859)

Crowder, Martha A. to William R. Johnson 3-15-1870

Cupp, Sarah C. to Charles D. Chamberlain 10-9-1855

Cupples, Rebecca to Goodman Richardson 7-14-1849

Currie, Elizabeth Caroline to William M. Ewing 4-29-1857

Currie, Mary Ann to Wm. D. Winchester 2-6-1858

Currie, Roena J. to John R. Dodd 2-12-1867

Dalton, Lizzie to Z. Haas 4-8-1869

Daniel, Judy to Harbert Ferrell 2-22-1841 (3-2-1841)

Darby, Mary Jane to Wilson C. Jones 12-29-1845 (1-1-1845?)

Darby, Matilda A. to Thomas V. Burns 4-28-1868

Darby, Sibella A. to Elias Cook 5-22-1843 (5-24-1843)

Darmon, Jane to John Wilson 9-22-1842 (9-?-1842)

Darnell, Mary Elvira to James M. Cook 10-12-1841 (10-13-1841)

Davidson, Eliza F. to Atlas J. Cate 8-7-1866 (8-9-1866)

Davidson, Nancy A. to James D. Nevill 12-22-1866 (12-23-1866)

Davidson, Susan J. to Bennett W. McDade 2-13-1858 (2-17-1858)

Davie, Cornelia J. to James B. Davie 7-21-1853

Davie, Elizabeth J. to Lacy L. Brown 12-4-1857 (12-6-1857)

Davie, Emily H. to James White 9-19-1855

Davie, Louisa to Benjamin F. Elder 12-6-1858

Davie, Mary R. to Edward Telfair 10-28-1850

Davie, Sarah A. to John L. Fly 12-19-1853 (12-21-1853)

Davie, Sarah J. to Alexander Bowling 11-29-1850

Davis, Amanda Harris to George Carson Gattis 6-11-1853

Davis, Amanda J. to Elijah H. Williams 12-23-1867 (12-27-1867)

Davis, Artela F. to Joshua M. Reams 12-2-1868 (12-4-1868)

Davis, Bazilla Jane to Elam Richardson 1-11-1853

Davis, Catherine to John A. Gladney 3-27-1869 (4-1-1869)

Davis, Dicey (Mrs.) to Solomon Godfrey 12-18-1860

Davis, Elizabeth B. to Benjamin J. Powell 2-2-1848

Davis, Elizabeth Jane to Arthur Deloach 11-3-1846

Davis, Elizabeth T. (Mrs.) to William J. McKinney 8-9-1858 (8-10-1858)

Davis, Emilina to John Rodenhizer 8-21-1858 (8-22-1858)

Davis, Harriet to Hiram (of Illinois) Crow 9-19-1862

Davis, Jane B. to William A. Davie 11-8-1841

Davis, Lou Jane to Felix G. Sherrod 5-4-1868 (5-18-1868)

Davis, Lucy to James L. Davis 6-26-1848 (6-29-1848)

Davis, Lucy to John Dickie 11-1-1851 (11-2-1851)

Davis, Lucy to William Sparks 4-16-1855 (4-10?-1855)

Davis, Maggie to Wm. A. Dismukes 8-20-1870 (8-21-1870)

Davis, Margaret A. to James A. Dodd 1-7-1853 (1-11-1853)

Davis, Martha Ann to James S. Jester 1-20-1854 (1-26-1854)

Davis, Martha Ann to William H. Henning 10-15-1839

Davis, Martha to Thomas Taylor 11-18-1850 (11-19-1850)

Davis, Mary A. to William L. Gattis 12-21-1847 (12-22-1847)

Davis, Mary Ann to Robert A. Campbell 8-11-1847 (8-12-1847)

Davis, Mary Daniel to Samuel Clark Davis 10-7-1850

Davis, Mary E. to Reubin Buntin 12-16-1850 (1-1-1851)

Davis, Mary K. to Tinsly W. Halliburton 2-23-1843

Davis, Mary to James F. Guinn 6-21-1862 (6-22-1862)

Davis, Mary to Samuel Jackson 5-22-1839 (5-25-1839)

Davis, Nancy Susan to Pitt C. Browder 12-9-1867 (12-10-1868?)

Davis, Nancy to Leander Alford 1-30-1844

Davis, Rachael to Louis Elkins 7-1-1840 (7-2-1840)

Davis, Rebecca Jane to Drury B. Williams 10-20-1857 (10-22-1857)

Davis, Sarah E. to Dempney Ellington 5-28-1861 (5-30-1861)

Davis, Sarah F. to William Latham 7-21-1856 (7-24-1856)

Davis, Sarah Francis to Edmund Haltom 12-17-1856 (12-18-1856)
Davis, Sarah T. to Washington R. Browder 10-17-1857 (10-18-1857)
Davis, Sarah to Elias Lawrence 12-3-1840 (12-8-1840)
Davis, Susan T. to Council Buntin 1-28-1867
Davis, Susan to Benjamin F. Croom 12-12-1862 (12-13-1862)
Davis, Susan to Robert G. Adams 3-17-1862
Davis, Susan to William J. Ragsdale 8-14-1847 (8-17-1847)
Dawkins, Martha to Calvin Langston 2-2-1839
Dawson, Martha J. to Wm. C. Quinly 9-3-1842 (9-4-1842)
Dawson, Minerva C. to Wm. H. Fogarty 9-10-1866 (9-11-1866)
Day, Clara to John Shane 9-4-1866
Day, Elizabeth J. to John W. Grant 9-25-1850
Day, Harriett R. to John J. Oliver 6-2-1853 (6-3-1853)
Day, I. Virginia to John s. Fenner 2-27-1867
Day, Janetta J. to Francis J. Baber 10-6-1859
Day, Luvina M. to Flavius Fly 11-9-1852 (11-12-1852)
Day, Malvina H. to Henry C. Watkins 11-5-1845
Day, Martha A. to Robert P. Ford 1-23-1850 (1-25-1850)
Day, Mary E. to Calvin C. Vesser 9-30-1867
Day, Mary E. to James T. Willett 11-15-1862 (11-19-1862)
Day, Mary Elizabeth to Henry L. Bray 3-15-1859 (not executed)
Day, Nancy J. to Isaac Parlow 2-8-1868 (2-13-1868)
Day, Olivia to James McRoe 10-10-1842
Day, Sallie Cornelia to Albert Talmedge Lovallette 10-6-1855
    (10-9-1855)
Dean, Mattie C. to Wm. T. Teague 3-9-1870 (3-10-1870)
Dean, Minnie to William Holdsworth 11-21-1870
Dearmore, Ann to Zachariah Holliday 3-21-1846 (4-2-1846)
Dearmore, Mary Jane to Powhattan B. Littlepage 4-20-1841
Dearmore, Perlina W. to Enoch Gaskins 9-17-1849
Dearmore, Susan P. to Lea H. Johnson 1-24-1853 (1-30-1853)
Deaton, Amanda C. to James F. Baker 7-26-1869 (7-28-1869)
Deaton, Senna A. (Mrs.) to Peter F. Crowel 7-1-1867
Deberry, Anna M. to W. T. Nelson 12-20-1870 (12-21-1870)
Deberry, Elizabeth F. (Mrs.) to Wm. R. Cunningham 6-30-1859
Deberry, Lizzie to James G. Meriwether 1-24-1871 (1-25-1871)
Deberry, Rebecca F. to William H. Meriwether 12-15-1838
Deberry, Susan A. to Robert H. Hurt 6-1-1843 (6-3-1843)
Delapp, Jane to James M. Wilie 4-11-1853 (4-12-1853)
Delapp, Lucy to William l. Trask 6-19-1858 (6-21-1858)
Delda, Susan to Thomas Archa 11-15-1838
Delf, Margaret T. to Peter P. Puckett 10-8-1849 (10-9-1849)
Deloach, Ann R. to Gideon Hicks 12-19-1860 (12-20-1860)
Deloach, Lou to George L. Harding 12-12-1866 (12-20-1866)
Deloach, Martha to Josiah F. Clanton 9-6-1847 (9-9-1847)
Deloach, Susan A. to Eugene R. Willoughby 12-3-1866 (12-6-1866)
Delph, Elizabeth A. to Calvin Gardner 2-26-1856 (2-27-1856)
Delph, Mary to Joseph Blackwell 12-2-1856 (12-7-1856)
Delph, Sarah Eveline to Hartwell M. Stone 3-31-1856
Denmark, Catherine to Edmund J. Eddington 8-24-1852 (8-25-1852)
Denny, Liley to Kingsberry German 4-1-1856 (4-11-1856)
Denny, Mary J. to Miles P. Chandler 10-18-1842
Dent, Frances to James Caradine 12-27-1843 (12-28-1843)
Dent, Martha E. to John Nash 10-31-1847 (11-1-1847)
Denton, Nancy (Mrs.) to Arnold Winston 11-9-1857 (11-10-1857)
Derrah, Ann Caroline to George C. Rogers 12-17-1840
Detherage, Eliza to Chapman Williams 11-28-1838
Dew, Joanna to William J. Sturdevant 1-15-1861 (1-16-1861)
Dew, Joannah to William G. Cardwell 5-4-1860
Dew, Narcissa to Jefferson Anderson 5-11-1855
Dick, Elizabeth to Benjamin W. Perry 12-22-1854
Dick, Martha C. to Iverson Burton 10-16-1850 (10-17-1850)
Dick, Martha M. to Wade Byrum 5-9-1861
Dick, Mary E. J. to William L. Copeland 3-19-1853
Dickens, Sarah C. to Avery Hunt 12-18-1841 (12-23-1841)
Dickerson, Mary M. to Alvin R. Williams 12-14-1859 (12-15-1859)
Dickey, Elizabeth to William Pope 2-8-1841
Dickie, Katie E. to John Deloach 3-14-1871
Dickinson, Eliz. R. to Joseph A. Fogg 10-9-1860
Dickinson, Elizabeth to Herod Kirby 12-27-1853
Dickinson, L. A. to Sampson Deaton 2-22-1854 (2-23-1854)
Dickinson, M. Caroline to Wm. J. Anderson 1-29-1867 (1-31-1867)
Dickinson, M. D. to William P. Ripley 9-18-1849 (9-20-1849)
Dickinson, Rutha Jane to Rufus A. Weatherly 12-12-1859
Dickinson, Sarah Ann to John West 1-13-1853

Dickison, Rachel L. to John H. Harber 9-26-1859
Dickson, Ann Eliza to William R. Howlett 10-7-1843 (10-12-1843)
Dickson, Celia to Calvin Goforth 2-4-1854 (2-5-1854)
Dickson, Isabella M. to John D. Smith 12-19-1840
Dickson, Mary E. to Edwin J. McAdams 1-21-1870 (1-30-1870)
Dickson, Mary E. to Gabriel Hardin 6-5-1858 (6-6-1858)
Dickson, Mary Jane to William Goforth 1-28-1854 (1-31-1854)
Dickson, Nancy to Philip D. Carly 10-27-1840 (10-29-1840)
Dickson, Zelpha to Jesse Pugh 5-26-1842 (5-27-1842)
Diffy, Sarah to Stephen Moore 3-6-1840
Digg, Malinda D. to Randolph Hazlewood 8-12-1839 (8-13-1839)
Dillard, Holland P. to Samuel Luckey 10-15-1838 (10-16-1838)
Dis?, Eliza to Frnaklin J. Parker 6-17-1871 (6-18-1871)
Dismuke, Sarah A. to Joseph B. Jones 8-4-1849
Dixon, Fannie to William H. Ursery 9-13-1867 (9-15-1867)
Dixon, Susan J. to Joel T. Justice 8-14-1849
Doak, Amanda M. to Christopher C. Fly 3-6-1841 (3-7-1841)
Doak, Margarett H. to George H. Wright 11-26-1839
Doak, Mary Jane to John W. Lile 5-27-1843
Doake, Eunica A. to Rufus M. Mason 10-5-1850
Doake, Mary Jane to John E. Clark 1-25-1849 (1-30-1849)
Dobbs, Kitty to Joseph T. Rankin 11-10-1854 (11-12-1854)
Dockins, Cynthia to David G. Mason 7-3-1849
Dodd, Rachel (Mrs.) to Robert H. Givens 12-13-1867
Dodds, Julia A. to Edward F. Alexander 6-22-1870
Dodson, Nancy Jane to Elipha Z. Robinson 4-21-1857 (4-26-1857)
Doherty, Rutha J. to Joseph D. Askew 12-19-1857
Dollar, Angy to Daniel A. Young 4-8-1868
Dollar, Martha A. L. to Arthur Forbis 7-19-1847 (7-20-1847)
Dollar, Mary C. to Samuel Duffey 7-4-1854
Dollar, Sarah E. to George Belue 6-7-1854 (6-8-1854)
Donald, L. M. to Thos. I. Person 9-20-1842 (9-29-1842)
Donald, Levina to Robert A. Atkison 10-30-1840
Dougan, Nancy A. to James M. Baxter 10-2-1850 (10-3-1850)
Dougan, Nancy A. to William F. Joyner 10-22-1849
Douglass, Emily E. to Jesse W. Lassiter 2-6-1871 (2-7-1871)
Dowin, Margarett to Daniel White 8-20-1838
Downing, Elizabeth to Valentine McMillan 1-25-1843 (1-27-1843)
Downing, Narcissa to John Croom 8-27-1842 (8-28-1842)
Drake, Catherine to Nathan Francis 1-29-1859
Drake, Elizabeth T. to Martin Davis 10-3-1853
Drake, Mariah to E. G. Harris 2-13-1855 (2-14-1855)
Drake, Mary H. to James E. Harris 11-7-1857 (11-10-1857)
Drake, Mary to Richard Johnson 2-27-1845
Draper, Polly A. N. E. to William H. Cassels 8-24-1853 (8-25-1853)
Duffer, Susan Ann to Richard M. Price 11-13-1869 (11-14-1869)
Duffery, Kedie H. (Mrs.) to Daniel A. Young 1-4-1870 (1-6-1870)
Duffey, Elizabeth to William Lassiter 4-3-1852 (4-7-1852)
Duffey, Malvina to David T. Phillips 4-17-1869 (4-25-1869)
Duffey, Malvina to David T. Phillips 5-7-1866 (not executed)
Duffey, Patsey to Patrick M. Duffey 10-27-1862 (10-28-1862)
Duffy, Eliza to John H. Dollar 1-?-1847 (1-14-1847)
Duffy, Elizabeth B. to William E. Stewart 3-7-1853 (3-8-1853)
Duffy, Lucy J. to Lewis Dollar 4-18-1854 (4-20-1854)
Dugan, Margarett to William Yancey 12-23-1841
Dugan, Mary to John L. Shelton 9-12-1870
Dumanet, Martha W. to Benj. F. Epperson 11-13-1861 (11-17-1861)
Dunaway, Ellen B. to James W. Anderson 5-8-1861
Duncan, Amacivil to James Gillikin 2-17-1844
Duncan, Celia A. to James K. Webb 11-19-1847 (11-20-1848?)
Duncan, Elizabeth Ellen to Andrew J. Miller 6-20-1866
Duncan, Fannie T. to John R. Hicks 9-18-1866 (9-19-1866)
Duncan, Lotty L. to James Gillikins 5-27-1850
Duncan, Louisa to William H. Parrot 12-22-1841 (12-23-1841)
Duncan, Mary Jane to William L. Gregory 3-18-1852
Duncan, Neoma to Lewis Gregory 9-18-1841
Duncan, Perline to Joseph S. Utley 5-14-1849 (5-17-1849)
Duncan, Ruth A. to Washington D. Shuffield 7-31-1850 (8-1-1850)
Duncan, Sallie J. to Henry T. Allison 10-12-1871
Duncan, Sallie J. to Wm. M. Shelton 10-4-1870
Duncan, Sally Ann to Benjamin Replogle 9-19-1854 (9-21-1854)
Dungan, Mary A. E. to Julius Edwards 11-6-1852 (11-11-1852)
Dungan, Mary Jane to Robert H. Burns 12-11-1862
Dungan, Parthenia A. E. to William J. McFarland 2-23-1856
(12-25-1856)

Dunn, Jane C. to Charles W. Ferguson 12-2-1869
Dunnaway, Sallie E. to Wm. R. (Dr.) Cole 11-12-1870 (11-17-1870)
Dupriest, Francis to John Wright 1-3-1848
Duvall, Nannie J. to William H. McAdoo 12-20-1858 (12-21-1858)
Dyer, Rebecca J. to Henry B. Claridge 9-8-1853
Dyson, Mary E. to Thomas Ingram 8-16-1847
Eastwood, Lucy to George Using 10-16-1839
Eaton, Lizzie M. to Peter C. Winne 12-23-1869
Eddins, Ann R. to Leonidas J. Hill 2-27-1856
Eddins, Margarett L. to Anthony T. Williams 3-27-1850
Eddins, Martha Jane to George W. McGuire 11-11-1856
Edmondson, Eliza K. to Charles H. Blacknall 11-23-1852 (11-25-1852)
Edmonson, Charlotte to Rufus W. Dickinson 1-20-1845
Edmonston, Elvira to Thomas M. Meriwether 7-16-1845
Edward, Elizabeth to C. I. Huntsman 2-10-1844
Edwards, Ann to Matthew Glidewell 4-6-1857 (4-8-1857)
Edwards, Caroline to Wyatt Oates 11-24-1858 (11-25-1858)
Edwards, Elizabeth to Enoch W. Levy 10-11-1842 (10-13-1842)
Edwards, Elvy Jane to James T. Ward 8-16-1854 (8-18-1854)
Edwards, Julia Ann Eliza to W. P. Williams 11-22-1860 (11-25-1860)
Edwards, Mariah L. to James A. Fitz (Fith?) 9-4-1843 (9-6-1843)
Edwards, Mary E. to Joseph Marley 9-20-1853 (9-22-1853)
Edwards, Mary to William Perry 2-19-1870
Edwards, Nancy L. to James T. Watson 1-27-1869 (1-28-1869)
Edwards, Rebecca to James Stobaugh 5-24-1838
Edwards, S. J. (Mrs.) to Samuel J. Morrow 2-6-1868
Edwards, Sarah F. to Obidiah Gravitt 12-22-1845
Edwards, Sarah Jane to James N. White 9-7-1868
Edwards, Sarah to William Trice 12-19-1868
Edwards, Sophronia to William Thedford 10-4-1849 (1-8-1849?)
Elizabeth?, Sarah to James Y. Kirk 11-9-1848
Ellington, Eliza Jane to Thomas T. Thompson 5-13-1861 (5-17-1861)
Ellington, Frances to Berry H. Williams 12-22-1868 (12-23-1868)
Ellington, Mary Ann to Edward Davis 12-21-1838 (12-25-1838)
Ellington, Mary D. to Willis Haughton 10-23-1867 (10-24-1867)
Ellington, Sarah Elizabeth to Wm. R. Pettigrew 9-18-1867 (9-20-1867)
Ellington, Sophie to Milton Cook 7-28-1838 (7-29-1838)
Ellington, Sophronia to Newton Williams 12-15-1850 (12-17-1850)
Elliot, Cynthia Ann to William R. Webb 12-22-1866 (12-26-1866)
Elliott, Paralee M. to Jasper Holliday 6-16-1852
Elrod, Mary Eliza to John T. Oates 5-7-1856 (5-8-1856)
Elrod, Sarah R. to Benjamin Barr 1-4-1843
Elvill, Ann to Thos. I. Tuggle 11-6-1841 (11-12-1841)
Emerson, Mary Ann to Archibald Boyd 9-22-1858 (9-23-1858)
Emerson, Mary E. to Joel A. Thomas 1-27-1869 (1-28-1869)
Emerson, Mary Jane to Ralph Williams 12-15-1868 (12-17-1868)
Emerson, Nancy Ann to Francis M. Leggett 8-7-1867 (8-11-1867)
Emerson, Rebecca to Daniel Hershaw 3-4-1850 (3-7-1850)
Emerson, Sarah Jane to Dempsey Bird 7-15-1848 (7-20-1848)
Emmerson, Sarah E. to William K. Stone 11-25-1844
Epperson, Elenore to B. Alexr. Person 5-9-1866
Epperson, Mary Ann to William H. Edwards 3-22-1854 (3-3?-1854)
Epperson, Susan to John F. Newsom 5-4-1853
Eppes, Orleana T. to William H. Hunt 4-23-1860 (4-24-1860)
Ervin, Angie C. to John Darr 7-25-1839
Estes, Louisa to Columbus C. Sharp 12-22-1857
Estes, Margaret to S. Lafayette Allen 7-9-1862
Estes, Martha to James A. Wilkins 9-1-1845 (9-4-1845)
Estes, Mary Elizah to James D. Rooks 11-24-1870
Estes, Penelope to James W. Tomlin 12-14-1861 (12-15-1861)
Estes, Rachel to Jno. H. McGee 11-11-1868
Estes, Roxannah to Peter McCollum 1-28-1854
Estes, Sophronia to Joseph Pope 5-17-1859 (5-18-1859)
Estes, Virginia to James R. Anderson 10-8-1870 (10-13-1870)
Estis, Martha to Grandonfield Lambert 9-14-1839 (9-15-1839)
Estridge, Sarah R. to Archibald R. Harris 2-12-1848
Evans, Louisa to Marion Goodwin 12-7-1853
Evans, Lucinda to David J. Wrenn 7-5-1841 (7-6-1841)
Ewell, Bettie to W. B. Langford 7-26-1870
Ewing, Jane to James N. Steed 1-11-1859
Ewing, Rebecca to Duncan McMellon 11-21-1840
Exum, Eliza A. to William W. Garland 1-13-1841 (1-15-1841)
Exum, Martha A. (Mrs.) to Dudley C. Talley 1-13-1870
Exum, Martha to Lytle Newton 3-20-1871
Exum, Rebecca A. to Robert A. Cathey 11-12-1856

Fagg, Martha Jane to Thomas D. Blanchet 11-4-1850
Fairless, Penelope to James C. Teal 3-10-1838
Falden, Ann Eliza to Thomas Eason 8-31-1853
Fancher, Mollie E. to Wm. T. Morton 5-8-1871 (5-9-1871)
Fanner, Margaret E. to J. N. Cooper 11-16-1859 (11-17-1859)
Farmer, Ann M. to Benj. R. Pettus 4-6-1866 (3?-7-1866)
Farris, Sarah to Isaac Miller 6-11-1853
Faucett, Lucinda C. to James W. Lowdermilk 5-7-1870 (5-8-1870)
Faucett, Margarett E. to William A. Glass 10-29-1845 (10-30-1845)
Faulkner, Abagail to James Lawry 6-27-1859 (6-28-1859)
Faulkner, Catherine to John W. Blurton 12-16-1870 (12-18-1870)
Fawcett, Eliza Jane (Mrs.) to Bartholomew C. Britton 7-27-1870 (7-28-1870)
Fearless, Martha to Fullington Rooks 1-30-1847
Fenner, Ann to Francis M. Whitlow 2-2-1857 (2-5-1857)
Fenner, Ella to Frank Monroe 11-24-1869
Fenner, Eunice B. to Alexander Jackson 10-21-1850 (10-22-1850)
Fenner, Lizzie V. to Henry D. (of Ala.) Smith 4-28-1869 (4-29-1869)
Fenner, Lucy Ann to Isaac D. Walton 3-1-1859 (3-2-1859)
Fenner, Rebecca Ann to Etheldred L. Smith 12-17-1856
Ferguson, Ellen to James Carnatzer 12-26-1860
Ferrel, Mattie U. to Samuel B. Boykin 12-12-1870 (12-14-1870)
Ferrell, Maletta to Josiah Young 6-28-1838
Ferri, Ann E. to J. G. McGowan 9-26-1866 (9-27-1866)
Ferrill, Eliza Jane to Alfred P. Moore 10-19-1870 (10-20-1870)
Ferris, Sarah A. to Daniel W. Burton 12-9-1854 (12-10-1854)
Finger, Julianne C. to Coleman H. Tucker 7-14-1845 (7-15-1845)
Fisher, Lucinda to William Golden 8-14-1845
Fisher, Mahulda to Andrew M. Davidson 11-13-1844
Fitts, Marianna to Wm. G. (Gibson Co.) Hollowell 8-3-1870 (8-4-1870)
Fitz, Caroline to Robert L. McCracken 2-2-1858
Fitz, Harriet E. to Thomas J. Jett 3-23-1846 (4-9-1846)
Fitz, Minerva to William D. Gravette 12-30-1847 (12-31-1847)
Fitzgerald, Ann Elizbeth to William Jarrett 12-21-1854 (12-23-1854)
Fitzhugh, Mary T. to Jestice Byrum 12-15-1852
Fitzhugh, Susan M. to Jarrod Harston 10-21-1871
Fitzmorris, Maria to William Delaney 2-18-1871
Fleming, Mariah T. to Benjamin Hayley 11-24-1846 (11-25-1846)
Flemming, Mattie J. to Joseph D. Ewell 1-8-1868
Florence, Ann to James West 10-25-1858 (11-7-1858)
Flowers, Mariah to John S. Russell 8-4-1846 (8-6-1846)
Flowers, Mary Eliza to Claudius B. Hall 4-11-1859 (4-13-1859)
Fly, Almira E. to William H. Higden 6-21-1858 (6-22-1858)
Fly, Frances M. to Tarlton H. Graves 1-27-1844 (1-30-1844)
Fly, Mary A. to Calvin C. Clements (Gibson Co) 11-10-1849 (11-13-1849)
Fly, Rebecca C. to John A. Williamson 6-30-1857 (7-1-1857)
Fly, Rebeccah to David Gill 10-12-1840
Fly, Sarah E. to William Hall 12-31-1838
Fly, Sarah J. to Thomas J. Senter 11-1-1848 (11-2-1848)
Fly, Virginia Ann to L. G. B Seat 1-5-1854
Fogg, Archelius Ann (Mrs.) to Samuel Neely 6-29-1858 (7-1-1858)
Fogg, L. Annie to Mark Hodges 2-5-1867
Fogg, Mary L. to Samuel D. Barnett 5-25-1857
Follis, Rebecca M. to William J. Oliver 3-12-1853 (3-17-1853)
Follis, Salina E. to William C. Young 10-2-1857 (10-5-1857)
Fonner, Mary to Vincent Garrett 2-6-1841
Ford, Martha J. to Ezekiel Fitzhugh 1-20-1852 (1-21-1852)
Ford, Mary Ann to Washington Sturdivant 7-21-1852 (7-23-1852)
Ford, Mary E. to Rowan Bridges 11-20-1866
Forsythe, Elizabeth to William Armstrong 2-21-1850
Fortner, Elizabeth (Mrs.) to William A. Lewis 3-19-1870 (3-24-1870)
Fortune, Laura V. to Samuel McClanahan 12-28-1858 (12-29-1858)
Fortune, Mary Jane to James M. Townes 4-26-1870 (4-27-1870)
Fortune, Sarah Marcella to Andrew J. Jones 10-5-1868 (10-6-1868)
Fossett, Bettie to Wm. H. Long 12-25-1869 (12-20?-1869)
Fowler, Laura Ann to John Hayley 11-9-1842
Foxwell, Kittura to James M. Hammons 12-16-1847
Frances, Susan A. to Alexander Jackson 1-24-1843 (1-28-1843)
Francis, Sarah D. to John C. Singler 12-24-1870 (12-25-1870)
Franklin, Fannie E. to Almarine Simmons 11-12-1867 (11-14-1867)
Franklin, Martha A. to William T. Browder 10-29-1860 (10-30-1860)
Franklin, Susan E. to Logan J. Anderson 12-8-1862 (12-9-1862)
Fransioli, Guiseppa A. to Giovanni Dado 7-6-1870

Frazier, Elizabeth T. to Alex. A. Bumpass 9-4-1848
Frazier, Marcha A. to James M. Bumpus 3-15-1842 (3-17-1842)
Frederick, Caroline to Edward L. Birmingham 7-6-1859 (7-7-1859)
Fredericks, Eveline V. to John H. Norwood 6-5-1860 (6-7-1860)
Freding, Mary E. (Mrs.) to Wm. D. Wilkerson 8-8-1870 (8-9-1870)
Freeling, Sarah to Hinton Bryan 4-4-1842 (4-7-1842)
Freeling, Susan G. to Phillip A. Donlin 8-3-1842 (8-4-1842)
Freeling, Tennessee to Alfred D. Garrett 1-23-1849 (1-24-1849)
Freeman, Emily A. to Charles Phillips 11-13-1848
Freeman, Martha to Joseph H. Talbot 8-16-1842
Freeman, Neely A. M. to Terrel Thompson 9-1-1845 (9-4-1845)
Freeman, Sarah E. to John C. Murphy 9-30-1868
Freno, Mary Ritty to Berry H. Williams 2-4-1857 (2-5-1857)
Frieles, Frances (Mrs.) to Joseph F. Alexander 12-10-1868
   (12-13-1868)
Fry, Ann to Wm. S. Kincaid 5-23-1871
Fry, Catherine E. to John W. Rowsey 11-12-1861 (11-14-1861)
Fry, Jane to Asa P. Holtsford 8-23-1855
Fry, Lacy J. to Lawson D. Taylor 11-26-1849 (11-29-1849)
Fry, Margaret E. to Archibald S. Rogers 7-15-1856 (7-17-1856)
Fry, Mary E. to Robert N. Gillispie 11-12-1845
Fulbright, Adeliza to Lawrence T. Hudson 12-21-1846 (12-22-1846)
Fulbright, Margaret E. to James M. Davis 2-9-1858
Fulbright, Nancy A. to John G. Lea 5-17-1854 (5-?-1854)
Fulgham, Louisa R. to John H. Deberry 11-25-1856
Fulghum, Idotha to Saml. Sharpe 6-19-1866
Fulghum, Sophronia A. to Benjamin E. Lewis 8-23-1854 (8-25-1854)
Fuller, Gilla to James Hundley 10-23-1849 (10-25-1849)
Funderburk, Mary to W. James Martin 3-4-1868 (3-8-1868)
Fussel, Susan to Jonas Mayo 3-8-1848 (3-9-1848)
Fussell, Elizabeth to James W. Boren 12-12-1867
Fussell, Matilda W. to John J. Anderson 9-8-1847
Fussell, Minerva to Robert Harris 8-6-1846 (8-20-1846)
Fussell, Susan to William Smith 6-12-1860
Futrell, Arella to James W. Warren 10-6-1847 (10-6-1847)
Gabriele, Carmela to Carmelo Rando 1-10-1856
Gallant, Mollie to Jerome Herndon 12-28-1867 (1-2-1868)
Gallop, Mary to Thomas Grubbs 1-13-1845 (1-23-1845)
Gamewell, Leonilla E. to Thomas S. Vincent 12-1-1869
Gannaway, Sarah E. F. to William Adkins 11-24-1866 (11-25-1866)
Gardner, Mary to Jonas M. Waller 2-26-1862 (2-27-1862)
Garland, Eliza to John R. Rowlett 11-11-1841
Garland, Harriett to Stephen Miller 2-27-1838
Garland, Margaret C. to N. B. Winston 9-13-1856 (9-17-1856)
Garland, Martha C. to John L. Walsh 11-18-1856 (11-30-1856)
Garland, Rebecca L. to John C. Simmons 10-21-1867 (10-22-1867)
Garland, Sarah M. to Ira M. McJones 8-22-1839
Garner, Dionca Ann to David Poindexter 4-4-1842 (4-7-1842)
Garrett, M. A. to W. L. Maxwell 5-10-1848
Garrett, Mahala V. E. to Peter B. Barnett 12-3-1860 (12-5-1860)
Garrett, Mary Ann A. to Thomas J. Sturdevant 9-14-1858
Garrett, Mary E. to John H. Clay 1-30-1868
Garrett, Mary to Peter Rainey 6-10-1846
Garrett, Stachey to William Jarrett 2-19-1842 (2-?-1842)
Garrison, Geraldine to Sanders Williams 11-21-1870 (11-23-1870)
Garrison, Mary Malina to James Shivers 3-27-1843
Gaskins, Harriet M. to Wm. A. Stephens 11-19-1866 (11-21-1866)
Gaskins, Vicey Ann to William J. Dearmore 2-20-1850 (2-21-1850)
Gastings, Drucilla to N. Roe 1-7-1840 (2-2-1840)
Gaston, Nancy to John H. Billington 10-29-1866 (10-31-1866)
Gateley, Nancy to William C. Childress 4-7-1856 (4-10-1856)
Gateley, Phebe to Wm. F. West 8-6-1850 (8-7-1850)
Gately, Jemima J. to James M. Lewis 10-25-1853
Gates, Eugenia to Thos. T. Butler 6-1-1870 (6-11-1870)
Gatlin, Eveline to Elijah, jr. Jones 4-11-1850
Gattis, Mary F. to C. B. Russell 11-8-1859 (11-9-1859)
Gattis, Mattie A. to Richd. W. Fisher 12-8-1866 (12-11-1866)
Gattis, Rebecca Ann to Thomas R. Warren 12-15-1848 (12-20-1848)
Geyle, P. E. to Lemuel B. Haughton 5-8-1860 (5-9-1860)
Gholson, Frances to John Dodd 8-16-1853 (8-?-1853)
Gholson, Margarett to Samuel G. Ganaway 10-12-1843
Gholson, Mary Ann to William Carson 12-10-1839 (12-12-1839)
Gibbs, Martha G. to David D. Bell 4-9-1846
Gibson, Mary Ann to John Behns 2-5-1870
Gibson, Ruth to Robert W. Burns 7-17-1839 (7-19-1839)

Gill, Caroline T. to William Hazlewood 2-11-1856
Gill, Cynthia A. to Kenneth G. Hicks 9-28-1858 (9-29-1858)
Gill, Fannie E. to Handsel W. Burrow 10-12-1857 (10-13-1857)
Gill, Martha J. to J. Frank Jones 12-14-1870 (12-15-1870)
Gill, Mollie F. to William H. Bruton 12-18-1866 (12-20-1866)
Gilliam, Cynthia to Andrew Derryberry 4-8-1853
Gilliam, Martha Ann to John E. Gilliam 11-19-1866 (11-20-1866)
Gilliland, Margaret E. to Bartholomew C. Britton 4-11-1861
Gillum, Sarah E. to William A. Biddle 10-22-1866 (10-30-1866)
Given, Caroline to Washington Eddins 1-24-1857 (1-28-1857)
Givens, Amanda to John M. Johnson 6-14-1848 (6-15-1848)
Givens, Nannie to John T. Harrison 5-6-1867 (5-16-1867)
Givens, Sarah to Hardy Mayo 3-31-1853
Givens, Winnefred H. to Harrison Johnson 9-25-1845
Gizzard, Elizabeth B. to Gabriel Chandler 1-22-1855 (1-25-1855)
Gladney, Ann to Joseph W. McClohm 5-10-1842 (5-12-1842)
Gladney, Elizabet L. to Joseph J. Cooper 11-20-1845
Gladney, Jane R. to Jesse Currie 10-29-1860
Gladney, Louisa Jane to Stephen Miller 9-28-1849 (10-2-1849)
Gladney, Margarett M. to James L. Longhorn 11-22-1842
Glass, Mary Jane to Geo. E. Armstead 2-8-1870 (2-9-1870)
Gleeson, Martha K. to George A. Smith 12-8-1847 (12-9-1847)
Glenn, Bettie H. to Jno. W. Fitzhugh 1-2-1869
Glenn, Elizabeth to James H. Baker 12-27-1849 (12-29-1849)
Glenn, Elizabeth to William Perciful 3-16-1854
Glenn, Lydia to John T. Byrum 11-1-1866
Glenn, Maie to Henry C. Brown 5-19-1871 (5-22-1871)
Glenn, Mary to F. M. Davis 12-1-1856 (12-2-1856)
Glidewell, Eliza to George W. Miller 8-4-1846 (8-5-1846)
Glidewell, Elizabeth J. to William Cox 8-3-1846
Glidewell, Martha to Eliazer Sullivan 9-26-1870 (9-28-1870)
Glidewell, Martha to Isaac McCarver 8-6-1849
Glidewell, Mary to William Tims 8-6-1852
Glidwell, Catherine to Jesse Edwards 10-25-1856
Glidwell, Evalina L. to Nathaniel Miller 8-27-1856
Glidwell, Jane (Mrs.) to John T. Tims 9-7-1858 (9-9-1858)
Glidwell, Sarah to Thomas Percival 11-27-1840
Glover, Elizabeth H. to Jacob Parker 9-22-1850
Glover, Mary M. to Robert D. Morris 12-3-1850 (12-5-1850)
Goad, M. Mary to Manoah F. Jones 7-23-1853 (7-24-1853)
Goad, Margarett to George W. Lumpkins 8-2-1848 (8-3-1848)
Golden, Berneta R. to John C. Dearmore 7-19-1848 (7-20-1848)
Golden, Lucinda to David B. Porter 8-7-1848 (8-?-1848)
Golden, Lucy A. to Elias W. May 12-2-1846 (12-3-1846)
Golden, Susanna to E. Hadson 8-16-1842 (8-18-1842)
Goldzinsky, Rachel to Louis Solomon 8-17-1871
Goodall, Mary Ann to William R. Hughes 10-28-1868 (10-29-1868)
Goode, Sarah to James H. Johnson 6-19-1857
Goodrich, Caroline (Mrs.) to Wm. A. Barnhill 2-16-1871
Goodrich, Elizabeth M. to John Burrus 1-9-1849
Goodrich, Elizabeth to Andrew I. Bailey 2-8-1842
Goodrich, Jane, jr. to John Harris 4-6-1849 (4-17-1849)
Goodrich, Margarett L. to John H. Lintchicum 8-19-1841
Goodrich, Mary A. to B. G. Stewart 12-19-1839 (12-23-1839)
Goodrich, Mary Ann to George P. McAlelley 12-12-1850
Goodrich, Nancy to Nathan Johnson 9-7-1847 (9-14-1847)
Goodrick, Mary M. to Caswell C. Cock 11-4-1857 (11-5-1857)
Goodwin, Emma C. to John W. Harris 1-4-1870 (1-5-1870)
Goodwin, Mary to Charles S. Ball 7-30-1860
Gopher, Jemima to George W. Johnson 3-22-1853
Gordan, Emma T. to James H. Moss 1-18-1869 (1-20-1869)
Gordon, Eliza to Robt. M. Rutherford 12-13-1866
Gordon, Isabella to Joseph T. Howard 3-2-1869 (3-4-1869)
Gordon, Lizzie to Jno. C. Spencer 2-28-1871 (3-2-1871)
Gordon, Naomi to Leroy Barnett 9-25-1850 (10-1-1850)
Gordon, Queen A. to Thomas Spears 12-18-1856 (12-22-1856)
Gordon, Sarah to Andrew Burge 4-27-1838
Gossett, Amanda to James Smith 12-24-1860
Gowan, Mary Susan to Wm. Andrew Poteete 5-28-1870 (5-29-1870)
Gowen, Mary to Lemuel Day 7-21-1849 (7-26-1849)
Graham, Martha J. to Freeman H. Seeley 5-19-1866 (5-20-1866)
Graham, Rosa T. to William C. York 12-18-1867
Graham, Rosa to John W. Herridge 10-20-1866
Grant, Eliza to Stephen Maphey 6-6-1838
Grant, Elizabeth T. to William W. Boyet 10-6-1851 (10-9-1851)

Grant, Mary H. to Ethan H. Parrot 12-3-1855 (12-24-1855)
Grant, Mary to Thomas Chatten 8-7-1853 (9-8-1853)
Grant, Milly to James E. Wood 11-15-1858 (11-16-1858)
Grant, Minerva to Daniel M. Gaston 12-22-1866 (12-23-1866)
Grant, Mlda? B. to Elijah Bennet 7-3-1855 (7-4-1855)
Grant, Nancy to Mathias Harrington 4-1-1856
Grant, Nancy to Thomas Jackson 1-15-1845 (1-16-1845)
Graves, Eliza J. to Andrew J. Harrison 9-9-1845 (9-11-1845)
Graves, Mariah to John M. Spears 4-28-1846 (4-29-1846)
Graves, Mary Ann to Samuel Gordin 11-6-1838 (12-3-1838)
Graves, Mary to Noel Jackson 9-11-1841 (9-15-1841)
Graves, Musidora to Francis M. Harrison 8-10-1853
Graves, Naomie Jane to Jno. Frankliln King 5-23-1868 (5-26-1868)
Graves, Samantha L. to George W. Freeman 1-17-1859
Graves, Sarah A. to Henry C. Baker 6-23-1866 (6-24-1866)
Graves, Sarah Emeline to Cornelius Ruddle 7-23-1849 (7-12?-1849)
Graves, Sarah to Hudson J. Spears 6-3-1850 (6-30-1850)
Graves, Susan P. to Albert A. Rains 12-22-1859
Gravit, Sarah Jane to John Wadlington 8-15-1859 (8-16-1859)
Gray, Lydia to James Herron 1-29-1839
Greeds, Mary Ann to John McCarrus 10-22-1838
Green, Catharine (Mrs.) to Lorenzo D. Stout 2-18-1858 (7-15-1858)
Green, Eliza I. to William Scott 10-20-1843
Green, Susan E. to Benjamin B. Person 10-20-1842
Green, Susan to Minus M. Ward 11-8-1856 (11-11-1856)
Greenwell, Martha M. to Matthew Tetterton 1-31-1849 (2-1-1849)
Greer, Lide A. to John Reid 10-1-1867 (10-2-1867)
Gregory, Elizabeth t. to John S. Appleton 3-11-1870
Gregory, Harriet J. to James H. Harbert 1-24-1859 (1-27-1859)
Gregory, Martha Ann to Richard B. Vaughter 12-4-1854 (12-7-1854)
Griffin, Drusilla to Anthony Bledsoe 7-4-1842 (7-7-1842)
Griffin, Mary Jane to Wilson R. Gilbert 11-10-1871 (11-12-1871)
Griffin, Minerva Jane to Andrew Stephens 8-21-1860
Griffith, Sarah Ann to Foster Perry 12-9-1857 (12-10-1857)
Guin, Emery to Benjamin R. Perron 1-2-1844 (1-9-1844)
Guinn, Emily E. to Jno. W. Chandler 3-14-1871
Guinn, Jane to Philip D. Alexander 12-22-1869 (12-23-1869)
Guinn, Nancy N. to William Alexander 3-18-1868
Guinn, Sarah E. to Elijah Alexander 12-22-1868 (12-23-1868)
Guthrie, Fannie M. to Absolem D. Hunt 1-1-1868 (1-2-1868)
Guthrie, Mary Ann to John B. Cobb 5-27-1862
Guthrie, Susan to Benjamin L. Thompson 3-15-1840 (3-25-1840)
Hadaway, Rachel to Augustus W. Johnson 8-17-1866
Hafflabower, Ella V. to George C. Corbitt 11-17-1869 (11-18-1869)
Haislip, Lucinda to Samuel J. Patterson 11-1-1852 (11-2-1852)
Haislip, Rebecca to Andrew J. Pounds 12-7-1860
Haislip, Rebecca to Nathan C. Smith 7-31-1854 (8-1-1854)
Hale, Mary A. to R. A. Edwards 12-11-1855 (12-12-1855)
Hale, Mary D. to Robert Taylor 5-12-1842
Hale, Rebecca M. to James E. Ruff 10-26-1847 (10-28-1847)
Hall, Aly to William H. Williams 9-12-1840 (9-25-1840)
Hall, Mattie to John R. Wilbon 12-22-1869
Hall, Parmelia W. to Robert W. Jenning 2-21-1848 (2-22-1848)
Hall, Rebecca Jane to James A. Kirby 12-21-1853 (12-22-1853)
Hallian, Mariah to Patrick Joyce 7-29-1869
Halliburton, Mary to Augustine Carter 9-28-1848 (10-10-1848)
Haltom, Amanda to Francis M. Johnson 9-30-1847
Haltom, Deborah to John R. Blair 11-21-1855
Haltom, Frances M to Edwin R. Johnson 8-31-1842
Haltom, Helen to Jep. Johnston 4-7-1840 (4-30-1840)
Haltom, Jane Elizabeth to William F. Gardner 6-4-1855
Haltom, Margaret R. to Robert F. Cain 5-18-1858 (5-19-1858)
Haltom, Marinda C. to Jesse D. Tucker 12-2-1869 (12-5-1869)
Haltom, Rebecca E. to Daniel B. Cooper 11-20-1866 (11-21-1866)
Halton, Hannah to James T. Maroney 8-24-1854
Halton, Hester Ann to George R. Scott 2-7-1839 (2-14-1839)
Halton, Mary Jane to Mathew Williamson 1-22-1868 (1-26-1868)
Ham, Dicey to John J. Taylor 3-19-1850
Ham, Visy to John Handly 11-29-1842
Hamerly, Mollie to Claudius E. Chappell 5-22-1867
Hamilton, J. Lou to C. B. Stewart 6-13-1871
Hamilton, Louisa to Cyrus Wilson 1-21-1840
Hamilton, Martha (Mrs.) to Henry J. Pearson 8-8-1867
Hamilton, Mary J. to William L. Fox 4-21-1852 (4-27-1852)
Hamilton, Mary Jane to William C. Cason 6-26-1860 (6-27-1860)

Hamilton, Sarah E. to Saml. S. Johnson 3-24-1857
Hamilton, T. N. to John S. Wadkin 12-13-1839
Hamlett, Elizabeth to Thomas B. Thompson 10-25-1856 (10-26-1856)
Hammon, Margaret to David Huddleston 5-4-1842 (5-5-1842)
Hammond, Adeline to Jesse Mask 5-16-1855
Hammond, Amanda F. to George W. King 2-24-1869 (2-25-1869)
Hammond, Elizabeth to William P. Howard 4-23-1856
Hammond, Martha to John Pennington 8-16-1842 (8-18-1842)
Hammond, Mary K. to William P. Howard 4-24-1869
Hammond, Nancy J. to Wm. S. King 1-4-1870 (1-5-1870)
Hamner, Jane to James King 11-2-1839 (11-3-1839)
Hampton, Elenora H. to William P. James 10-28-1868
Hampton, Harriet Caroline to John S. Conger 5-20-1861
Hampton, Marianna to Joseph H. Sewell 5-8-1871 (5-9-1871)
Hanes, Sarah Margaret to Robt. E. Newton 12-10-1867
Harbert, Adelia E. to Rufus W. Rice 4-5-1853
Harbert, L. S. to Wm. W. Bond 4-27-1854 (5-3-1854)
Harbert, Sarah W. to John F. Hicks 12-5-1853 (12-6-1853)
Harbert, Senia A. to David S. Nicholson 2-1-1859
Hardage, Eliza J. to John B. Long 12-7-1847 (12-?-1847)
Hardage, Margaret A. to Wm. F. Hudson 11-17-1870
Hardage, Nancy A. to Jerome B. Tate 12-24-1859
Hardgrave, Louissanna to L. B. Mitchell 6-24-1839 (6-26-1839)
Hardgraves, America E. to William M. Avery 8-26-1867
Hardgraves, Nancy B. (Mrs.) to Robert O. Lowry 1-19-1867 (1-20-1867)
Hardgrove, Lavinia B. to Neil M. Gardner 6-18-1857 (6-23-1857)
Hardin, Eliza to Charles W. Carrington 3-12-1868
Hardin, Misoura Ann to Patterson Graves 12-17-1853
Hardin, Sarah to George Vinson 6-24-1852
Hardin, Sarah to Nathaniel Timms 1-20-1849 (1-21-1849)
Hardin, Sophronia to John Drake 10-16-1848 (3-10-1850)
Harding, Mary Jane to Henry A. Welsh 9-11-1854 (9-13-1854)
Harding, Sarah P. to Benjamin F. Watkins 1-19-1857
Hardy, Lucinda to Thomas Campbell 12-13-1852
Hardy, Mary E. to Jesse H. Lewis 12-30-1848
Hardy, Nancy to John N. Franklin 2-8-1852
Harns, Elizabeth to Augustin Rollins 3-29-1843
Harp, Jackey J. to John M. Barnet 2-21-1855 (2-27-1855)
Harp, Virginia to Green C. Howlett 9-15-1842 (9-13?-1842)
Harpool, Susan B. to Andrew J. Patrick 11-2-1846
Harrell, F. J. to J. G. McMahan 9-26-1855 (9-27-1855)
Harris, Amanda A. to Vinson Edwards 12-4-1866 (12-5-1866)
Harris, Ann C. to Duke J. Beadles 11-18-1857
Harris, Aurelia to Whitman H. Hearn 1-11-1847
Harris, Eliza A. to Joseph D. Tidwell 10-31-1866
Harris, Eliza W. to David J. Kenaday 3-8-1838
Harris, Eliza to John C. Goodrich 3-27-1844 (3-28-1844)
Harris, Elizabeth H. to William N. Butt 6-20-1856
Harris, Elizabeth to Thomas Boyett 12-15-1839 (12-19-1839)
Harris, Ellen to Marion Mills 5-25-1868 (5-26-1868)
Harris, Emeline to Hampton Liggett 11-21-1838 (11-25-1838)
Harris, Emma G. to William E. Tomlinson 11-19-1866 (11-21-1866)
Harris, Helen to William N. Butts 7-15-1852
Harris, Jane L. to John M. Phillips 6-7-1855
Harris, Jerome W. to James R. West 9-4-1841
Harris, Louanna to William P. Robertson 9-3-1867 (9-4-1867)
Harris, Louisa C. to Samuel S. Watkins 12-20-1847 (12-21-1847)
Harris, Lucinda B. to Charles M. Jackson 2-15-1859
Harris, M. Alice to James H. Clayton 3-6-1866 (3-7-1866)
Harris, Margaret D. to General M. Francis 6-23-1866 (6-24-1866)
Harris, Mary A. E. to Pleasant A. Gowan 7-30-1849
Harris, Mary A. to David A. Jones 11-10-1868 (11-11-1868)
Harris, Mary E. to Gastin Rollins 5-27-1846 (6-4-1846)
Harris, Melvina to Thomas H. Winslow 10-5-1866 (10-7-1866)
Harris, Melvina to William Holloman 1-7-1863 (1-?-1863)
Harris, Miranda A. to Andrew Mills 12-17-1853
Harris, Nancy C. to Lemuel Newsom 1-4-1856
Harris, Narcissa D. to James M. Alexander 8-29-1844
Harris, Narcissus to Robert Newsom 10-15-1850
Harris, Phalba M. to William Hammon 2-28-1867
Harris, Thera to Charles Chamberlin 1-7-1847 (1-10-1847)
Harrison, Aurora to John Peterson 6-26-1866
Harrison, Eliza Jane to Thomas Anderson 8-7-1854
Harrison, Lydia Wheaton to W. R. Kendall 12-27-1869

Harrison, Mary to Thomas F. Mosley 5-29-1871
Harrison, Missouri to David L. Fulbright 11-12-1866 (11-14-1866)
Harrison, Sarah C. to John A. Pemberton 6-17-1846
Harrison, Sarah E. to Geo. B. Black 12-22-1868 (12-24-1868)
Harrison, Sarah Jane to James A. Sweeny 1-11-1848
Harrison, Susan E. to Peter S. Duncan 9-30-1847
Harrison, Virginia B. to Daniel McIver 1-10-1843 (1-11-1843)
Harston, Barbara A. to Stephen R. Bryan 12-8-1856 (12-10-1856)
Harston, Louisa J. to David C. Woodelle 9-5-1849
Hart, Eliza Jane to William McDaniel 11-7-1857 (11-11-1857)
Hart, Elizabeth R. to Hugh Nanny 11-26-1853 (11-29-1853)
Hart, Hannah E. to John McIntosh 3-6-1839 (3-7-1839)
Hart, Margaret J. to Thomas A. Simmons 12-21-1848
Hart, Margaret to James Wesley Williams 9-28-1868
Hart, Martha to George Mathews 8-26-1867 (8-29-1867)
Hart, Mollie J. to Lemual J. Humphreys 1-10-1870 (1-12-1870)
Hart, Nancy L. to Robert S. Mathews 10-29-1866 (10-30-1866)
Hart, Nannie M. to Joel Buntin 1-18-1871 (1-19-1871)
Hart, Susan P. to John Dearmore 12-14-1846 (12-15-1846)
Hartgrave, Minerva to Noah G. Hearn 1-15-1839
Harton, Julia P. to William Carrington 6-4-1842
Harton, Sarah A. E. to Claibourne Weaver 7-19-1843 (7-20-1843)
Haskell, Ellen N. to Wallace C. Claiborne 11-12-1853
Haskins, Annie E. to Jno. A. Steadman 11-8-1869 (11-11-1869)
Haskins, George R. to George Williamson 4-15-1844
Haskins, Mary E. to Wm. H. Harris 12-14-1870
Haslip, Sarah to Daniel Rust 1-21-1841
Hastings, Catherine to Henry L. Mooring 1-4-1858
Haston, Sarah P. to Vicent Moon 7-3-1839 (7-9-1839)
Hathaway, Ann E. to Robert E. Armstrong 8-4-1858
Hathaway, Elizabeth F. to Elisha Rains 10-10-1862 (10-23-1862)
Hathaway, Elizabeth to Thomas T. Taylor 12-21-1859
Hathaway, Mahulda A. to Thomas Laman 12-14-1867 (12-18-1867)
Hathaway, Mary to Milton A. Brown 10-4-1866 (10-9-1866)
Hathaway, Nancy J. to George W. Boals 7-19-1859 (7-21-1859)
Hattom, Sarah F. to Geo. W. Richardson 12-10-1866
Hatton, Sophronia to James M. Nolin 8-16-1842
Haughton, Emma to Alonzo F. Love 4-25-1871 *
Haughton, Sally B. to Jonathan W. Crook 10-2-1855 (10-3-1855)
Hawkins, L. R. to Lewis B. Bond 7-3-1860 (7-4-1860)
Hawse, Martha E. to George A. Sharp 12-14-1852 (12-15-1852)
Hayley, Harriet (Mrs.) to George Hayley 8-15-1871 (8-17-1871)
Hayley, Martha I. to William Vantrice 1-10-1845 (SB 1843?)
Hayley, Susan Catherine to William T. Pearce 3-9-1857 (3-10-1857)
Haynes, Elizabeth to E. W. Lea 3-4-1850 (3-7-1850)
Haynes, Jane C. to Jesse B. Ward 11-24-1866
Haynes, Julia B. to Wm. W. Bain 12-18-1866 (12-20-1866)
Haynes, Mary S. to Andrew L. Finger 12-15-1843 (12-20-1843)
Haynes, Matilda to Thomas B. Williams 5-21-1861
Haynes, Mollie L. to William H. Latham 11-24-1870 (12-1-1870)
Haynes, Saluda J. to Isaac E. Dickie 9-25-1848
Haynes, Sarah A. to Robert H. Perry 12-24-1849 (12-25-1849)
Haynes, Susan A. to William H. McAdoo 3-18-1856
Haynie, Sarah Jane to Robert L. Rogers 1-17-1843
Hays, Fannie Middleton to Walter E. Preston 3-9-1858 (3-10-1858)
Hays, Frances (Mrs.) to William H. Jackson 1-20-1858 (1-21-1858)
Hays, Hannah to Thomas Daily 10-24-1861
Hays, Jane D. to Burkie A. Fossett 8-23-1867 (8-25-1867)
Hays, Josephine C. to Jesse B. Gordon 1-9-1871
Hays, Martha to Allen A. Bruce 11-4-1850
Hays, Mattie to James G. Oliver 5-7-1868
Hays, Rachel J. to William Pitt Deadrick 5-9-1855
Hays, Rebecca J. to Lucius J. Thomas 7-27-1859
Hearn, Elsey to William Hammond 9-13-1845 (9-14-1845)
Hearn, Jane P. to Allen W. Morgan 3-18-1859
Hearn, Jearn to John W. Hearn 12-9-1854 (12-10-1854)
Hearn, Letitia F. to James M. Moore 10-5-1860 (10-9-1860)
Hedleburg, Eveline to William Bryant 11-4-1840
Hefley, Mary J. to William D. Rainey 7-18-1859 (7-20-1859)
Hefley, Sarah A. to John A. Kennedy 10-28-1858 (10-30-1858)
Heidleburg, Jane to Jesse Hooten 2-13-1843 (2-14-1843)
Heidleburg, Louisa to Nowes Miller 10-11-1842 (10-12-1842)
Hellard, Mary C. to Burrell W. Utley 12-11-1855 (12-12-1855)
Henderson, Amanda to Dempsey N. Sewell 2-1-1849
Henderson, Ann Eliza to David W. Jamison 12-6-1856

Henderson, Bettie to Wm. W. Durham 12-21-1869
Henderson, Corriana A. to Henry W. McCorry 12-11-1838
Henderson, Elizabeth to Memory Wooten 12-31-1868
Henderson, Lucinda J. to Enos H. Barnett 8-17-1846 (8-20-1846)
Henderson, M. E. to Charles F. Boon 8-24-1869
Henderson, Margarett A. to Alonzo M. Chamberlin 4-14-1842
Henderson, Mary A. to William A. Hudson 10-5-1841
Henderson, Mary E. to Williams H. Bradley 1-15-1850 (1-17-1850)
Henderson, Nancy Minerva to James W. Barclay 3-10-1857 (3-11-1857)
Henderson, Susan B. to Thomas H. Garrett 11-30-1859 (12-1-1859)
Hendricks, Cassa Ann to George W. Watson 2-8-1854
Henning, Judie A. to Wm. P. Merriwether 12-20-1859 (12-21-1860)
Henning, Sallie F. to Robert W. Bond 2-17-1869
Henning, Sarah Thomas to John N. Arnold 1-5-1844 (1-2?-1844)
Henry, Amy to Richard Parks 10-28-1867 B
Henry, Caroline to James L. Chisum 12-2-1867
Henry, Margarett M. to Alpha R. Bumpus 1-3-1843
Hensler, Sallie E. to S. U. Howell 10-4-1857
Herndon, Arabella to Hugh B. Robinson 8-8-1868 (9-3-1868)
Herndon, Mary E. to Wm. F. Duffy 10-14-1871 (10-18-1871)
Herrington, Elizabeth to Willis Langford 9-24-1850 (9-25-1850)
Herron, Emily Jane to Thomas A. McNail 11-5-1855 (11-7-1855)
Herron, Malinda to William Scarborough 4-14-1841
Herron, Mariah to Francis Parmer 1-16-1844
Herron, Martha C. to Robert W. Mason 3-30-1859 (3-31-1859)
Herse, Matilda to Asa Patterson 5-3-1852
Hewett, Emily to William W. Sexton 8-16-1867 (8-18-1867)
Hewett, Malinda C. to Phineas T. Scruggs 5-22-1861 (5-23-1861)
Hewitt, Mary E. to Asbury Pegues 1-27-1843 (2-1-1843)
Hickman, Mary C. to William Thomas Baldridge 12-24-1853 (12-27-1853)
Hickman, Nancy J. to Milton D. Norvell 7-10-1849
Hicks, Cherry A. to Turner P. Holmes 8-30-1854
Hicks, Ella J. to J. T. Obenchain 6-8-1868
Hicks, Hulda to William M. Allen 3-15-1870 (3-16-1870)
Hicks, Jane M. to Silas Deloach 1-14-1857 (1-15-1857)
Hicks, Martha Ann to Thos. H. Leake 7-14-1846
Hicks, Martha E. to James B. Pearcy 12-4-1849
Hicks, Nancy to John Vantreese 10-2-1847 (10-6-1847)
Hicks, Sophronia to Campbell Price 2-9-1867 (2-10-1867)
Hicks, Susan T. to John J. Clanton 5-11-1870 (5-12-1870)
Hicox, Sarah E. to Eldridge L. Fisher 9-21-1857
Higginbottom, Pamina to John Foreman 11-23-1842
Hight, Amelia Jane to Conrad Seuberth 11-22-1855
Hight, Milla to John S. York 11-20-1838
Hightower, Betsy Jane to Edward Owen 3-4-1871 (3-5-1871)
Hill, Anna to James Lacy 12-14-1850
Hill, Eliza Ann to Thos. Lacy 10-25-1841 (10-28-1841)
Hill, Elizabeth A. to Darius D. Newbern 3-25-1850
Hill, Elizabeth H. to Samuel Epperson 11-18-1844
Hill, Harriet to Leander D. Edwards 12-8-1866 (12-9-1866)
Hill, Louisa C. to George W. Newbern 8-10-1852
Hill, Mary Jane to Samuel Williams 12-13-1842 (12-15-1842)
Hill, Sally H. to George G. Hughes 5-8-1860 (5-9-1860)
Hill, Sarah E. to Joseph C. Sharp 2-16-1857 (2-17-1857)
Hill, Sarah P. to David Lacy 8-10-1842
Hilliard, R. F. to Albert C. White 12-22-1869
Hobb, Esther to Archibald M. Nicholson 2-25-1856 (2-26-1856)
Hobbs, Caroline C. to George W. Turner 1-18-1848 (1-19-1848)
Hobbs, Isabella to Robert Whitworth 10-15-1857 (10-16-1857)
Hobbs, Martha W. to Robert M. Dickinson 12-4-1844 (12-5-1844)
Hodgson, Amanda to William M. Allen 6-15-1839 (6-18-1839)
Hogan, Sarah to John Harvey Ursery 8-22-1866
Hogsett, Donia C. to William T. Henderson 12-2-1867
Hogsett, Mary Ann to Mark C. Henderson 2-6-1867 (2-7-1867)
Holderfield, Nancy Jane to Henry N. Simpson 7-28-1868
Holderfield, Sarah M. to Hiriam Hall 7-26-1843 (7-27-1843)
Holland, Martha A. to Martin L. Chandler 2-9-1869 (2-11-1869)
Holland, Mary to Archibald Thompson 3-9-1840 (3-12-1840)
Hollingsworth, Frances A. to James P. Blankinship 11-12-1866 (11-13-1866)
Holloman, Mary to Charles H. Weathers 12-11-1867 (12-12-1867)
Holloman, Nancy to Arthur Williams 2-16-1869 (2-17-1869)
Hollyfield, Emsey to Louis Rider 7-12-1839 (7-2?-1839)

Hollyman, Elizabeth to James H. Short 12-14-1847 (12-25-1847)
Holmes, Martha M. to Henry W. Davis 12-25-1844
Holmes, Mary A. to Louis McNeely 1-31-1854 (2-1-1854)
Holt, Ann Eliza to George W. Rooker 9-15-1856 (9-17-1856)
Holt, Judith F. to Augustus B. Alston 3-14-1854 (3-15-1854)
Holt, Martha J. to William T. Blackard 2-11-1850
Holyfield, Frances J. to Green Castles 9-3-1846 (8?-3-1846)
Holyfield, Lydia to Green B. Moore 1-26-1847
Holyfield, Susan A. to James L. Medlin 4-16-1850
Hopkins, Emily to Joseph Gallaway 1-24-1855
Hopkins, Logan to Josephine Brock 11-16-1857
Hopkins, Olive to Mason Gilliam 2-27-1854 (2-28-1854)
Hopper, Emeline to Daniel O. March 4-6-1852
Hopper, Lucinda to James M. Bumpass 8-9-1853 (8-10-1853)
Hopper, Margaret L. to Geo. W. Price 12-24-1869
Hopper, Mary Ann to John R. Weakes 12-21-1869 (12-23-1869)
Hopper, Mary Jane to Samuel S. S. Smithwick 1-27-1862 (1-29-1862)
Hopper, Prudence T. to James T. Gill 1-8-1850 (1-19-1850)
Hopper, Rachel J. to Josephus Sims 12-28-1852 (12-29-1852)
Hopper, Sarah A. to O. K. Carpenter 12-10-1855 (12-11-1855)
Hopper, Susanna to William Parker Day 4-8-1845
Hopper, Tabitha E. to Hugh A. Montgomery 2-21-1848 (2-23-1848)
Hoppers, Mariah Frances (Mrs) to Thos. D. Hoppers 8-26-1868 (8-27-1868)
Hoppers, Rebecca to William G. Smithwich 1-5-1850 (1-9-1850)
Horn, Martha to Valentine Tims 12-23-1846
Horn, Mary Jane to Thomas Barber 1-11-1849
Horn, Sarah to Anderson Horn 3-18-1846
Horne, Elizabeth to Jonathan Boswell 10-30-1849
Horton, Mary A. to George W. Cooper 11-12-1866 (11-13-1866)
Horton, Mary to Samuel Huntsman 10-3-1840
Hotchkiss, Martha to William G. Black 1-10-1850
Houghton, Martha to Elizabeth J.? Barnett 10-20-1845 (10-21-1845)
Howard, Ann Eliza to Arthur J. Hedgepath 8-20-1846
Howell, Elizabeth (Mrs.) to Owen Pickens 4-26-1871
Howell, Lumisa to James M. Gately 9-22-1857 (10-1-1857)
Howell, Margaret A. (Mrs.) to I.L.. Reneow 9-9-1870
Howell, Mary Ann to Henry J. Austin 9-30-1857 (10-1-1857)
Howell, Rachel to Martin Sewell 2-8-1867 (2-10-1867)
Howlett, Mary M. to Herbert Perry 11-27-1848 (11-30-1848)
Howlett, Virginia to Edwin L. Wingrove 1-8-1862 (1-9-1862)
Hubbard, Alice to John Jay Lane 2-28-1859 (3-2-1859)
Hubbard, Nannie B. to Thomas C. Salter 8-7-1866 (8-8-1866)
Hudgens, Laura to Wm. H. Mason 6-19-1871 (6-22-1871)
Hudgins, Mary T. to Charles W. Wright 2-24-1869 (2-25-1869)
Hudson, Amanda E. to Benjamin F. Dickinson 3-26-1857
Hudson, Eliza I. to William W. Deberry 1-4-1839
Hudson, Elizabeth to W. N. Hearn 12-21-1846
Hudson, Euginia J. to George R. Scott 10-27-1866 (10-30-1866)
Hudson, Laura to Henry H. Dean 1-23-1854 (1-26-1854) *
Hudson, Lucinda A. to John M. Neal 11-23-1841 (11-25-1841)
Hudson, Martha Ann to John N. Walker 10-26-1867 (11-7-1867)
Hudson, Susan F. to James G. House 12-5-1866 (12-6-1866)
Hudson, Susanna B. to John Bostick 2-22-1841 (2-24-1841)
Hugh, Eunice B. to John M. Fenner 7-25-1844
Hughes, M. K. to H. H. Rogers 2-1-1870 (2-2-1870)
Hulsey, Mary Ann to Oliver Butler 8-5-1848
Humphrey, Martha to Joseph M. Green 10-11-1852
Humphreys, Azalee M. to Hinton J. Jelks 1-22-1845
Humphreys, Clara R. to Levin Hill Harris 11-15-1871 (11-22-1871)
Humphreys, Margaret J. to Thomas G. Arnold 9-14-1853 (9-15-1853)
Humphreys, Margaret J. to Thos. G. Arnold 9-4-1853
Humphreys, Margarett to James Baxter 7-20-1849
Hundley, Gilly to Arthur Williams 11-4-1857
Hunt, Lucy Eugenie to Jas. G. Glenn 10-5-1868 (10-6-1868)
Hunter, Elizabeth M. to James R. Glenn 4-3-1854 (4-5-1854)
Hunter, Frances F. to Oren A. Hearn 12-9-1859 (12-11-1859)
Hunter, Margaret A. to Wm. H. Bray 5-15-1866
Hunter, Martha E. to Newton A. McCoy 11-7-1855 (11-?-1855)
Hunter, Mary to James W. Perry 12-22-1838
Huntsman, Ann to Timothy P. Spurlock 12-21-1840 (12-22-1840)
Huntsman, Paradise to Nathiel W. Williams 3-30-1855
Huntsman, Sarah L. to Isaac D. Parker 12-27-1845 (12-28-1845)
Hurt, Harriett C. to Archibold W. O. Toten 3-29-1843
Hurt, Lizzie J. to Guy Leeper 1-6-1869

Hurt, Pattie to Joseph D. Neilson 4-30-1867 (5-1-1867)
Hutcherson, Addie C. to Harvey N. Milligan 11-16-1870
Hutcherson, Ida to Benj. A. (of AR) Word 2-22-1870
Hutchings, Mary C. to John H. Cross 11-30-1848
Hutchison, Laura to Thomas A. Reid 11-16-1869 (11-18-1869)
Hutchison, Nancy Wilmoth to Levi B. Herron 12-29-1858 (12-30-1858)
Hutchison, Tempee to Thomas C. Harbut 5-11-1870
Ingram, Ann to Matthias Deberry 11-3-1847
Ingram, Jane to Thomas H. Taylor 5-1-1849
Ingram, Louisa to John A. Greer 5-21-1859 (5-22-1859)
Ingram, Lydia to James Johnson 12-8-1858
Ingram, Mattie to Peter Combs 10-10-1871 (10-14-1871)
Inman, Martha E. to Jno. W. Leonard 2-6-1871
Inman, Mary Ann to Wm. D. Neff 12-27-1869 (12-29-1869)
Irvin, Adriadna to T. G. Osburn 1-10-1870 (1-11-1870)
Irvin, Julian to Newton Butes 7-5-1841
Irvin, Malvina to Nathan W. Whittington 9-6-1842
Irvin, Suzy Ann to William A. Alexander 3-21-1843 (3-23-1843)
Irvine, Hannah to Eli C. Chandler 6-5-1850
Isom, Harriott to John M. Marsh 6-27-1839
Jabasford?, ___ to Moses Harden 12-15-1842
Jackson, Almedia L. to W. P. Williams 10-19-1870 (10-20-1870)
Jackson, Angelina to Hugh S. King 3-26-1850
Jackson, Anna to John Jackson 12-13-1838 (12-20-1838)
Jackson, Caroline (Mrs.) to John Davis 4-29-1871 (4-20?-1871)
Jackson, Caroline to M. B. Sherman 9-22-1856
Jackson, Elizabeth to Samuel Irvey 5-23-1857
Jackson, Emily to William King 7-2-1861 (7-3-1861)
Jackson, Eugenia Lafayette to William H. Hunt 12-22-1846
Jackson, Frances C. to John A. Tomlinson 4-25-1848
Jackson, Harriet M. to Joseph Bailey 12-18-1847 (12-20-1847)
Jackson, Louisa E. to Solomon Smith 7-16-1856 (7-17-1856)
Jackson, Louisa to William H. Morris 1-25-1859
Jackson, Louisa to William Tomlinson 10-1-1839 (10-2-1839)
Jackson, Margaret to Asa McAfee 12-6-1866
Jackson, Martha C. to Elisha Baly 1-14-1852 (1-15-1852)
Jackson, Martha J. to Francis Gamewell 5-17-1849
Jackson, Martha Jane to James N. Jackson 10-10-1868 (10-14-1868)
Jackson, Mary C. to Wm. B. Hays 11-9-1868 (11-12-1868)
Jackson, Mary to George B. Moore 1-30-1839
Jackson, Nancy F. to John J. Evans 12-31-1867
Jackson, Rebecca to Jacob Baker 11-4-1850
Jackson, Sallie A to Anderson P. Selph 12-24-1867 (12-29-1867)
Jackson, Sally to Patrick Harper 1-5-1841 (1-10-1841)
Jackson, Sarah A. to James A. Lackie 2-29-1868
Jackson, Sarah L. to Andrew J. King 1-27-1868 (1-30-1868)
Jackson, Viola to Peter Williams 12-14-1849 (12-19-1849)
Jacobs, Gertie to Edward J. Griffin 4-18-1868 (4-20-1868)
Jarnagin, Martha L. to Amphias Smith 12-16-1844 (12-19-1844)
Jarratt, Mary to Henry Warmath 11-3-1842 (11-5-1842)
Jayne, Mary E. to John Coats 6-21-1849
Jayne, Orva Ann to Geo. W. Talbot 6-25-1849 (6-27-1849)
Jeffries, Mary to Parminue Strans 8-1-1840 (8-4-1840)
Jeffries, Permelia J. to Wm. A. Boren 12-12-1870 (12-13-1870)
Jeffrys, Sarah B. to William Y. Newbern 7-2-1840 (7-7-1840)
Jelks, Alice to Erasmus F. Hicks 3-16-1858 (3-17-1858)
Jelks, Louisa C. to John F. Sinclair 10-29-1849 (10-31-1849)
Jenkins, Elizabeth to James Hicks 10-11-1852 (10-13-1852)
Jenkins, Sarah Elizabeth to Radford Booe 1-24-1857
Jerman, Eliza to John Wilkerson 1-27-1843 (1-30-1843)
Jester, Callie J. to Robert Gates 10-29-1867
Jester, Margarett to John Lowden 3-1-1841
Jett, Elizabeth A. to Finis E. Bryan 12-7-1868
Johnson, Alsey Jane to Josiah L. Lacy 12-5-1843
Johnson, Amanda to Elijah H. Spencer 7-26-1851 (7-31-1851)
Johnson, Ann Elizabeth to Noah Nelson 9-24-1850 (9-25-1850)
Johnson, Annis to William H. Nobles 4-4-1844
Johnson, Caroline to Council B. Mayo 11-8-1843
Johnson, Catherine to William B. Haltom 3-3-1853
Johnson, Celia to Elias G. B. Cook 10-26-1840
Johnson, Eliza J. to William B. Manley 10-21-1850
Johnson, Elizabeth E. to Neal Carrington 4-24-1852
Johnson, Elizabeth M. to William W. Hart 1-5-1857 (1-6-1857)
Johnson, Elizabeth to Alexander Story 2-10-1843

Johnson, Elizabeth to William Hogan 10-8-1866 (10-11-1866)
Johnson, Elvira Catherine to Isham H. Brower 12-28-1855 (12-29-1855)
Johnson, Emily to Dempsey Ursery 3-22-1852 (3-23-1852)
Johnson, Emily to Winston Ellington 8-22-1868 (8-25-1868)
Johnson, Jane to Caswell Hogans 8-3-1845
Johnson, Jemima to George A. (of Miss.) Bagley 7-16-1861
Johnson, Leonora to John P. Day 1-17-1870 (1-19-1870)
Johnson, Lydia A. to Matt D. Meriwether 11-14-1860 (11-15-1860)
Johnson, Lydia A. to William W. Manley 6-15-1860 (6-17-1860)
Johnson, Madelena to John Hobbs 7-12-1843 (7-13-1843)
Johnson, Margaret E. to James M. Johnson 10-6-1869
Johnson, Margarett to Littleton Storey 3-5-1844
Johnson, Marianna to Richard J. Fenner 3-23-1841 (3-24-1841)
Johnson, Martha A. to Reuben Sewell 9-29-1841
Johnson, Martha Ann to Olen West 11-1-1841
Johnson, Martha E to John J. Boon 7-10-1850
Johnson, Martha F. to Whitson H. Wilson 10-4-1858 (10-6-1858)
Johnson, Martha J. to Robert J. Williams 12-22-1852
Johnson, Martha Jnae to Andrew J. McClish 12-27-1856 (12-28-1856)
Johnson, Martha P. to John T. Anderson 7-15-1850
Johnson, Martha Sarah to John T. Cherry 1-28-1858
Johnson, Martha to Wilson Tolley 3-28-1840 (3-1?-1840)
Johnson, Mary A. T. to T. F. Amos 12-2-1867 (12-5-1867)
Johnson, Mary E. to John C. Ledbetter 11-27-1852 (11-28-1852)
Johnson, Mary Frances to Joseph Allison 7-16-1839
Johnson, Mary S. to C. (Dr.) Harris 8-23-1845 (8-25-1845)
Johnson, Mary to Alscy Jordon 7-3-1841 (7-8-1841)
Johnson, Mary to H. W. Cotter, jr. 6-5-1867 (6-6-1867)
Johnson, Nancy to Crred B. Haskins 12-26-1848 (12-27-1848)
Johnson, Nancy to James Henry White 5-23-1866
Johnson, Narcissa to James L. Storey 5-15-1841 (5-19-1841)
Johnson, Sarah A. to John W. Brown 7-9-1846
Johnson, Sarah Ann to Wm. J. Dearmore 10-4-1871 (10-5-1871)
Johnson, Sarah to Isiah Hogan 12-20-1849
Johnson, Sarah to William Loftin 12-8-1852
Johnson, Sideous I. to James H. Nelson 11-1-1842 (11-3-1842)
Johnson, Susana Maria to John F. N. Sypes 11-6-1868 (11-8-1868)
Johnson, Tempy S. to Leroy C. Gillaspie 10-29-1852 (10-30-1852)
Johnson, Winney to Calvin Sauls 10-4-1847
Johnston, Ann C. to James M. White 10-2-1838
Johnston, Mary Elizabeth to Robert Evans 9-28-1867
Johnston, Sarah A. to William L. Slack 8-21-1843 (8-24-1843)
Johnston, Sarah Jane to Bedford M. Estes 4-24-1854 (5-4-1854)
Johnston, Tempie to Farrington B. Snipes 11-30-1868 (12-3-1868)
Joiner, Malvina to James M. Lusk 1-12-1871
Jones, Amanda M. to Thomas P. Morgan 11-2-1850 (11-3-1850)
Jones, Ann Eliza to John R. Boals 12-17-1860 (12-19-1860)
Jones, Arcady F. to Henry Bayley 6-12-1848
Jones, Clotilda to John F. Crawford 6-21-1838
Jones, Daruishia Belmont to William Van Pelt 7-22-1868 (7-17?-1868)
Jones, Eliza to Noel Spragins 1-30-1844 (2-1-1844)
Jones, Elizabeth A. to Thomas H. Follis 12-21-1859 (12-22-1859)
Jones, Elizabeth E. to Henry Caskins 7-29-1844
Jones, Emelina C. to Joseph M. Dickson 1-5-1849 (1-8-1849)
Jones, Emily B. to William K. Love 3-14-1840 (3-17-1840)
Jones, Emily to Wiley Medlin 9-9-1868 (9-10-1868)
Jones, Frances L. to Alfred L. Lunsford 12-20-1843 (12-21-1843)
Jones, H. (Mrs.) to W. F. Kizer 10-5-1870
Jones, Harriett E. to Lenoir Bruton 11-16-1843
Jones, Hellen to Lincefield Sexton 7-16-1844 (7-4?-1844)
Jones, Jane M. to Thomas Rawlings 1-29-1855 (2-1-1855)
Jones, Laviney to John M. Irvin 10-20-1853
Jones, Lucinda P. to Francis A. Follis 10-23-1860 (10-25-1860)
Jones, Margarett Ann to Andrew J. Goodlow 8-17-1843
Jones, Maring to John Stephens 5-5-1841 (5-17-1841)
Jones, Martha J. to William Grimes 2-6-1846
Jones, Martha M. to James H. Winston 1-11-1843 (1-12-1843)
Jones, Mary Abagail to Wm. H. C. McDurmit 4-27-1859
Jones, Mary Ann to George Chipman 12-18-1852
Jones, Mary Anna to W. Bond Dashill 9-28-1871
Jones, Mary E. to George W. Day 10-12-1848 (10-15-1848)
Jones, Mary H. to John J. Donnell 9-18-1866 (9-19-1866)
Jones, Mary to Thomas Pearce 9-9-1871 (9-10-1871)
Jones, Matilda to John Jones 2-5-1844 (2-8-1844)

Jones, Nancy A. to Jno. T. Medlin 4-12-1871 (4-13-1871)
Jones, Nancy Emily to William Vanpelt 7-28-1866 (7-29-1866)
Jones, Nancy M. to Albert B. S. Johnson 4-13-1848 (4-18-1848)
Jones, Octavia H.? to Joseph T. Phillips 12-18-1860 (12-19-1860)
Jones, Sallie R. to George W. Moore 3-19-1868
Jones, Sarah C. to Geo. L. Jones 1-16-1869 (1-17-1869)
Jones, Sarah M. to Blythe McCorkle 12-13-1855
Jones, Sarah W. to Stephen D. Ross 2-16-1838 (2-23-1838)
Jones, Sophia P. to John W. Mooring 1-15-1858 (1-18-1858)
Jones, Sophronia Cathy to Alfred Britton Jones 7-13-1867 (7-14-1867)
Jordan, Mahala A. to Jno. M. Ursery 1-13-1869
Jordon, Susan M. to Irvin Finch 12-2-1843 (12-3-1843)
Joyce, Elizabeth to Harbird K. Joyce 9-14-1853
Joyce, Mary E. to Snowden H. Davis 10-21-1850
Karr, Mary to Alfred Pool 9-15-1843 (9-17-1843)
Kell, Nancy P. to Jimms P. Alexander 10-24-1871 (10-25-1871)
Kelly, Margaret J. to David T. Hodge 8-28-1848 (8-31-1848)
Kelly, Sally to John Miller 2-18-1846
Kendrick, Catherine to Thomas N. Stephenson 3-15-1848
Kendrick, E. S. to James A. Dodds 12-15-1839 (12-18-1839)
Kendrick, Fanny to William Pasmose 1-10-1843 (1-12-1843)
Kendrick, Martha to Felix G. Gibbs 1-10-1845
Kennon, Arabella L. to William J. Sykes 1-31-1848
Kerby, Rebecca to Anthony Haywood Cazort 3-8-1848 (3-9-1848)
Kerksey, Emily to Silas Lassiter 1-1-1857 (1-2-1857)
Kerr, Celia to William Long 6-16-1845
Kerr, Martha to Willoughby Pugh 10-8-1840
Kershaw, Sarah A. to Wm. H. Rush 6-14-1871 (6-15-1871)
Key, Almira N. to Elias D. Barnett 3-22-1848 (3-28-1848)
Key, Rebecca Elizabeth to James H. Ezell 12-28-1858
Kile, Margaret O. to John N. Harris 4-19-1870 (4-21-1870)
Kilpatrick, Cynthia C. to Christopher Glenn 12-4-1848
Kilpatrick, Hannah J. to William A. Glenn 1-21-1867
Kilpatrick, Margaret A. to Henry A. Piffin 9-18-1866
Kilpatrick, Rebecca to Medlin Stone 2-17-1869 (2-21-1869)
Kilpatrick, Sarah to William Pentecost 12-29-1846
Kimball, Sarah J. to Edmond J. Orgain 2-5-1850 (2-7-1850)
Kimble, Mary T. to Edward Lad 10-6-1866 (not executed)
Kincaid, Nancy Amanda to David Patterson 9-30-1857 (10-1-1857)
Kincaide, Lucinda E. to John Milling 5-11-1869
Kind, Mary to Green Moore 1-17-1855
King, Ann to James M. Hart 7-28-1854 *
King, Dicey to Seaborn J. Stewart 1-14-1845 (1-19-1845)
King, Eady to Samuel Duffey 10-22-1862 (10-23-1862)
King, Harriet to Daniel Hicks 5-1-1871
King, Isabella Clemintine to Dawson D. Newman 12-15-1843 (12-21-1843)
King, Julia A. E. to Thomas A. Cock 5-14-1849 (5-15-1849)
King, Keady to William A. Duffie 12-17-1846 (12-20-1846)
King, Margaret Ann to Benj. C. Long 5-28-1868
King, Margaret to John S. Duffey 2-12-1852
King, Martha Ann to Julius C. Harris 2-28-1859 (3-3-1859)
King, Martha Jane to William N. Fussell 9-11-1866 (9-13-1866)
King, Mary Ann to William I. G. King 10-11-1838
King, Mary F. to Jno. W. Walters 1-1-1869 (1-3-1869)
King, Mary L. to Alfred King 11-27-1839 (11-28-1839)
King, May Ann to Lafayette Moize 7-4-1850 (7-10-1850)
King, Paralee F. to William J. McFarland 10-29-1850
King, Rebecca to William T. Lyon 1-1-1842 (1-3-1842)
King, Sarah E. to Robert W. Sims 10-10-1862 (10-23-1862)
King, Sarah to Thos. F. Mosley 1-4-1870
King, Susan to Joseph McFarlin 4-15-1861 (4-16-1861)
Kirby, Ann E. (Mrs.) to Henry C. Johnson 11-8-1869
Kirby, Elizabeth W. to John Glover 1-5-1845 (1-8-1846)
Kirby, Henretta J. to Sylvanus Taylor 10-12-1850 *
Kirby, Laura L. to Timothy J. Barnes 10-5-1869 (10-6-1869)
Kirby, Martha to Owen J. Busick 9-25-1847
Kirby, Mary to George M. Bennett 4-15-1857 (4-16-1857)
Kirby, Mary to Gilbert Cozart 1-1-1845 (1-7-1845)
Kirby, Mattie E. to George W. Collins 12-14-1870 (12-15-1870)
Kirby, Mollie to Andrew H. Bevill 12-13-1866
Kirby, Rebecca to John Elam 11-24-1866 (11-29-1866)
Kirk, Emma C. to William J. Calloway 10-8-1867
Kirkpatrick, Cynthia J. to John W. McElwee 8-28-1847
Kirkpatrick, Mary H. to George T. Mahon 2-7-1848 (2-?-1848)

Kirkpatrick, Rebecca J. to Joseph Wilks 12-6-1847 (12-7-1847)
Kirkpatrick, Synthia Jane to Samuel R. N. Pendergrast 12-6-1843
Kirksey, Martha Ann to James Pinckney Jones 7-13-1858
Kittrell, Nancy M. to James A. Newsom 9-14-1854 (9-19-1854)
Knight, Jane to George C. Medlin 1-20-1852 (1-21-1852)
Knight, Mary E. to Ashley Midgett 5-6-1850 (5-8-1850)
Knott, Sallie to Josiah W. Brown 8-20-1867 (8-22-1867)
Kollinsworth, Elizabeth to James Haddon 1-25-1867
Kyle, Margaret Ellen to John W. Hill 3-28-1867
Kyle, Mary S. to James G. Perry 11-20-1851
Kyle, Sarah C. to Charles H. Brown 8-9-1854
Lacey, Margarett to Lemuel Stone 1-23-1849 (1-24-1849)
Lackey, Mary Ann to William Y. Carter 3-12-1859
Lackey, Matilda to Stephen Brooks 2-8-1840 (2-16-1840)
Lackey, Permelia J. to William H. Guthrie 10-6-1853
Lackie, Bettie to J. Polk Harston 11-28-1868
Lackie, Bettie to Thomas L. Carter 12-24-1867 (12-25-1867)
Lacy, Lucretia L. to John J. Boon 3-28-1866 (3-29-1866)
Lacy, Margaret to John B. Johnson 2-1-1858 (2-2-1858)
Lambert, Anna to Lewis Acre 1-3-1839 (1-6-1839)
Lambert, Delilah to William K. Steepleton 11-8-1850
Lambert, Eliza to Jerimiah Sullivan 1-17-1843
Lambert, Emily Ann to Eugene Campbell 10-27-1866 (10-30-1866)
Lambert, Martha J. to Daniel R. Burn 12-31-1849 (12-16?-1849)
Lancaster, Ann Eliza to Thomas Henderson 7-25-1848
Lane, Charity to George Patterson 11-27-1852
Lane, Martha J. to William O. Boykin 11-17-1852
Lane, Mary E. to John R. Jelks 1-18-1845 (1-22-1845)
Lane, Nancy B. to William H. Ellenton 9-22-1855 (10-4-1855)
Lane, Prior A. J. to Franklin B. Tidwell 11-23-1842 (11-24-1842)
Laney, Victoria to Wm. M. Mallory 10-26-1870 (10-28-1870)
Langford, Jane M. W. to Omer H. Stanley 12-22-1852 (12-23-1852)
Langford, Martha E. to Armstead P. Pool 8-17-1848
Langford, May Ann to John Munn 5-20-1841
Langston, Jane to Silas Tettleton 10-14-1841
Langston, Margaret E. to Robert M. Brooks 9-6-1866
Lanier, Bettie to Jno. R. (Dr.) Atkinson 12-6-1869 (12-8-1869)
Lanier, Lucy V. to James N. Parrish 12-9-1868 (12-16-1868)
Lanier, Mollie J. to A. R. Waynick 10-13-1856 (10-30-1856)
Lanier, Sarah A. to Newett N. May 11-3-1858
Lankford, Gabella to James R. Heas 9-1-1841
Lassiter, Lucy A. to Boker C. Jarrall 4-3-1849
Lassiter, Mary Ann to M. T. Cock 9-21-1852 (9-22-1852)
Latham, Elizabeth to Francis Wright 8-21-1853 (8-23-1853)
Latham, Elizabeth to William P. Lacy 9-13-1858
Latham, Lucretia Paralee to Samuel Richardson 11-19-1855
Latham, Martha Ann to Wm. T. Herbert 3-11-1871 (3-15-1871)
Latham, Mary Ann to William H. Wells 12-23-1850 (12-24-1850)
Lathrick, Catherine to John L. Crews 2-4-1856
Lattimer, Margaret to Mark Mitchell 9-13-1853
Lawrence, Ann Eliza B. to William R. Lacy 12-17-1867 (12-18-1867)
Lawrence, Exalina to David M. Quinley 2-12-1850
Lawrence, Jane to Cader Piercy 7-19-1845 (7-20-1845)
Lawrence, Lydia to James Dawson 1-30-1856
Lawrence, Martha to Elisha T. Harbour 8-22-1868 (8-26-1868)
Lawrence, Martha to James Dawson 4-12-1854
Lawrence, Moniza to David T. Thurman 10-28-1858
Lawrence, Sally M. to Jno. S. Lacy 12-1-1868 (12-2-1868)
Laws, Nancy P. to Lemuel M. Jelks 5-4-1850 (5-7-1850)
Laxton, Martha M. to William F. Privett 8-31-1843
Lcy, Mary Jane to Henry J. Jackson 6-15-1861 (6-16-1861)
Lea, Georgiana H. to John M. Morrill 4-23-1855
Lea, Mary E. to William Pool 8-21-1849 (8-23-1849)
Lea, Mary L. to Calvin Graus 2-11-1859
Leadbetter, Eloner to Joshua Price 12-3-1838
Leake, Lucinda to William Robert Wilson 1-18-1856
Ledbetter, Betsy Ann to John S. Burrow 12-21-1842
Lee, Sarah Lucinda to J. T. Conner 2-8-1871
Lemond, Mary S. L. J. to William Jackson 12-10-1857 (12-31-1857)
Lemons, Mary to Hugh Boyd 2-5-1855 (2-7-1855)
Lester, Louiser C. to Wm. H. Justice 5-1-1866 (5-3-1866)
Lester, Mary E. to William F. McKnight 4-15-1856
Lett, Elizabeth to John D. West 2-10-1871 (2-11-1871)
Lewis, Jennie to Eli Smith 11-14-1871 (11-15-1871)

Lewis, Martha Ann Tennessee to Edward L. M. Smith 7-18-1860 (7-19-1860)
Lewis, Martha Ann to James G. Futrell 9-3-1866 (9-5-1866)
Lewis, Martha Rebecca Ann to John Woodson 8-26-1867 (8-28-1867)
Lewis, Mary B. to John N. Walker 5-14-1870 (5-19-1870)
Lewis, Mary E. to Calvin C. Clement 7-10-1866
Lewis, Mary Elizabeth to Gardner Lytle 11-12-1867 (11-13-1867)
Lewis, Olivia J. (Mrs.) to James R. Bourland 2-20-1871 (2-21-1871)
Linton, Martha D. to Thomas B. Carroll 11-1-1866 (11-8-1866)
Little, Jane to Elijah Jean 10-8-1850 (10-10-1850)
Little, Mary E. to John W. Baker 7-3-1852 (7-8-1852)
Littlepage, Lamira Ann to Thomas Clark 12-8-1866 (12-16-1866)
Lock, Adeline E. to Andrew T. Brown 12-2-1850 (12-5-1850)
Lock, Martha E. to John P. Simmons 9-30-1848
Locke, Frances A. to William J. Jones 1-20-1852
Locke, Sarah A. to Robert F. Brown 7-12-1855
Lofte, Catherine I. to George F. Jones 10-14-1840 (10-15-1840)
Logan, Sarah B. to Thomas Christian 8-25-1841 (8-26-1841)
London, Eveline to Lemuel Leake 3-30-1849 (4-1-1849)
London, Sarah N. to Parmenias Fifer 1-3-1860
Londu, Cynthia to Jesse Johnson 8-25-1846 (8-26-1846)
Long, Caroline D. to James Elrod 3-15-1855
Long, Eliza P. to John P. Pryor 9-19-1845
Long, Harriet Ann to John G. Mann 6-27-1860 (6-28-1860)
Long, Mary J. to Robert H. Chester 11-1-1853
Long, Rhoda to Robt. H. Nichols 2-19-1870 (2-20-1870)
Long, Susie to Robt. A. Treadwell 2-9-1869
Love, Caroline to James Burton 10-1-1855
Love, Mary F. to Richard M. Whitfield 1-1-1855
Lovelace, Caroline to William H. Newton 1-10-1871
Lovelace, Eugenia V. to Francis E. Hudson 2-13-1856 (2-14-1856)
Lovelace, Sabetha W. to William C. Vantreese 6-8-1840 (6-10-1840)
Lovelace, Susan V. to Stephen M. Johnson 1-6-1859
Lovell, California to Sandford M. Bickerstaff 4-13-1869 (4-14-1869)
Lovill, Mary Jane to James M. Gately 11-9-1852 (12-22-1852)
Lovin, Lavicy to William W. Holliday 12-9-1847
Loving, Elizabeth to Cullud Lane 1-6-1841 (2-16-1841)
Lovitt, Sarah to William Munn 11-13-1839
Lowell, Sarah to Robert W. Gordon 1-7-1848 (1-20-1848)
Luckey, Caroline to Stephen B. Goodrich 7-24-1858 (7-29-1858)
Luster, Susan E. to F. M. Robinson 12-29-1853 (12-29-1853)
Lynch, Kate to John Ohanlon 11-4-1869
Lynch, Milly Ann to Robert Foster 10-6-1866
Lyon, Julia A. to John J. Cash 12-28-1859
Lyon, Lizzie C. to B. L. Rozell 2-26-1855 (2-27-1855)
Lyon, Nancy E. to Thomas J. Watt 9-4-1867 (9-5-1867)
Lyon, Sarah A. to Thomas J. Watt 1-4-1854 (1-12-1854)
Lyon, Sarah J. to Lemuel K. Clifton 11-6-1845
Lyon, Sarah Jane to James N. Watt, jr. 3-16-1850
Lyons, Margaret E. to William J. Oakes 4-11-1859
Macon, Jane to Christinberry Russell 11-14-1849
Madders, Labertha to Bennet Drake 1-5-1858 (1-6-1858)
Maddind, Sarah C. to James M. McDonald 11-27-1844 (11-28-1844)
Maddox, Mary Elizabeth to Wyatt Fussell 4-20-1842 (4-21-1842)
Maddox, Mary S. to Hugh C. Henderson 4-28-1852
Maddox, Nancy to Robert H. Henderson 5-3-1855
Maddox, Rachel A. to Joel W. Altman 2-19-1849 (12-20-1849)
Maginis, Mary to James C. Chandler 11-22-1842 (11-23-1842)
Mahon, Mary Nany to Johnson Faulkland 2-14-1838
Mainord, Sarah A. to George A. Scarborough 5-2-1870 (5-5-1870)
Mallory, Virginia to Andrew Percifull 9-25-1855
Malone, Caroline A. to James W. Boyd 2-6-1845 (2-8-1845)
Mangrum, Elizabeth to Arthur Bland 5-8-1841 (5-9-1841)
Mangrum, Hawkins to Alfred N. Weaver 11-12-1860 (11-13-1860)
Manley, Louisa N. W. to John Carroll 12-30-1847
Manley, Martha E. to Robert B. Williams 7-19-1853
Manley, Sarah J. to Pleasant R. Davis 9-18-1861 (9-19-1861)
Manley, Sarah to Wesley Anderson 1-27-1858
Manly, Harriet to George Hudson 1-26-1869 (1-27-1869)
Mann, Elizabeth P. to William A. Nobles 12-11-1847 (12-14-1847)
Manus, Louisa F. to George N. Brogdon 6-17-1868 (12-3-1868)
March, Leminda Clementine to James J. Jacobs 7-10-1866 (7-12-1866)
March, Rachael to Jacob A. Norton 6-28-1845 (7-1-1845)
Margrave, Susan Ellen to Freeman Patterson 9-22-1855 (9-23-1855)
Marks, Anna to D. C. Neal 6-26-1867

Marks, Kate to William Bradley 3-8-1870 (3-9-1870)
Marlow, Amanda C. to John Faulkner 9-25-1850 (9-26-1850)
Marlow, Emelina to Madison Cozort 12-29-1847 (12-30-1847)
Marlow, Julia Frances to Joshua M. Cozart 2-13-1858 (2-17-1858)
Marlow, Mary Jane to James McMillan 2-26-1850
Maroney, Elizabeth to Haywood Williamson 1-3-1856
Maroney, Martha Ann to Andrew M. Eagan 9-2-1856
Marsh, Drusilla T. to John H. Johnson 12-17-1853 (12-20-1853)
Marsh, Elizabeth S. to John I. Temples 3-24-1869 (3-28-1869)
Marsh, Elizabeth to Coleman Toone 7-26-1852
Marsh, Mary to Granville Mathews 12-17-1840 (12-19-1840)
Marsh, Nancy to Spencer Epps 1-4-1848 (1-5-1848)
Marshall, Asenith M. to Andrew D. Weatherly 12-7-1858 (12-8-1858)
Marshall, Nancy T. to James F. Holloway 1-27-1859
Marshall, Susan to John F. Williams 6-13-1842 (6-16-1842)
Mary, Nancy to William Brookshire 12-29-1841 (12-30-1841)
Mason, Abigail F. to William Ursery 8-3-1837 (8-3-1847?)
Mason, Ann to Nathan Johnson 1-10-1857 (1-13-1856?)
Mason, Eliza F. to James T. Devore 9-7-1866 (9-9-1866)
Mason, M. P. E. to Green Wortham 11-26-1860 (11-27-1860)
Mason, Margaret to R. W. Wood 3-14-1870 (3-15-1870)
Mason, Margaret to William H. Piercy 3-7-1849 (3-8-1849)
Mason, Maria E. to Nolen S. White 9-19-1871 (9-20-1871)
Mason, Martha Ann to William Cleavis 6-1-1842 (6-9-1842)
Mason, Mary J. to John T. Pounds 7-5-1859 (7-7-1859)
Mason, Rachael to Joshua J. Sanders 12-22-1840 (12-23-1840)
Mason, Rebecca to Matthew M. Goodridge 2-12-1848 (2-17-1848)
Massey, Caroline to Narcus R. Campbell 7-28-1852
Massey, Catherine to Collin Williams 1-10-1854 (1-11-1854)
Massey, Eliza Jane to Ezekiel Boyett 5-6-1848 (5-18-1848)
Massey, Jane to John Brimingham 9-8-1852
Massey, Lucy E. to James H. Passmore 1-2-1855
Massey, Miranda Jane to William Henry Adams 2-10-1859 (2-17-1859)
Matcik, P. A. to John Dorsey 11-28-1870
Mathews, Fidelia E. to Miles F. Sloan 9-10-1866 (9-12-1866)
Mathis, Emma J. to David W. Turner 3-2-1870 (3-8-1870)
Mathis, Martha to John Newson 2-10-1845
Mathis, Mary M. to Chasteen Ellington 9-17-1845 (9-18-1845)
Matthews, Alice to William H. Nelson 12-5-1867 (12-8-1867)
Matthews, Catherine E. to Benjamin W. Clement 12-21-1858 (12-22-1858)
Matthews, Elizabeth J. to Robert C. Wyatt 3-13-1858 (3-18-1858)
Matthews, Margaret E. to Robert Hunt 4-28-1857 (4-29-1857)
Matthews, Martha Ann to William C. Stovall 10-30-1847 (11-4-1847)
Matthews, Mary E. to Carren E. Boykin 4-17-1854 (4-18-1854)
Matthews, Mattie to Wm. M. Teahen 12-20-1870 (12-21-1870)
Matthews, Nancy E. to John Bunyan Sloan 6-25-1869 (6-27-1869)
Matthews, Sue to Powhatton P. Bennett 12-16-1868 (12-19-1868)
Mauldin, Elizabeth to George Morphis 1-10-1842 (1-11-1842)
Maxey, Betty A. to Robert N. Hill 9-10-1856
Maxwell, Matilda A. to Tilman D. Corum 11-19-1847 (11-21-1847)
May, Elizabeth to John Parmer 1-7-1841
May, Elizabeth to John R. Clark 2-13-1844 (2-15-1844)
May, Ellen to Robert D. Hart 10-1-1862 (10-2-1862)
May, Fannie H. to Nathan I. Mainor 2-10-1868 (2-12-1868)
May, Harriet D. to S. C. Benjamin 12-9-1857 (12-10-1857)
May, Harriett to Edward Cock 12-9-1858
May, Julia to James Kindrick 5-6-1844 (5-7-1844)
May, Lucy to Bailey G. Rooks 9-24-1840
May, Mary C. to Doddridge Trader 8-2-1859 (8-3-1859)
May, Nancy to John J. Pearcy 11-25-1857 (2-5-1857?)
May, Sarah to Reuben Johnson 1-20-1846 (1-21-1846)
Maynard, Malinda to Harvey M. Alexander 12-16-1869 (12-17-1869)
Maynard, Mary F. to William R. Rooks 9-19-1863 (9-20-1862?)
Mayo, Martha S. to James N. Hart 11-22-1869
Mayo, Sarah Jane to Jackson Smith 2-23-1858
Mays, Ella B. to Archibald J. Sneed 1-19-1869 (1-20-1869)
Mays, Malinda to Alexander C. Shane 6-26-1861
Mays, Malinda to Harrison L. H. Stanley 3-7-1861
Mays, Mary F. to Isaac N. Croom 5-19-1856
Mays, Nancy Jane to Frederick Blake 4-21-1870 (4-24-1870)
Mays, Sarah A. to James Swink 11-2-1852 (12-2-1852)
McAdoo, Frances E. to Elijah Robinson 12-8-1858 (12-12-1858)
McAdoo, Lavenia J. to Davie McCree 1-20-1858

McAfee, Elizabeth S. to William H. Nelson 11-22-1856 (12-1-1856)
McAfee, Ruth C. to John Nelson, jr. 12-22-1845
McAfee, Sarah A. to Jesse Inman 8-16-1869
McAlexander, Jennie to Thomas Fry 1-31-1871
McAlfee, Mary Jane to Christopher L., jr. Johnson 3-31-1849
McAlfee, Minerva H. to Jarrett Hollinsworth 10-7-1848
McBryde, Sarah (Mrs.) to James Scarbrough 4-13-1869 (4-14-1869)
McCabe, Mary M. to Moses E. Pratt 12-23-1867 (12-24-1867)
McCaig, Eliza Ann to Jno. W. Harris 12-16-1869
McCaig, Emily J. to James R. Denton 12-6-1862
McCaig, Julia F. to John W. Winston 5-28-1870 (5-31-1870)
McCain, Mary (Mrs.) to Nat Mickens 5-23-1861 (5-28-1861)
McCain, Polly to John Stephens 2-10-1848 (2-11-1848)
McCallister, Elizabeth to Stanly Rushing 1-9-1847
McCarver, Nicey to William R. Groves 11-17-1858
McCarver, Susan to James Kelly 9-16-1846
McCauley, Mary Jane to James J. Thompson 12-?-1858 (12-9-1858)
McChord, Margaret to James Sellers 9-17-1855
McClabahan, Susan to John McGevany 10-30-1838 (11-1-1838)
McClaland, Basora to George Wade 11-15-1854 (11-18-1854)
McClanahan, Mary F. to Wm. F. Henry 12-9-1868
McClellan, Eliza J. to George B. Hicks 10-9-1849 (10-10-1849)
McClellan, Mary C. to Benjamin M. Hicks 10-26-1847 (10-28-1847)
McClelland, Lida to Jno. J. W. Ingram 10-26-1868 (10-27-1868)
McClellen, Martha A. to James W. Tomlin 2-17-1852
McClish, Caroline to Jno. Alex Kirkpatrick 10-9-1848
McClish, Martha E. to Robert M. Neely 10-12-1859
McClish, Mary A. to John F. Lea 5-14-1855 (5-16-1855)
McCollough, Mary Ann to Jacob J. R. Reeves 12-7-1855
McCombs, Sinay to Edwin P. Shipes 9-4-1854 (9-5-1854)
McCord, Nancy A. to Wm. R. Durrett 8-16-1870
McCorkle, Mary Jane to Charles T. Strain 12-26-1860 (1-2-1860?)
McCorkle, Rachel to James H. Oneal 5-16-1859
McCorry, Mary P. to William F. Henderson 11-8-1847
McCoy, Ann E. to Alfred H. Mays 11-7-1859 (11-8-1859)
McCoy, Jane to O. D. Ward 3-5-1849 (3-14-1849)
McCrory, Anna R. to Alexander Ragan 9-3-1861
McCrory, Eleanor (Mrs.) to Richard Bess 4-30-1857
McCrory, Sarah L. to Jordan D. James 10-31-1859 (11-2-1859)
McCrory, Susan J. to Claiborne Webb 2-4-1856
McCullock, Jennett to Peyton S. Hamilton 1-13-1849 (1-23-1849)
McCullough, Mary A. T. to Edward R. Clement 8-10-1859
McDaniel, E. J. (Mrs.) to Benj. R. Calloway 1-25-1869 (1-27-1869)
McDonal, Lou T. to Joel T. Evans 12-9-1867 (12-10-1867)
McDonald, Emma C. (Mrs.) to Saml. D. McDonald 11-3-1869
McDonald, Irena to John C. McKoy 9-7-1852 (9-9-1852)
McDonald, Mary C. to Samuel B. Forrest 1-17-1852
McDurmit, Mollie to George A. Mayfield 3-22-1869 (3-24-1869)
McElever, Martha to Nashville Dolson 5-26-1843
McElver, Eliza S. to Joseph Scott 2-18-1840
McElwee, Sarah A. to James Jackson 11-19-1850
McFarlan, Rhosha to Andrew Dewberry 5-3-1859
McFarland, Mary to Richard McGowan 11-21-1842
McFarland, Rutha to William Taylor 3-13-1838 (3-22-1838)
McFarland, Sarah to James M. Woodard 12-19-1840 (12-14?-1840)
McFarland, Susie (Mrs.) to Robt. H. Adams 8-22-1871 (8-22-1871)
McFarlin, Mary to John Nelson 2-14-1846
McGee, Elda to Stephen Rains 11-2-1839
McGee, Nancy C. to William N. Harrison 9-16-1846
McGee, Trangnella A. to Alfred P. Powell 4-1-1859
McGlothlin, Nancy E. to Wesley Dixon 10-12-1853
McGown, Susan to James P. Skillern 12-28-1841
McGraw, Sarah to John C. Langston 11-8-1841
McGroom, Rebecca to William Anderson 6-22-1852
McGuire, Martha to George D. Blair 2-9-1846
McGuire, Susan F. to John C. Flin 8-12-1856 (8-13-1856)
McIntosh, Mary to Rollin J. Locke 11-30-1848
McIver, Betsy Ann to John R. Bowles 1-30-1856 (2-5-1856)
McIver, Louisa A. to Nicholas L. Midyett 11-1-1856 (11-2-1856)
McIver, Mary C. to John R. Reed 3-18-1841 (3-19-1841)
McIver, Sarah Jane to John J. Thomas 12-8-1845 (12-9-1845)
McKnight, Catherine B. to John Harton 6-8-1843
McKnight, Eleathia J. to Josephus Perkins 1-24-1852
McKnight, Elizabeth to John Carter 1-3-1848 (1-6-1848)
McKnight, Harrell to Nathaniel M. Price 10-2-1843 (10-5-1843)

McKnight, Lucy E. to Joseph E. Fortner 12-17-1850
McKnight, Margaret Jane to Henry F. Parker 9-10-1859 (9-11-1859)
McKnight, Mary E. to William W. Garland 12-18-1854 (12-19-1854)
McKnight, Mary Q. to James E. Newsom 8-29-1854
McKnight, Nancy Ann to Benj. F. Branch 10-13-1858 (10-14-1858)
McKnight, Sallie K. to Wm. A. McGill 3-9-1867
McKnight, Sarah F. to Samuel J. Morrow 1-27-1852
McLary, Frances H. to Jno. B. Smith 7-27-1858
McLeary, Eliza to Thomas Barnett 2-8-1843
McLemore, Dora E. to John E. Boyd 5-12-1870 *
McLemore, Margaret B. to John W. Turner 2-10-1855 (2-13-1855)
McLemore, Mary N. to Samuel H. Blaydes 11-23-1852 (11-25-1852)
McLemore, Nannie D. to Thomas B. Cole 5-13-1856 (5-14-1856)
McLeod, Bettie C. to Hiram Johnson 8-14-1855 (8-15-1855)
McMahon, Martha (Mrs.) to L. R. Harrison 12-6-1854
McMillan, Adeline to John T. Rodgers 4-30-1866 (5-4-1866)
McMillan, Mary Ann to Henry L. Guion 12-18-1838
McMillan, Nancy M. to Joshua McMillan 8-1-1839 (8-7-1839)
McMillen, Amanda P. to William G. Cockrill 7-1-1857
McNaion, Eliza Jane to Turner M. Anderson 8-3-1869
McNeill, Margaret E. to Joseph S. Hamlett 9-11-1854 (9-12-1854)
McVey, Cynthia to Nathan Francis 5-1-1848
McVey, Mary Jane to Elias T. Butler 7-10-1848 (7-13-1848)
McWhirter, Julia C. to Alexander Wells 12-18-1868
McWilliams, Jane to Aulsey D. Roark 12-29-1845 (1-1-1846)
McWilliams, Rebecca M. to James H. Medlin 10-9-1847 (10-13-1847)
Mcclish, Jane M. to James W. B. Thomas 3-13-1844
Meacham, Caroline to William C. Neely 4-2-1852 (2-5-1852?)
Meacham, Nancy to Hays Stanley 6-2-1853 (7-2-1853)
Meacham, Sarah to Thos. Morse 2-11-1841
Meadows, Elizabeth Ann to John W. Newsom 3-6-1855 (3-7-1855)
Meadows, Mary F. to Richard R. Croom 4-21-1857 (4-29-1857)
Meadows, Parthenia to William S. Hardin 5-7-1853 (5-10-1853)
Meaxey, Margaret to James V. Haskins 7-19-1865
Medlin, Agnes to William F. Young 7-31-1848 (8-1-1848)
Medlin, Elizabeth to Willis W. Evans 3-19-1845 (3-23-1845)
Medlin, Harriett to Mathew Williams 5-16-1840 (5-17-1840)
Medlin, Lucy to William Phelps 3-9-1871
Medlin, Martha S. to Thomas Pierce 1-4-1856 (1-6-1856)
Medlin, Missouri E. to Meekins N. Jackson 8-2-1869 (8-8-1869)
Medlin, Rebecca (Mrs.) to Nelson Davie 1-8-1862 (1-9-1862)
Medlin, Rebecca to C. D. Edington 12-8-1840
Medlin, Siddy Ann M. to W. D. Williams 12-16-1859 (12-18-1859)
Medling, Weltha to Benjamin Niel 5-11-1838 (5-17-1838)
Medly, Peggy to Benjamin Williams 9-4-1839 (9-1?-1839)
Melley, Mary (Mrs.) to James N. Acres 6-6-1857
Meriweather, Parasade M. to Edmond Taylor 3-23-1843 (3-28-1843)
Meriwether, Fannie to Gaither Tyson 12-11-1866 (12-12-1866)
Meriwether, Jane Caroline to James A. Taylor 12-5-1839
Meriwether, Sarah Elizabeth to George W. Trotter 4-28-1857
Mews, Isabella to Samuel D. Kenneday 1-2-1840
Micheal, Nancy to Samuel B. Brown 7-31-1847 (8-4-1847)
Midgett, Eleanor to David T. Moody 12-19-1848 (12-20-1848)
Miles, Curlin to William H. Curlin 7-27-1842
Millen, Minerva to Green Berry Long 7-24-1843 (11-27-1843)
Miller, Barbara to William H. Stephens 12-31-1838 (1-2-1839)
Miller, Catharine to Howell Short 10-24-1842
Miller, Louise to Thomas H. Drake 11-12-1867
Miller, Malsina to William Thurman 6-11-1849 (6-12-1849)
Miller, Margaret to Milton Elsten 2-15-1858
Miller, Martha P. to Archibald H. Harper 11-4-1871
Miller, Nancy to Nicholas Perry 9-18-1849 (9-20-1849)
Miller, Sarah Eliza to Isaac M. Jackson 5-25-1858 (5-26-1858)
Miller, Valery to Alexander Ragsdale 10-12-1843
Miller, Willie to Lamuel F. Grayson 12-30-1868 (12-31-1868)
Mills, Amanda to Daniel M. Allison 2-19-1870 (2-20-1870)
Mills, Eliza to Simeon M. Jones 7-2-1848
Mills, Lucy to John J. Taylor 11-16-1857
Mills, Malvina to James H. Norton 12-8-1856 (12-9-1856)
Mills, Minerva to Thomas M. Norton 9-15-1860 (9-17-1860)
Mills, Polly to William G. Ingram 7-2-1848
Mitchell, Ann A. to Robert H. Boon 11-1-1858 (11-4-1858)
Mitchell, Elizabeth P. to John W. Chrisp 12-23-1847 (12-25-1847)
Mitchell, Elizabeth to Hinson Lunnon 11-27-1843
Mitchell, Emoline to Marcus H. Cline 9-14-1839 (9-15-1839)

Mitchell, Louisana to George Hill 12-28-1848
Mitchell, Margarett to ___ Davenport 12-15-1838 (12-17-1838)
Mitchell, Martha to John Willett 4-4-1842 (4-7-1842)
Mitchell, Mary (Mrs.) to Alonzo O. Green 3-15-1867 (3-17-1867)
Mitchell, May L. B. to Josiah W. King 12-12-1840
Mitchell, Nancy to Robert W. Sims 8-1-1853 (8-3-1853)
Mizell, Martha to Joseph G. Sharp 11-16-1843
Mizell, Mary E. A. to Calvin Spivey 1-28-1847
Montgomery, Ann Cornelia to Stephen L. Shelton 8-16-1869 (8-19-1869)
Montgomery, Elenora to Edmond Outland 10-10-1866 (10-11-1866)
Montgomery, Elizabeth E. to Wm. D. Fletcher 12-12-1870
Montgomery, Emma to Asa Buntin 4-28-1866
Montgomery, Frances B. to Samuel J. Bell 1-16-1849
Montgomery, Martha K. to Alexander M. Jones 1-26-1848
Montgomery, Mary Jane to Joseph Bell 12-28-1840
Moody, Mary to Lemuel Sanderlin 12-24-1850
Mooney, Elizabeth to John Trousdale 12-26-1842 (12-27-1842)
Mooney, Louisianna to Christopher Hamlett 1-2-1867 (1-6-1867)
Moore, Auzal Inza to William W. Dollar 12-15-1858 (12-16-1858)
Moore, Bettie to Alfred Moize 12-16-1867 (12-19-1867)
Moore, Caroline to William Dickinson 3-11-1858 (3-12-1858)
Moore, Elizabeth C. (Mrs.) to Joseph J. Pardue 5-6-1861 (5-7-1861)
Moore, Ella V. to William C. Coats 1-7-1867 (1-8-1866?)
Moore, Emma to Lewis Z. T. Bolen 11-16-1870 (11-17-1870)
Moore, Frances to Richard Hardin 4-29-1843 (4-30-1843)
Moore, Frances to Robert J. Lewellen 9-4-1850
Moore, Holtan to James B. Richards 9-18-1866 (9-20-1866)
Moore, Josephine to Banister Terrell 12-20-1856
Moore, M. F. to Jasper N. Walker 12-2-1867 (12-3-1867)
Moore, Malinda to William H. Latham 10-31-1871
Moore, Martha F. to John M. Bradbury 3-16-1857 (3-18-1857)
Moore, Martha to Ezekiel Faris 10-18-1841
Moore, Mary America to Harry B. Christian 7-22-1839 (7-23-1839)
Moore, Mary to Robert R. McWilliams 2-29-1839
Moore, Mattie A. to James M. Whittenton 1-6-1870
Moore, Mollie A. to Marshall E. Smith 12-6-1866
Moore, Mollie H. to Hugh Delass 7-6-1868 (7-7-1868)
Moore, Rebecca to Ezekiel Haltom 12-10-1855 (12-18-1855)
Moore, Rebecca to Robert M. Compton 11-26-1840
Moore, Sarah Jane to James W. McKey 9-28-1857 (10-1-1857)
Moore, Sylvia L. to David M. Quinly 6-29-1846
Mooring, Caroline to Jesse Gray 12-25-1847
Mooring, E. F. to Geo. T. Harrison 4-21-1866 (4-22-1866)
Mooring, Eliza Jane to John W. Haley 4-1-1850 (4-4-1850)
Mooring, Elizabeth to James S. Coates 11-9-1852 (11-11-1852)
Mooring, Margaret C. to Robert C. Algee 12-27-1855
Mooring, Mary J. E. to Benjamin F. Fly 1-17-1846 (1-21-1846)
Morgan, Ellen to James N. Hall 4-4-1860
Morgan, Lou to James Turner Perry 12-17-1866 (12-20-1866)
Morgan, Lucinda to Joshua C. Hatton no date
Morgan, Mary Ann to Burtis Innsford 9-23-1869 (9-24-1870?)
Morgan, Mary Ruth to Kinsey Harrison 11-1-1839 (11-7-1839)
Morgan, Nancy Jane to Elijah Turner 4-8-1867 (4-9-1867)
Morphis, Elizabeth to Charles McCoy 12-26-1838 (12-29-1838)
Morphis, Mary Jane to Joseph Patterson 12-13-1845
Morphis, Milly Ann to William Manly 11-6-1841 (11-14-1841)
Morrell, Louis S. to Charles A. Bland 4-11-1846 (4-12-1846)
Morrill, Mary E. (Mrs.) to Willis W. Williams 2-25-1867 (2-27-1867)
Morris, Amelia Ann to John Hensley 4-8-1858
Morris, Hanah to I. Thornton 12-28-1839 (12-30-1839)
Morrison, Margarett L. to David Williams 2-10-1849
Morrow, B. H. to G. W. Mayfield 9-12-1853 (9-13-1853)
Morrow, Elizabeth E. to John M. Meals 12-3-1846 (12-24-1846)
Morrow, Lavica Parker to Andrew Jackson Lewis 2-25-1859 (3-1-1859)
Morrow, Martha J. to Archy Y. Douglas 3-31-1845 (4-1-1845)
Morrow, Mary Ann to James W. Carruthers 5-28-1846
Morrow, Sarah H. to Daniel J. Meals 12-6-1843 (12-7-1843)
Moser, Lourana to Moses Holt 9-13-1869
Moses, Martha Ann to Richmond N. Shackleford 11-9-1854
Mosly, Minerva M. to George W. Grafford 11-26-1840
Moss, Almeda to Markens Williams 12-21-1842
Moxley, Emily C. to John A. Sturkie 4-9-1866 (4-10-1866)
Moxley, Mary E. to James Hayley 1-23-1869 (1-24-1869)

Mullen, Mary to James Johnson 11-16-1842 (11-20-1842)
Mullins, Sarah Jane to Neil Thompson 9-11-1866 (9-13-1866)
Munn, Sarah Jane to Amos W. Barron 10-25-1859 (11-1-1859)
Murchison, Ann E. to Caleb Woods 8-5-1846 (8-13-1846)
Murchison, Isabela to James F. Haddoway 4-23-1842 (4-24-1842)
Murchison, Isabella M. to James W. Harris 11-16-1858 (11-18-1858)
Murchison, Martha J. to John L. Walsh 2-16-1849
Murchison, Mary Jane to James C. Whaton 9-2-1841 (9-?-1841)
Murchison, Sallie I. to John A. Givens 11-4-1871 (11-6-1871)
Murrell, Leander Jane to William P. Davis 3-12-1853 (3-15-1853)
Murrell, Missouri E. to Benjamin T. Hardy 4-17-1853 (4-21-1853)
Murrell, Sarah A. to Edmond A. Edmonson 3-20-1866
Muse, Nancy L. to B. O. Bryant 8-27-1870 (9-4-1870)
Mylor, Julia R. (Mrs.) to James M. Wollard 5-21-1868
Nabors, Jane to Nathaniel Guy 11-4-1871 (11-5-1871)
Nabors, Mary Ann to Nathaniel Guy 4-10-1869 (4-15-1869)
Nail, Elizabeth A. to E. N. Simmons 1-6-1840
Nail, Margarett to James W. Nanny 6-21-1840 (6-22-1840)
Nance, Mary A. to James P. Ince 10-22-1855 (10-23-1855)
Nance, Mary to Jamerson Bledsoe 1-31-1843
Nanny, Barbara to James J. Edwards 9-27-1845
Nanny, Margaret to Ezekiel Case 7-14-1856 (7-15-1856)
Nanny, Martha A. to William Vantrees 4-16-1850 (4-17-1850)
Nanny, Martha E. to Charles T. Wyatt 7-27-1869 (7-28-1869)
Neal, Mary E. to William L. Casey 1-11-1867 (1-15-1867)
Neely, Eliza Jane to John Coates 2-26-1857
Neely, Elizabeth to William Willis 6-9-1866 (6-10-1866)
Neely, Margaret Ann to Floridore A. Keelen 7-15-1856 (7-16-1856)
Neely, Minnie to John T. Carthel 5-13-1857
Neil, Elizabeth R. to William H. Smithern 2-4-1843
Neill, Martha Ann to Christopher C. May 4-22-1852 (4-28-1852)
Nelson, Eliza J. to William T. Allen 12-30-1844
Nelson, Elizabeth to Ben Franklin Bona 9-11-1838
Nelson, Frances to W. T. Allen 4-16-1853
Nelson, Martha to John H. Allen 12-10-1839 (12-12-1839)
Nelson, Mary E. to Theron B. Barnett 4-15-1861 (4-18-1861)
Nelson, Mary Elizabeth to Charles A. Hill 5-14-1839 (5-16-1839)
Nelson, Mary Elizabeth to Charles W. Reeves 12-7-1869
Nelson, Mary Jane to John Nelson 8-20-1859 (8-21-1859)
Nelson, Mary to Benjamin Lewis 11-2-1856
Nelson, Nancy to William Slaton 8-8-1859 (8-11-1859)
Nelson, Rebecca to Alexander Mullins 11-21-1870 (11-22-1870)
Nelson, Rhoda Ann to Tomlin P. Allen 12-22-1840 (12-24-1840)
Nelson, Sarah J. to Raleigh Moore 9-22-1852
Nesbitt, Tenie J. to Mark C. Henderson 12-29-1870 (12-30-1870)
Nevill, Elizabeth to Thomas Barnes 8-20-1852
Neville, Caroline C. to Robert W. Brinson 3-22-1845
Neville, Sarah to Robert Brinson 10-20-1853
Neville, Susan Jane to John Vincent King 1-31-1856 (2-7-1856)
Nevils, Julia Ann to John Brinson 2-10-1850
Newbern, Anna to Wesley Yarnell 11-6-1862 (11-7-1862)
Newbern, Julia E. to Moses S. Neely 10-25-1859 (10-30-1859)
Newbern, Pauline A. to Cyrus C. Shipps 12-13-1858 (12-14-1858)
Newel, Sudie to Jas. T. Amos 11-14-1871 (11-15-1871)
Newsom, Amanda F. to William A. Phillips 1-26-1858 (1-27-1858)
Newsom, Eliza to Eli Ray 12-15-1866 (12-16-1866)
Newsom, Lucinda to Moses J. Hardin 1-11-1858 (1-12-1858)
Newsom, Martha E. to Stephen B. Irvin 8-18-1860 (8-19-1860)
Newsom, Mary A. to James B. Justice 1-12-1857
Newsom, Mary Ann to Austin Goodell 6-15-1855 (6-21-1855)
Newsom, Sarah C. to Moses T. Hardin 9-22-1846
Newsom, Susan C. to Thomas H. Smith 9-11-1862 (9-15-1862)
Newson, Tennessee to Benjamin Hays 12-22-1847
Newton, Nancy J. to Gabriel A. Henderson 8-15-1855 (8-16-1855)
Nichol, Adeline to Littleberry Langford 2-1-1855 (2-4-1855)
Nichols, Benvilla to James T. Ward 9-4-1839
Nicholson, Margaret to Joseph E. Winston 2-26-1848 (3-1-1848)
Nicholson, Nancy to James Turner 1-12-1856 (1-13-1856)
Nicks, Miriam to Henry Darr 5-28-1840 (5-31-1840)
Niel, Almera to John R. Woodfolk 2-23-1842 (2-24-1842)
Nipper, Cara to John Wesley McGhee 9-23-1856
Nipper, Sarah to James Griffin 7-13-1843
Nipper, Susan E. (Mrs.) to John Coats 1-12-1867 (1-13-1867)
Nix, Martha A. to James M. Shaw 1-27-1852
Nobles, Caroline M. to Andrew T. Brown 11-2-1846

Noel, Laura to Jacob Hill 2-24-1869 (3-2-1869)
Nolan, Sarah to James Garrett 1-27-1843
Nolen, Mary to John G. Stone 3-27-1838 (3-29-1838)
Norrow, Margaret to Benjamin Norrow 12-5-1842 (12-7-1842)
Norton, George Ann to Barney Burkes 2-18-1844 (12-24-1844)
Norton, Martha to De L. Carter 2-24-1859 (2-25-1859)
Norton, Mary to James McBride 12-15-1845 (12-18-1845)
Norton, Mourning to Addison Nanney 1-29-1852
Norvell, Elizabeth Jane to Wm. Alexr. Winn 12-15-1857 (12-17-1857)
Norvell, Martha E. to Joseph Edwards 11-29-1843
Norvell, Mary Eliza to Porter B. King 6-23-1857 (6-24-1857)
Norvell, Parnina H. to Francis Marion Craig 12-6-1859
Norvell, Susan A. to John E. Glass 11-2-1859 (11-3-1859)
Norwood, Sallie E. to Eli C. Johnson 5-24-1870 (5-25-1870)
Nowell, Elizabeth to Benjamin Harris 7-9-1858 (7-15-1858)
Nowell, Nancy to Dorsey Davis 3-21-1843
Nuttall, Lucy C. to Henry C. Davis 6-30-1858 (7-1-1858)
O'Conner, Mary to Thomas Kelley 8-22-1870 (8-23-1870)
O'Neal, Mary M. to Andrew J. Jordan 7-31-1857 (8-2-1857)
O'Neal, Talitha C. to Isaac W. Ballard 11-7-1866
O'Neil, Amanda to Atlas H. Jones 12-14-1858 (12-16-1858)
Odle, Elizabeth I. to Cader Sowell 2-27-1840
Olahan, Nancy H. to John McEwin 2-15-1838
Olds, Anne? Ragan to Albert A. Davis 2-26-1842
Oliver, Amanda M. to Joshua E. Brassfield 1-2-1854
Oliver, Barbara A. to Milton Climer 12-22-1854 (12-25-1854)
Oliver, Flora to Charles N. Roberts 9-11-1857 (9-10?-1857)
Oliver, Francis Lucinda to Albert Brassfield 3-2-1857 (3-5-1857)
Oliver, Lucinda D. to Jonathan Utley 5-23-1846
Oliver, Mary Jane to Moses E. Pratt 9-9-1871 (9-10-1871)
Oliver, Matilda (Mrs.) to Peyton S. Bell 8-4-1862 (8-10-1862)
Oliver, Nancy to Chester T. Adams 10-30-1860 (11-1-1860)
Oliver, Sally to William Adkins 11-26-1860 (11-27-1860)
Oliver, Sarah E. to Marma D. Anderson 12-23-1850
Oliver, Virginia M. to Tarlton H. Graves 8-3-1858 (9-7-1858)
Oniel, Martha Jane to Sydney Moore 12-14-1853 (12-15-1853)
Orgain, Louisa S. to Thomas C. Barham 2-28-1848 (3-1-1848)
Outland, Margaret A. to Wm. S. Wooten 12-15-1870
Overton, Ann to Willie Humble 6-8-1840
Overton, Willis to Mary I. Clark 11-28-1842
Owen, Delilah to Quintillian T. Whittenton 10-11-1862
Owen, Kaziah T. to Joseph H. Cooper 3-15-1867 (3-16-1867)
Owen, Sirena to Patrick M. Duffy 9-19-1844
Owens, Arcena to Simeon Duffy 7-31-1845
Owens, Letitia to Simeon Duffy 12-12-1866
Ozier, Elizabeth to William T. Watlington 8-5-1847
Ozier, Margaret A. to Matthew F. Latta 9-8-1852
Ozier, Marian to E. L. McAdoo 2-10-1846 (2-15-1846)
Pace, Fanny to Wm. R. Anderson 9-12-1866 (9-13-1866)
Pace, Martha E. to Elija Smith 12-19-1854
Paisley, M. J. to WM. A. Wilson 1-31-1854 (2-2-1854)
Panst, Jane R. to Preston L. Childress 3-6-1841 (3-7-1841)
Park, M. Jennie to James H. Graves 7-20-1868 (7-21-1868)
Parker, Elizabeth to Bryant Tettleton 12-30-1846
Parker, Elizabeth to Zelmon Voss 4-29-1857
Parker, Jane to David w. Bivins 2-2-1846 (2-6-1846)
Parker, Luroney B. to Robert S. Reeves 1-18-1847 (1-21-1847)
Parker, M. E. to With T. Oneal 1-7-1868
Parker, Mary to John A. Dean 2-25-1848 (3-2-1848)
Parker, Nancy to George A. Bolin 6-23-1856 (6-24-1856)
Parker, Sarah L. to Samuel S. Johnson 7-3-1854
Parker, Susan H. to Eli P. Jenkins 11-29-1859
Parkinson, Mary Elizabeth to William Crosby 4-15-1839
Parlow, Martha J. to George W. Upton 7-1-1867 (7-17-1867)
Parmer, May to John Butler 11-5-1838
Parrish, A. M. to James Matthews 7-14-1840 (7-16-1840)
Parrish, Alsa J. to William H. Bryant 12-30-1846
Parrish, Emelin to Shim Cook 2-19-1867 (2-21-1867)
Parrish, Mary Elizabeth to William E. Stewart 9-21-1860 (9-23-1860)
Parrish, Mattie J. to William C. Shelton 12-17-1867 (12-19-1867)
Parrott, Elmina to John L. Chappell 12-18-1838
Patrick, Sarah to Thomas Riden 7-2-1839
Patterson, Caroline to William Hughes 12-28-1840
Patterson, Ela to Calvin Henderson 3-18-1842
Patterson, Frances to Thomas Clark 8-19-1845

Patterson, Louisa to Ben Franklin Bosheers 8-14-1869 (3?-15-1869)
Patterson, Lucinda to William P. Howlett 10-1-1866 (10-2-1866)
Patterson, Margarett H. to Wiley W. Thomas 7-16-1849 (7-17-1849)
Patterson, Marina to Stephen Outerbridge 8-19-1845
Patterson, Marion to Thomas Henderson 11-2-1852
Patterson, Martha S. to Jabez Bingham 10-1-1855
Patterson, Matilda to Malachi Holloman 8-5-1857
Patterson, Permelia to Thomas Overton 10-5-1869
Patterson, Susan to Nathaniel Henderson 11-1-1859 (11-2-1859)
Patterson, Temperance A. to George C. Ayers 11-25-1868
Patterson, Vicey to Edward Covington 5-18-1859
Patton, Mary to Josiah Hodges 7-10-1839
Pearce, Elizabeth to Samuel Crowell 5-13-1852 (5-18-1852)
Pearson, Mary E. to George W. Duncan 11-22-1852 (11-25-1852)
Pearson, Mary T. to Edward T. Transau 12-7-1855 (12-13-1854?)
Pearson, Mary to Thomas F. Berry 3-10-1870
Pearson, Sallie A. to Henry Yarbrough 11-10-1858
Pearson, Sue to John G. Woolfolk 11-3-1868 (11-5-1868)
Peirce, Annie C. A. (Mrs.) to J. H. D. Evans 9-24-1870 (9-25-1870)
Pemberton, Jane to Reuben McVey 6-6-1844 (6-11-1844)
Pendergrast, Lucinda to James Eason 6-11-1856
Penn, Bell to Eaton Bond, jr. 12-9-1867
Penny, Caroline to C. H. Hailey 5-18-1870
Pentecost, Mary E. to Robt. W. Taylor 6-22-1866
Pentecost, Nannie C. to Jason L. Wood 1-4-1870
Percy, Martha Ann to William R. Baker 12-13-1843 (12-15-1843)
Perkins, Mary R. to Petser Medlin 11-3-1853 *
Permator, Mary H. to Benjamin Emison 11-20-1854 (11-22-1854)
Perry, Adaline to Benjamin S. Brooks 5-23-1850
Perry, Ann Eliza F. O. to John C. M. Garland 9-5-1854
Perry, Celicia to John T. Coleman 7-30-1855 (7-31-1855)
Perry, Eliza to William T. Deloach 9-9-1850
Perry, Elizabeth to William P. Hopper 1-4-1845
Perry, Francis A. to William N. Coleburn 8-14-1854 (8-15-1854)
Perry, Helen M. to Gale H. Kyle 7-25-1843
Perry, Hesperan A. to James P. Hudson 7-8-1867
Perry, Lucretia to Joshua Baker 5-11-1839
Perry, Martha to Jacob Ing 2-17-1844
Perry, Mary E. D. to Charles E. Carnatzan 9-9-1857 (9-10-1857)
Perry, Mattie J. to David M. Hampton 12-19-1866 (12-20-1866)
Perry, Maudy to Chas. D. Carroll 6-2-1869
Perry, Mollie H. to Gillam J. Moore 11-15-1871
Perry, Sarah A. to Wm. L. Rutherford 11-28-1866 (11-29-1866)
Person, Ann E. to James A. Mason 5-15-1871 (5-16-1871)
Person, Hibernia A. to Gilbreth Neill 12-8-1869
Person, Martha E. to Thomas D. Tomlinson 8-27-1866 (8-28-1866)
Person, Mary to William M. Tidwell 6-17-1841
Peters, Harriet A. to Wesley S. Acree 1-4-1870 (1-6-1870)
Pettigrew, Eliza to John E. Davis 3-14-1868 (3-15-1868)
Pettigrew, Louisanna to Lafayette Smith 3-5-1866 (3-6-1866)
Pettus, Hannah Jane to Thomas B. Fenner 7-22-1853 (7-26-1853)
Pettus, Mary E. to John McDonald 11-10-1857
Peyton, Mary Jane to John Wells 6-6-1857 (6-7-1857)
Phelps, Judith to Fetus Baker 11-8-1842 (11-9-1842)
Phelps, May T. to Allen K. Jones 12-23-1854 (12-26-1854)
Phifer, Martha J. to William J. Bratton 6-27-1852
Phillips, Nettie to Peter J. Allen 9-8-1866 (9-9-1866)
Phillips, Susan Jane to William J. Rooker 1-3-1860 (1-5-1860)
Pickens, Eliza to Martin Pearce 8-14-1869 (8-15-1869)
Pierce, Della to James Dunn 7-26-1871 (7-28-1871)
Pierce, Elizabeth to Malden Y. Goad 2-22-1841 (3-14-1841)
Pierce, Manerva to Redmond Richards 10-9-1850 (10-10-1850)
Pierce, Mary to Dudley Alexander 5-5-1858
Pierce, Rachel to Whitmill P. Adams 11-16-1853
Pierce, Tabitha to William Harrell 10-20-1846 (10-29-1846)
Piercey, Nancy L. to Barzilla Hopper 4-22-1844
Piercifull, Mary to Shadrich Baker 1-14-1850 (1-17-1849?)
Piercy, Catherine to Abner W. Mason 1-9-1850
Piercy, Jane to Elisha Lawrence 12-26-1848
Piercy, Lucinda to John Goad 8-17-1838
Piercy, Nancy C. to Elias Langford 3-6-1850 (3-8-1850)
Piercy, Sarah to Burrell Jones 12-26-1853
Piercy, Susan A. to John O. Glover 3-7-1850 (3-8-1850)
Piercy, Telitha to James Canaven 12-17-1856 (12-18-1856)
Pipkin, Jane C. to William Todd 1-12-1858 (1-14-1858)

Pipkin, Luan to Thomas Harrell 5-15-1848 (5-18-1848)
Pippin, Frances to David T. Thurman 1-30-1854
Poindexter, America C. to James V. McFarlin 7-5-1859 (7-7-1859)
Pole, Emily (Mrs.) to Denning Presley 2-8-1868
Pollock, Eliza Jane to Alexander Settle 7-30-1870 (8-5-1870)
Pool, Nancy Ann to Granberry Daniel 8-16-1842
Pope, Arabella to John T. Moore 12-28-1867
Pope, Frances N. to Robert J. Strayhorn 1-26-1859 (1-27-1859)
Potts, Helen P. to James H. Price 12-15-1868 (12-16-1868)
Pounds, Melissa Elizabeth to Henry Bennet Jones 6-8-1866
Powel, Nancy to Bennet Woodward 10-25-1862 (10-26-1862)
Powell, Artimissa to John W. Shelton 11-2-1852
Powell, Lydia to Judithan C. Shelton 12-21-1859 (12-22-1859)
Powell, Mary F. to Porter Lanier 12-17-1867
Prendergrast, Cynthia J. to John W. McElwee 8-31-1847
Prendergrast, Mary Ann to Frederick Chipman 4-19-1852 (4-20-1853)
Presley, Arabella to Hartwell Patiller 1-27-1868
Preson, Elizabeth to Calvin Spivey 1-6-1842
Preston, Joanna A. to John H. Gordon 12-19-1861
Preston, Julia to John R. Woolfolk 2-18-1861 (6-18-1861)
Prewitt, Jane to Benjamin L. Norton 10-6-1841 (10-7-1841)
Prewitt, Malinda C. to John H. Clark 4-12-1860
Prewitt, Marietta H. to James E. Hogshead 11-3-1841
Prewitt, Sarah to Nathan Vick 1-5-1843
Price, Mary Ann to Elisha R. Hunt 10-11-1842 (10-13-1842)
Price, Sophronia to James M. Fullerton 9-8-1870
Priest, Harriet to Thomas Priest 7-9-1860 (7-10-1860)
Provine, Harrie A. to William R. Barton 11-4-1850 (11-6-1850)
Pruden, Elizabeth to John Powell 10-4-1847 (10-5-1847)
Puckett, Lizzie to James F. Scott 12-10-1868
Puckett, Vilet to Martin B. Key 2-8-1853 (2-10-1853)
Pullum, Sarah E. to Reuben M. May 2-15-1854
Pyles, Mary Louisa to Sion W. Boon 4-17-1856 (4-8?-1856)
Pyles, Virginia A. to Robt. M. Sharp 10-24-1866 (10-25-1866)
Quinley, Elizabeth J. to William Dawson 2-12-1849
Quinley, Nancy E. to Jackson Dawson 10-30-1841 (11-3-1841)
Quinley, Rebecca to Wilson Moore 1-22-1849 (2-3-1849)
Quinly, Martha C. to Samuel Watt 12-18-1841 (12-19-1841)
Raggin, Moody F. to Edward T. Pollard 10-3-1871 (10-4-1871)
Raines, Elizabeth to Joseph J. Lloyd 10-20-1845
Raines, Frances E. to William H. Dunaway 9-1-1866 (9-6-1866)
Raines, Margaret E. to William W. Newman 12-8-1857 (12-10-1857)
Raines, Martha to Freeman Patterson 11-30-1850 (12-3-1850)
Raines, Mary to George F. Sloan 11-21-1860 (11-22-1860)
Raines, Matilda to Thomas G. Gaskins 7-16-1858 (7-18-1858)
Raines, Sally A. to Jerome B. Hyde 4-24-1860 (4-26-1860)
Raines, Ursula P. to Blackmon G. Hays 11-30-1859
Rainey, Mary Francis to Harrison Simmons 1-15-1868
Rains, Susan to Bradley Medlin 10-14-1840
Randolph, Altimira to L. H. Johnson 8-17-1838 (8-19-1838)
Rasberry, Rebecca to Andrew Jackson 7-22-1841 (7-29-1841)
Rasberry, Tobitha to Dickson Jackson 5-13-1843 (5-14-1843)
Rasons, May Ann to Alfred Combs 9-24-1838 (9-25-1838)
Ray, Emily C. to Benjamin F. Brown 11-14-1846 (11-15-1846)
Ray, Margaret to Thomas Howell 11-22-1859 (11-25-1859)
Read, Ama L. to Charles L. Wood 4-5-1856 (4-6-1856)
Read, Eliza A. to William K. Bennett 3-1-1849 (3-5-1849)
Read, Elizabeth to Henry Baker 8-3-1858 (8-12-1858)
Read, Mary Irene to H. M. Clarke 12-23-1839 (12-25-1839)
Read, Nancy to Daniel Taylor 9-10-1857
Reavis, Elizabeth to Samuel M. Thomas 11-6-1849
Reavis, Mary Ann to Dempsey C. Neal 11-13-1856
Redden, Martha I. to Sidney I. Thompson 3-12-1842
Reddick, Arcenia to Alexander Clinard 4-5-1860 (4-6-1860)
Reddick, Sallie E. to John R. Wilkinson 3-7-1871
Reddin, Mary L. to George M. Rosamon 10-22-1866 (10-24-1866)
Redding, Levina to Boland Dodd 10-28-1841
Redding, Lydia F. to Henry Jackson 7-16-1856 (7-17-1856)
Reden, Elviva M. to Abram H. Harpole 10-19-1860 (10-21-1860)
Redwine, Maria to Thomas C. Shelly 6-14-1856
Reed, Nancy A. to Robert L. Wilson 1-17-1841 (1-18-1841)
Reese, Louisa to Allen Little 7-6-1847
Reevely, Mary Ann to William M. Weatherly 12-15-1856
Reevely, Mary Jane to Thomas D. Wright 11-13-1855
Reeves, Adeline to George G. Perkins 10-8-1845 (10-9-1845)

Reeves, Ann to James C. Bradford 7-24-1855
Reeves, Catherine to Richard T. McKnight 12-31-1844 (1-2-1845)
Reeves, Emeline to Calvell Wilson 1-12-1838 (12-13-1838)
Reeves, Frances A. E. to Wm. C. Baker 8-9-1869 (8-12-1869)
Reeves, Louisanna E. to Robert M. McKnight 4-13-1839
Reeves, Lourena (Mrs.) to James Thornton 5-17-1867 (5-19-1867)
Reeves, Lucenda to John Duncan 4-3-1839 (4-4-1839)
Reeves, Mariah T. D. to David H. Parker 5-24-1853
Reeves, Rebecca M. to Otis L. Story 3-5-1841 (3-1?-1841)
Reeves, Susan to Thomas Murtaugh 2-9-1869 (2-11-1869)
Reid, Charlotte Caonia to THomsa L. Kincaid 9-2-1856 (9-3-1856)
Reid, Eliza to John Blackmon 9-21-1842 (9-22-1842)
Reid, Mary to Thos. M Greer 1-1-1846
Reid, Mary to Wade W. Lyon 11-2-1869
Reid, Sophronia to Jesse Duncan 2-2-1850 (2-13-1850)
Replogle, Nancy Ann to Willie T. Harns 2-18-1845
Revely, Margaret to George Bishop 1-17-1853 (1-18-1853)
Revely, Martha E. to Boyce E. Sherman 10-15-1857 (10-18-1857)
Revely, Martha E. to Henry Butler 2-12-1845
Revely, Martha E. to Martin S. George 11-30-1857 (12-3-1857)
Revely, Susan E. to William J. Sipes 12-24-1862 (12-25-1862)
Reynolds, Lina to William C. Garrett 4-3-1844 (5-17-1844)
Rhodes, Leah F. to George Locke 6-10-1868 (6-11-1868)
Rice, Hallie to William Witherspoon, jr. 3-29-1868 (4-2-1868)
Rice, Joe May to Lawrence E. Talbot 2-16-1871
Richard, Bedy to William Emison 12-27-1850 (1-2-1851)
Richards, Elizabeth to Cullen W. Jackson 1-30-1856 (1-31-1856)
Richards, Mary Ann to Williford Williams 1-8-1862 (1-9-1862)
Richards, Mary to Newton Ellington 10-9-1866 (10-11-1866)
Richards, Rebecca to Thomas Pierce 12-27-1853 (12-29-1853)
Richardson, Mary C. to James W. Marsh 7-30-1847 (8-1-1847)
Richardson, Mollie to Milton Boon 3-25-1868 (3-31-1868)
Richarson, Martha E. to Samuel J. Matthews 12-7-1868 (12-8-1868)
Richerson, Tamey to Dudley Diggs 1-13-1857
Richetts, Eliza Ann to William F. Jones 9-15-1858
Rickman, Eliza to Samuel I. Garrett 2-7-1842 (2-8-1842)
Rider, Martha to Rolin Miller 10-14-1846 (10-15-1846)
Rider, Sarah R. to James R. White 12-22-1840 (12-24-1840)
Roach, Harriet Tennessee to William J. Gordon 11-2-1860 (11-5-1860)
Roach, Nancy Jane to James M. Stone 3-7-1866
Roach, Sarah Jane to James W. Mathis 6-19-1869
Roane, Emily B. to Malcolm H. Goodrich 2-11-1852 (2-12-1852)
Robbins, Lucy to Hubbard Cozart 7-23-1866 (7-24-1866)
Roberson, Eugenia to John M. Burkett 10-13-1869 (10-14-1869)
Roberson, Mary to Churchwell B. Ducker 11-7-1860 (11-8-1860)
Roberson, Sarah E. to Harbert H. Haynes 9-21-1843
Roberson, Tennessee to Wm. P. Woodard 12-24-1866 (12-25-1866)
Roberts, Adaline to Eli McCorkle 12-27-1847 (12-28-1847)
Roberts, Caroline to Willie S. Harris 4-17-1841
Roberts, Isabella to Harvey A. Roberts 4-3-1855
Roberts, Judy F. to Ellison T. Potts 9-19-1857 (9-20-1857)
Roberts, Mary to George Morphis 1-6-1849
Roberts, Rebecca to Larkin Tims 6-10-1843 (6-11-1843)
Roberts, Susan A. to Wesley B. Bevill 10-9-1856
Roberts, Zillah Syrena to Joseph Newton Walker 7-6-1866 (7-8-1866)
Robertson, Tranquilla to Henry Kirkpatrick 8-22-1843
Robinson, Amanda to William Leathers 6-21-1844
Robinson, Ann M. to John Jackson 1-29-1842 (2-3-1842)
Robinson, Bettie to John H. Matthews 12-29-1869 *
Robinson, Dicy Ann to Robt. E. Prewett 10-31-1868 (11-3-1868)
Robinson, Eliza A. to John C. Lanier 10-6-1853
Robinson, Eliza to Samuel L. Norwood 3-27-1867
Robinson, Elizabeth to William C. McCarlin 2-10-1862
Robinson, Hepsy Ann to Dennis McFarlin 8-5-1852
Robinson, Jane to Winfield Williams 12-11-1847 (12-22-1847)
Robinson, Malinda to Henry W. Shelton 1-5-1858
Robinson, Margaret M. to Joseph Gilliland 2-7-1848
Robinson, Mary A. to Thomas B. Thompson 2-2-1853
Robinson, Mary Virginia to Henry K. Hilderbrand 5-19-1869
Robinson, Mollie M. to John Young Dysart 11-15-1869 (11-16-1869)
Robinson, Rebecca to James G. Montgomery 9-16-1841
Robinson, Sarah A. E. to William Allison 8-20-1848
Robinson, Susan A. to Valentine S. Vann 1-3-1855 (1-4-1855)
Robison, Nancy C. to William W. Price 12-8-1841 (12-9-1841)

Robley, Mary to James M. McKnight 1-18-1845
Rocheld, Martha J. to William F. Forrester 10-23-1844 (10-24-1844)
Rochella, Mercina to James King 11-15-1847
Rodgers, Rhoda M. to Henry F. Clark 4-30-1870 (5-1-1870)
Roe, Caroline to John E. Robinson 10-11-1869 (10-14-1869)
Roger, Mary J. to George R. Brasfield 10-6-1848 (10-17-1848)
Rogers, Ann L. to William D. Waller 2-27-1862
Rogers, Edith E. to John H. Deberry 11-27-1867 (11-28-1867)
Rogers, Elizabeth W. to John P. Weir 5-5-1842
Rogers, Elizabeth to John H. McNeal 9-21-1850
Rogers, Fanny E. to Richard H. Fenner 8-29-1853 (8-30-1853)
Rogers, Martha to Z. T. Gaston 10-29-1866 (10-30-1866)
Rogers, Mildred C. to Job H. Goodlett 10-28-1856 (10-29-1856)
Rogers, Olivia J. to John T. Lewis 7-27-1857 (7-29-1857)
Rogers, Rebecca to Gidion Rocksey 7-22-1841
Rogers, Sophia A. to Joseph W. Moxley 11-10-1868 (11-11-1868)
Roland, Virginia to William C. Holloway 11-17-1858 (12-1-1858)
Rollings, Mary Elizabeth to James M. Alexander 3-15-1855
Rollins, Mary Ann to William T. Griffin 12-21-1866 (12-23-1866)
Rollins, Mary E. to James Adams 9-20-1854 (12-21-1854)
Rollins, Nancy R. to Edward H. Goodrich 6-2-1866 (6-3-1866)
Rone, Josephine to Hugh A. Thompson 11-21-1862 (12-3-1862)
Rone, Martha A. to William J. Seehorn 4-28-1860 (4-29-1860)
Rone, Menerva to Harvey D. Oneal 12-9-1868 (12-13-1868)
Rooks, Emily B. to Charles Nelson 9-9-1869
Rooks, Julia R. to Ansolem Stobaugh 8-31-1870 (9-1-1870)
Rooks, Martha A. to James M. Stephenson 3-16-1866 (3-18-1866)
Rooks, Mary A. to Norfleet Fairless 11-26-1840
Rosamon, Sarah N. to Wm. A. G. Avery 9-3-1866 (9-9-1866)
Rose, Mary Ann to James Stewart 6-29-1867 (7-1-1867)
Roseman, Mary Jane to Chesterfield Warmoth 1-10-1859 (1-11-1859)
Roseman, Nancy to William J. Bell 9-19-1855 (9-20-1855)
Roseman, Rutha L. to James M. Warren 12-9-1862
Rosemond, Margarett E. to William J. Henderson 12-17-1850
Rosenbum, Tennessee M. to William H. Germon 12-12-1853
Rosenthal, Caroline to Morris Jaretsky 9-16-1869
Ross, Amanda to George H. Todd 4-13-1852 (4-15-1852)
Ross, Catherine to James B. Ferrell 12-23-1850 (12-26-1850)
Ross, Eliza C. to Wm. J. Driggers 11-23-1854
Ross, Helen to James W. Daniel 8-5-1850 (8-8-1850)
Ross, Martha J. to William H. Bratton 2-8-1853 (2-10-1853)
Ross, Martha to John L. Henry 11-5-1840
Ross, Mary Jane to Jas. Carlington 12-23-1846
Ross, Nancy (Mrs.) to Robert N. Newsom 2-16-1867 (2-17-1867)
Ross, Sarah C. to Nicholson G. Dixon 8-5-1858
Rowsey, Elizabeth C. (Mrs.) to William N. Stoe 12-30-1868 (12-31-1868)
Rucker, Cynthia W. to William G. Stute 10-31-1842 (11-4-1842)
Ruddle, Mary E. to George G. Thompson 12-14-1870
Ruff, Lucenda to Andrew McMahan 5-4-1840
Ruff, Sarah to Daniel Harris 2-5-1842
Ruffin, Martha to Geor. W. Wilson 12-15-1842
Rushing, Lively to Benjamin McGhee 8-22-1846
Rushing, Minerva to James Robertson 10-27-1841 (10-28-1841)
Russell, Aley M. to W. A. Kendrick 12-28-1859
Russell, Elizabeth H. to John M. Prewett 11-30-1859
Russell, Elizabeth to James Kendrick 3-12-1856
Russell, Malinda C. to Goodwin Green 7-16-1846 (7-28-1846)
Russell, Margarett C. to James A. Marks 6-19-1845
Russell, Mary A. to Andrew J. Allen 1-25-1870
Russell, Nancy Elizabeth to James E. Davis 12-12-1859
Russell, Sarah E. to Reuben M. May 3-14-1855 (3-15-1855)
Russell, Sarah J. to William M. Barr 9-12-1859 (9-13-1859)
Rutherford, Mollie to John Dodd 11-9-1871
Rutherford, Sophia J. to Jesse Biggs 7-18-1867
Rutledge, Mary E. to William Henry 12-25-1856 (12-20?-1856)
Sallie, Elizabeth J. to Wm. C. Herndon 12-28-1867 (1-1-1868)
Samuel, Elizabeth G. to Jefferson Clark 11-24-1841
Sanders, Adaline to Thomas Allen 11-21-1870 (11-23-1870)
Sanders, Amanda to William C. Johnson 12-9-1842
Sanders, Eliza M. to James F. Johnson 6-19-1839
Sanders, Malisa to Robert C. Moore 10-31-1848
Sanders, Mary Ann to William A. Webb 4-9-1841 (4-13-1841)
Sanders, Mary E. to Henry F. Birdsong 3-19-1866
Sanders, Mary to Solomon Morphis 11-21-1846

Sanders, Nancy C. to Thomas J. Cupples 6-19-1868 (7-5-1868)
Sanderson, Martha Ann to James P. G. Garrett 1-3-1867
Saners, Lucy A. to Wm. M. Burkett 1-25-1870 (1-26-1870)
Sanford, Eliza J. to John S. Smithson 2-24-1853
Sanford, Lureny to Wm. O. Lovelace 12-26-1853 (1-11-1854)
Sanford, Sarah to Joseph A. Hardage 2-10-1846
Satterfield, Caroline to Henry L. Thues 2-12-1859 (2-13-1859)
Savage, Martha to John Hinson 4-16-1849
Sawrie, Martha H. to James M. Collingsworth 11-20-1855
    (11-22-1855)
Saxton, Mary F. to Thomas Hapgood 4-20-1867
Scarborough, Amanda J. to Jordan A. Houston 11-14-1859
    (11-15-1859)
Scott, Biddy (Mrs.) to Benjamin F. Bond 10-20-1858 (10-21-1858)
Scott, Sarah E. to William H. Terry 12-16-1852
Scott, Susan to Enoch Gaskins 12-10-1867 (12-24-1867)
Scurlock, Kate L. to William D. Clark 5-24-1869
Seaborn, Selina to Nathan Peeples 9-13-1867 (9-15-1867)
Seahorn, Rebecca L. to John F. Fouth 3-30-1867
Searcy, Ann Eliza to Moody Passmore 11-2-1854
Seats, Susan to Lawrence Butler 11-15-1860 (11-18-1860)
Seay, Ida R. to Nelson I. Hess, jr. 11-16-1867 (11-20-1867)
Sensemon, Malinda to Hazael Hewit 12-22-1849 (12-25-1849)
Senter, Elizabeth to Daniel Bancroft 8-22-1840 (8-23-1840)
Senter, Fannie to Wm. D. Thompson 12-11-1866 (12-12-1866)
Senter, Martha A. to Robert D. Boon 10-20-1856
Senter, Mary Jane to Samuel G. Turner 12-6-1852 (12-7-1852)
Sevier, Elizabeth to James Wilson 10-13-1841
Sewall, Mary M. to Henry Goad 12-23-1841
Sewell, Adeline to Thomas Lyon 6-20-1870 (7-3-1870)
Sewell, Elizabeth C. to Milton A. Henderson 11-9-1854
Sewell, Martha Parthenia to Lewis C. Cox 11-16-1867 (11-27-1867)
Sewell, Nancy Ann to Enoch R. Walker 11-18-1868 (11-19-1868)
Sewell, Rachel to Franklin Lambert 11-15-1855
Sewell, Reuben to Martha A. Johnson 9-29-1841
Sharp, Jamima C. to Charles Hogsett 3-18-1846
Sharp, Louisa J. to William J. Thomas 12-21-1858
Sharp, Margaret A. to James W. Caruthers 12-15-1856 (12-16-1856)
Sharp, Mary J. to W. A. Smith 12-10-1866 (12-12-1866)
Sharp, N. Jane to James H. Thomas 11-3-1868 (11-4-1868)
Sharp, Virgina A. (Mrs.) to John H. Thomas 1-26-1869
Sharrock, Fannie to Ransom E. Hopper 11-1-1866
Shaw, Emma W. to Perry G. Carter 11-9-1843 (11-14-1843)
Shaw, Fannie M. to John N. Smith 9-20-1854 (9-19?-1854)
Shaw, Laura to Ferd. Wood 5-8-1871 (5-9-1871)
Shaw, Margaret J. to Augustus C. Fasmyre 12-19-1848
Shaw, Nancy A. N. to Allen N. Massey 1-23-1867
Shaw, Rhoeba S. to David B. Owen 1-6-1868 (1-7-1868)
Shaw, Sarah E. to John W. Wooley 12-6-1858
Shelby, Olive V. (Mrs.) to Francis M. Tubbs 11-19-1870 (11-20-1870)
Shelly, Martha J. to Jacob Pittman 10-30-1845
Shelly, Mary Ann to William Reeves 9-18-1843
Shelton, Ann Frances to Aaron W. Harkins 2-4-1856
Shelton, Elizabeth W. to Henry Newton 5-22-1852
Shelton, Elizabeth to James T. Harper 12-7-1868 (12-10-1868)
Shelton, Mildred E. to Stephen M. Powell 11-7-1859 (11-8-1859)
Shelton, Sarah B. to John C. Pailey 3-24-1866 (3-26-1866)
Shepard, Bella to Drury (Fayette Co.) Carter 8-19-1848 (8-21-1848)
Sherl, Elizabeth to William S. Temple 11-27-1854 (11-30-1854) *
Sherman, Elizabeth to Loftin McKimon 3-4-1850
Sherman, Frances A. to Henry H. Hankins 9-23-1843 (9-28-1843)
Sherman, Mary R. to William A. Christian 1-15-1859 (1-20-1859)
Sherman, Narcissa C. to William W. Womble 3-9-1848
Sherrill, Lavinia F. to John S. Temple 9-15-1856
Sherwood, Anna B. to Henry D. Franklin 12-8-1869 (12-9-1869)
Shivers, Emma E. to James M. Spears 12-31-1869 (1-2-1870)
Shivers, Mary Paralee to Benj. Franklin Forsyth 8-22-1871 (8-23-1871)
Shoemaker, Mary to Jacob McCain 12-14-1844
Short, Elizabeth L. to Jordon B. Boone 1-8-1844 (1-11-1844)
Shuford, Eliza Jane to George W. Ashford 11-29-1856 (12-2-1856)
Shuford, Susan A. to William W. Nichols 10-16-1862 (10-22-1862)
Shumate, H. V. to Joshua C. Lee 12-1-1853
Shumate, Mary Jane to John L. Cock 2-26-1857
Simmons, Amanda to James H. Davis 9-1-1870 (9-24-1870)
Simmons, Hannah O. (Mrs.) to Benj. H. Blume 3-20-1867

Simmons, Martha J. to John W. Browder 9-3-1853 (9-5-1853)
Simmons, Mary F. to Edward L. Sanford 12-23-1857
Simmons, Paralee to John W. Mays 1-23-1869 (1-25-1869)
Simonton, Margaret A. to Miles M. Hammond 5-9-1853
Simpson, Gracy to John W. Climer 11-27-1843
Simpson, Jane M. to John M. White 8-4-1846
Simpson, Jane to Lorenzo D. Mathis 7-18-1868 (7-19-1868)
Sims, Jane to Jesse Glidwell 8-7-1841 (8-8-1841)
Sims, Jane to Thomas Glidwell 11-4-1840
Sims, Maggie J. to Wm. J. Thompson 12-10-1870 (12-11-1870)
Sims, Virginia M. to William J. G. Birdsong 7-26-1862 (7-30-1862)
Sipes, Elizabeth to Thomas Cupples 2-?-1848 (3-1-1848)
Sipes, Mary C. to Daniel Osben 12-26-1853 (12-27-1853)
Skillern, Rebecca? J. to Samuel H. Mulherin 8-2-1860
Sledge, M. E. to S. S. Robertson 8-15-1855
Slocum, Harriett to Alfred Crowell 6-14-1849
Small, Rebecca A. to S. P. Moore 11-14-1866 (11-15-1866)
Smart, Martha E. to W. J. Funderbunk 4-13-1869 (4-15-1869)
Smith, Addie to James C. Ray 12-21-1870 (12-22-1870)
Smith, Artie Caroline to Isaac Volentine Williams 11-20-1855
Smith, Elizabeth to Henry Whitlaw 4-28-1849 (4-29-1849)
Smith, Elizabeth to Jess Sturtivant 7-10-1841 (7-14-1841)
Smith, Elizabeth to Willis Wood 6-23-1846
Smith, Ella V. to H. P. (Dr.) Cotton 10-3-1870 (10-5-1870)
Smith, Emeline to William Burrow 12-12-1848 (12-13-1848)
Smith, Jane T. (Mrs.) to Thos. P. Clement (Weakley Co) 3-16-1870
Smith, Jane to James Stevenson 1-6-1855
Smith, Lucy A. to John H. Bell 10-9-1866
Smith, Lucy A. to Newell T. Strayhorn 1-3-1844
Smith, Martha Ann to William Simmons 12-10-1839
Smith, Martha to James H. Norton 6-21-1866 (6-22-1866)
Smith, Martha to James McAlexander 2-23-1852 (2-24-1852)
Smith, Martha to Richard Dawson 9-15-1842 (9-16-1842)
Smith, Martha to Samuel Craig 9-20-1862 (9-21-1862)
Smith, Mary A. E. to Samuel Singer 2-3-1859
Smith, Mary C. to Anthony Graham 2-2-1870 (2-3-1870)
Smith, Mary D. to Nathaniel C. Carpenter 10-29-1849 (11-1-1849)
Smith, Mary E. to Allen G. Gooch 4-27-1852 (4-28-1852)
Smith, Mary Jane to Sherwood R. Davis 4-2-1870 (4-3-1870)
Smith, Mattie A. to Edward Matthews 4-13-1859 (4-14-1859)
Smith, Nancy H. to George W. Harris 10-19-1839
Smith, Nancy to Beverly Anderson 1-6-1844
Smith, Pattie to Scott Wisdom 6-17-1870 (6-18-1870)
Smith, Ruena to Daniel P. Dickey 8-29-1843
Smith, Sarah A. to Mark Hardy 8-22-1868 (8-23-1868)
Smith, Susan C. to Julius C. Harris 11-18-1852
Smithdorch, James? to James G. Ritchy 1-15-1841
Smithwich, Elizabeth to William P. Lacy 7-19-1853 (7-21-1853)
Smithwick, Mary Ann to Gaston G. B. Freeman 7-6-1843 (7-7-1843)
Smithwick, Mmary to John McFarlen 11-25-1843
Smitoe, Alfred Sarah to William R. Pay 9-16-1839
Snider, Christiana E. to John L. Lancaster 10-30-1855 (10-31-1855)
Snider, Louisa J. to James R. Graves 7-31-1856
Snodgrass, Frances C. to William R. Bryant 8-3-1861 (8-5-1861)
Snodgrass, Sallie to Gilbert T. Christian 4-9-1866
Snowden, Cornelia A. to Richard F. Butts 1-1-1855
Snowden, Mary Ann to John Anderson 6-18-1846
Somers, Mary J. to Jesse W. Thomas 12-3-1845 (12-4-1845)
Sorrell, Frances to Lewis Battle 8-11-1860 (8-16-1860)
Southall, Mary to James Croom 10-19-1850
Sowell, Mary to Habon Kirby 1-3-1849
Speh, Mary Ann to John H. McMillan 10-9-1871 (10-10-1871)
Spence, Fanny A. to James H. Bray 8-14-1869
Spencer, Jane to Andrew J. Hardage 7-24-1839
Spencer, Lidy E. to Thos. J. McMaster 1-12-1869
Spencer, Mary Ann to Henry Jane 6-15-1840
Spencer, Mary to Frederick Klenk 1-3-1853
Spencer, Minerva to James L. Brogdon 3-20-1839
Spivey, Mattie to Thomas, jr. Ingram 5-29-1871 (5-31-1871)
Spratt, Mary T. to William D. Brigance 3-14-1842
Spring, Elizabeth to John H. Albritton 3-31-1852
Springfield, Charity to Thomas I. Neely 1-29-1840
Springfield, Mary E. to James M. Creps (Cress?) 11-14-1871
Springfield, Temperance to Anderson S. Skillern 1-25-1847
Sprows, Mary to Preston Sullivan 4-3-1841 (5-5-1841)

Spurlock, Mary to Washington Parrot 12-17-1846
Stanley, Sarah A. (Mrs.) to Joseph A. Brooks 8-1-1860 (8-2-1860)
Stanly, Rebecca C. to John W. Furgerson 8-19-1856 (8-20-1856)
Starkey, Annie to Jerry T. Glidewell 12-24-1867 (12-25-1867)
Starkey, Eliza J. to John A. Roach 8-13-1867 (8-16-1867)
Staton, Nancy (Mrs.) to Charles B. Robley 3-31-1870
Steadman, Mary E. to Hughs Pipkins 9-25-1855 (10-10-1855)
Stegall, Harriet Ann to James R. Waldrup 12-7-1867 (12-10-1867)
Stephens, Argenta Rebecca to Robert Ferguson 8-2-1848
Stephens, Jane M. to Amos Black 10-26-1857
Stephens, Mary Jane to Alexander H. Claridge 8-21-1854
Stevenson, Sarah J. E. to Atlas M. Hogan 8-1-1866
Steward, Cynthia E. to Montgomery Anderson 8-8-1849 (8-16-1849)
Steward, Martha D. to Nelson C. Jordan 2-26-1859 (3-1-1859)
Steward, Mollie to William Keith 11-27-1869
Steward, Nancy E. to William L. Brent 12-9-1849
Stewart, Amanda to John C. Black 2-6-1854
Stewart, Angeline Frances to Anderson Bailey 1-7-1867 (1-8-1867)
Stewart, Eliza J. to James A. Faucett 6-2-1858 (6-6-1858)
Stewart, Elmena L. to William H. Jackson 7-25-1838 (7-26-1838)
Stewart, Jane to John Golden 12-27-1845
Stewart, Julia A. E. to Joseph Cromm 10-13-1856 (10-15-1856)
Stewart, Julia A. to John J. Collins 3-3-1866 (3-8-1866)
Stewart, Lavinia E. to D. H. Selph 12-27-1845
Stewart, Mahala L. to William J. Taylor 7-18-1870 (7-21-1870)
Stewart, Maria to William R. Moore 12-22-1847 (12-23-1847)
Stewart, Martha E. (Mrs.) to Jess Box 3-11-1870 (3-13-1870)
Stewart, Martha Jane to Atlas H. Jones 10-11-1855
Stewart, Martha to William D. Peterson 12-20-1842 (12-22-1842)
Stewart, Mary A. to Solomon Johnson 1-12-1847 (1-13-1847)
Stewart, Nancy to Nathan W. Steadman 12-19-1855
Stewart, Parthenia to John B. Morris 5-4-1854
Stewart, Sarah J. to William P. Hamilton 11-1-1858 (11-3-1858)
Stewart, Thurza Ann to Benjamin Talley 2-28-1841
Stier, Elizabeth to Isaac Croom 7-22-1840 (8-13-1840)
Stoddert, Mary Jane to William Caruthers 6-6-1859 (6-7-1859)
Stone, Agnes A. to John S. Rochell 11-29-1854
Stone, Eliza to John Blair 9-19-1845
Stone, Frances to William Humble 5-25-1841 (5-26-1841)
Stone, Louis A. to James V. Tupell 10-3-1844
Stone, Margaret C. to Caleb D. Bryant 4-10-1854 (4-18-1854)
Stone, Mary A. to William Vantress 4-22-1848 (4-26-1848)
Stone, Mary to Marian Emerson 7-4-1867 (7-7-1867)
Stone, Narcissa M. (Mrs.) to Benjamin F. Gates 5-4-1859
Stone, Ophelia to Saml. Craig 4-3-1871
Stone, Sarah Ann to Merlin Perry 12-5-1854
Stone, Sarah Ann to Watt Cash 6-29-1850 (7-1-1850)
Stout, Mary P. to John A. Austin 5-25-1866 (5-27-1866)
Strain, Elizabeth to Hardy Harrington 7-28-1840
Strain, Frances J. to Cardy Warrel 7-3-1852
Stratton, Virginia C. (Mrs.) to Lucius L. Weatherly 5-4-1869 (5-6-1869)
Strayhorn, Ann to William Pope 8-20-1838 (8-25-1838)
Strayhorn, Orabella to Oswill Newby 12-18-1841 (12-22-1841)
Strayhorn, Sarah Jane to Thaddeus D. Cooper 10-12-1859
Stribling, Mary Elizabeth to Thadeus Pope 12-13-1853
Stribling, Nancy A. to Nathaniel Benton 9-12-1848 (9-13-1848)
Stricklin, Catherine to Willington Keefe 3-20-1868
Sturdevant, Lucinda R. to Thomas D. Day 3-4-1868
Sturdevant, Martila to William Bradford 2-18-1868 (2-20-1868)
Sturdivant, Catherine to Feereby Wilkins 12-9-1850 (12-11-1850)
Sturdivant, Elizabeth to William G. L. Harrell 1-16-1850 (1-17-1850)
Sullivan, S. to A. C. Sullivan 11-9-1839
Summers, Eliza A. to Edward A. Mullins 12-10-1849
Summers, Rachael to Hickerson L. Doyle 8-13-1841 (8-18-1841)
Sumner, Frances to James Boman 4-24-1860 (4-25-1860)
Sutton, Anna Bell to James P. Robinson 12-30-1868 (1-19-1869)
Swan, Archebia Ann to Francis A. Fogg 12-17-1839 (12-20-1839)
Swan, Catherine to George W. Birch 12-13-1858 (12-16-1858)
Swan, Mary Jane to Samuel C. Lynch 1-7-1846
Sweeny, Anne to Adolphus Britton 11-30-1852 (12-2-1852)
Sweeny, Mary Louisa to Samuel W. McKnight 4-10-1856
Sweeny, Sarah to Adolpha Britten 8-26-1841
Swink, Lavinia to Alexander C. Murrell 9-9-1871 (9-13-1871)
Swink, Mariah G. to John Evans 7-16-1839

Swink, Mary C. to Thomas J. Butler 1-19-1869 (1-21-1869)
Swink, Mary S. to Elijah (Memphis TN) Price 4-17-1853
Swink, Sarah E. to John B. Scarborough 7-30-1856
Swink, Sophia E. to Thomas J. Nesbitt 4-20-1870 (4-21-1870)
Sykes, Callie A. to Simeon B. Rushing 12-28-1870 (12-29-1870)
Sykes, Elvira G. to Allen P. Vick 10-27-1869 (10-28-1869)
Sykes, Martha Ann to John D. Elam 12-8-1845
Sykes, Mary E. to John H. Hester 12-28-1869
Sykes, Sarah J. (Mrs.) to Danl. J. (Gibson Co) Birmingham 8-19-1869
Sypert, Mary L. to Horace H. Curtiss 8-31-1853
Talbot, Jane M. to Silas F. Field 4-24-1854 (4-25-1854)
Taliaferro, Victoria G. to Robert H. Green 4-23-1866
Tally, Fannie E. to S. A. Simmons 7-21-1870 (7-24-1870)
Tanner, Catherine to James E. Hopper 1-30-1841
Tanner, Evelina to Alexander Dudley 2-28-1854 (3-1-1854)
Tanner, Rosanna to Noel K. Johnson 2-14-1848
Tarbutton, Hanna H. to Arthur A. Jackson 3-31-1845 (4-1-1845)
Tarver, Elizabeth to David J. Merriwether 10-31-1849
Tarver, Fannie L. to Buren B. Waddell 6-9-1857
Tarver, Wilnoth C. (Mrs.) to Willie B. Dickinson 8-2-1871 (8-3-1871)
Tate, Susan to Turner J. Fuller 7-1-1841
Tatum, Mary M. to Thomas Carr 12-3-1853 (12-4?-1853)
Taylor, Apphia A. to John Chester 10-24-1848
Taylor, Betsy to Thomas Harrell 11-19-1838
Taylor, Charlotte to Bennett Burn 11-15-1844 (11-19-1844)
Taylor, Eliza Jane to Richard R. Dashiell 1-10-1850 (1-15-1850)
Taylor, Elizabeth E. to John R. Hicks 12-19-1854 (12-21-1854)
Taylor, Elizabeth to Henry Dunlap 12-17-1866 (12-20-1866)
Taylor, Elvina to Joseph B. White 8-3-1868
Taylor, Francis J. (Mrs.) to Jacob W. Welch 4-15-1862 (4-27-1862)
Taylor, Harriet to William Dunlap 10-20-1856
Taylor, L. J. (Mrs.) to Wm. L. Nooner 11-18-1869 (11-21-1869)
Taylor, Laura C. to J. W. C. Scharmahoran 1-1-1859 (1-7-1859)
Taylor, Laura to Augustus C. Reid 3-1-1869 (3-3-1869)
Taylor, Lizzie L. to Alex C. Caldwell 8-20-1868
Taylor, Lucinda M. to James M. Rose 8-1-1871 (8-2-1871)
Taylor, Lucy Ann to John G. Hargis 6-24-1840 (6-25-1840)
Taylor, M. E. A. to James L. Burton 8-1-1871 (8-2-1871)
Taylor, Maria L. to John C. Carpenter 12-23-1857 (12-24-1857)
Taylor, Martha A. to Andrew Friemmer 4-21-1866 (4-26-1866)
Taylor, Martha A. to John McCoy 5-5-1870 (5-8-1870)
Taylor, Martha to Drury B. Williams 8-31-1852 (9-5-1852)
Taylor, Mary Ann to Andrew Guthrie 4-12-1843
Taylor, Mary Ann to James C. Mote 9-12-1845
Taylor, Mary Ann to James G. Mahaffy 3-26-1838
Taylor, Mary C. to Baxter J. Williams 9-23-1841 (9-30-1841)
Taylor, Mary C. to John G. Bell 11-10-1856
Taylor, Mary E. to Robt. H. French 12-16-1867 (12-17-1867)
Taylor, Mary S. to Washington Currie 9-6-1853 (9-13-1853)
Taylor, Mollie R. to Lawriston Hardwicke 2-1-1871 (2-2-1871)
Taylor, N. E. to John H. Thomas 10-26-1857 (10-27-1857)
Taylor, Nancy G. to Phillip Weaver 11-15-1841
Taylor, Nancy Jane to Albert Stobaugh 2-10-1857
Taylor, Nancy S. to James W. Hicks 10-17-1860 (10-18-1860)
Taylor, Prescilla to Wm. W. Jones 9-19-1870 (9-22-1870)
Taylor, Rebecca Ann to John Price 3-30-1854
Taylor, Sarah Jane to Richard Sherrod 6-9-1856
Taylor, Sarah Jane to Samuel P. Caldwell 5-29-1855 (5-30-1855)
Taylor, Sarah Jane to William P. Wilson 12-27-1854
Taylor, Sarah to Willis Mann 9-10-1842 (9-11-1842)
Taylor, Sue M. to Andrew J. Hall 5-16-1866
Taylor, Susan to Hans Capell 1-18-1843
Taylor, Violet J. to Andrew M. Hart 6-12-1843 (6-13-1843)
Taylor, Zilpha L. to Sawnee B. Lawrence 10-22-1868
Teagart, Susan M. to Thomas I. Neely 7-31-1838 (8-4-1838)
Teague, Elizabeth C. to Moses S. Allen 4-17-1856
Teague, Peninah to James Alexander 12-25-1856
Teague, Sarah E. to Jesse Russell, jr. 4-22-1848
Tedford, Mary A. C. to Admiral G. Roach 10-21-1868 (10-22-1868)
Temple, Margaret W. to Robert W. Towns 11-27-1854 (11-30-1854)
Temple, Mary E. to Samuel Johnson 3-15-1855
Temple, Mary to William H. Little 7-12-1847
Temple, Nannie to Thomas J. Pearson 2-20-1869 (2-24-1869)
Temple, Susan M. to John F. Sherrill 10-12-1850
Templeton, Elizabeth to Benjamin Sturdivant 1-4-1848

Terrell, Elizabeth to William J. Davis 3-20-1841
Terrell, Sarah Ann E. to William J. Davis 9-1-1841 (9-2-1841)
Thasee, Ellen L. to John Hunter 11-9-1843
Thedford, Gemina to John C. Birdsong 11-23-1841
Thedford, Sarah F. to David W. Nevill 10-20-1871 (10-22-1871)
Theus, Elizabeth Lager to James G. Womack 12-24-1844
Thom, Dolloy to Samuel Harris 8-16-1838
Thom, Martha to Isaac Hasteto 3-3-1842
Thom, Mary to James M. Cobb 10-23-1842 (10-25-1842)
Thom, Theresa to James Bursh 4-13-1840 (4-1-1840)
Thomas, E. P. to John Christian 3-5-1838
Thomas, Eliza to James D. Arnold 12-17-1849 (12-17-1850?)
Thomas, Frances R. to Robert Billingsly 12-8-1846
Thomas, Georgian to Luther Turner 4-10-1858 (4-11-1858)
Thomas, Jane to Alonza White 6-22-1848
Thomas, Jane to William T. Johnson 1-8-1852
Thomas, Louisa to George Bethshares 3-19-1870
Thomas, Lydia R. to Wm. B. Drake 7-1-1871 (7-2-1871)
Thomas, Mahala to Francis N. Arnold 9-29-1858
Thomas, Martha M. to Nathe. C. Bailey 12-26-1870 (12-27-1870)
Thomas, Mary Ann to Jas. M. Irven 1-31-1850
Thomas, Mary E. to James W. Clark 1-2-1866 (1-3-1867?)
Thomas, Mary to William R. Chandler 7-21-1857 (7-2?-1857)
Thomas, P. M. to John M. Maynard 4-28-1855 (5-1-1855)
Thomas, Rachel to Nathan Johnson 7-29-1850 (7-30-1850)
Thomas, Sarah E. to Silas W. Edwards 12-3-1857
Thomas, Sarah Jane to Andrew J. Williams 9-26-1860 (10-2-1860)
Thomas, Tabitha J. to Joseph M. Bledsoe 12-29-1868 (12-31-1868)
Thompson, Christina to James H. Nelson 10-31-1859 (11-1-1859)
Thompson, Cynthia to Francis M. Pyles 9-7-1854
Thompson, Fannie C. to Jacob Shew 7-27-1870 (7-28-1870)
Thompson, Isabella to Robert Bickers 11-1-1847 (11-18-1847)
Thompson, Lydia to Baseley Jackson 8-27-1849 (8-28-1849)
Thompson, M. E. to Oscar F. Collins 3-20-1867 (3-28-1867)
Thompson, Malinda F. to Marion J. Holly 12-9-1869
Thompson, Margaret E. to John J. Barnett 4-6-1867 (4-9-1867)
Thompson, Maria L. to Avery Hunt 7-4-1844
Thompson, Martha to Raymond A. Blankenship 7-17-1855
Thompson, Mary Ann to Andrew H. Clark 11-4-1871 (11-6-1871)
Thompson, Mary to John Perciful 11-11-1856
Thompson, Rebecca to Jarrett Nelson 12-21-1846
Thompson, Sarah C. to William W. Hammonds 1-2-1850 (1-3-1850)
Thompson, Sarah J. to John H. Graves 11-8-1867 (11-10-1867)
Thompson, Susan E. to William K. Holmes 11-13-1845
Thompson, Susan R. to Lemuel L. Cherry 1-8-1859 (1-13-1859)
Thompson, Susan to George W. Cole 12-3-1849
Thompson, Susan to Lewis A. Bickers 11-1-1848
Thurman, Nancy to Vann Miller 4-20-1854
Tidwell, Sarah A. to Miners L. Thompson 4-29-1844 (5-7-1844)
Tigert, Mary C. to Washington M. Burrow 8-18-1844
Tigrett, Sarah M. to Hugh B. Robinson 12-19-1838
Timms, Leeana to James A. Nolen 12-17-1853 (12-18-1853)
Timms, Matilda to Vinson Timms 7-23-1849
Tims, Missouri Angeline to Robert Smith 5-2-1857 (5-1?-1857)
Tims, Missouri Ann to George W. Tims 2-27-1856 (2-28-1856)
Tims, Sarah to John Edwards 7-8-1839 (7-10-1839)
Tims, Sarah to William Glidewell 12-17-1840
Tims, Susan to Nash Glidewell 8-22-1838 (8-23-1838)
Tinsley, Sarah A. to Christopher Jackson 2-20-1867 (2-21-1867)
Tittleton, Maria to Zebina C. Ewing 3-18-1850 (3-?-1850)
Todd, Caroline to Williams Chapman 3-26-1850
Todd, Frizzy A. to James H. Lawrence 12-8-1846 (12-9-1846)
Todd, Jane S. to John S. Watkins 11-8-1843 (11-9-1843)
Todd, Mariah to William Daws 12-16-1840 (12-17-1840)
Todd, Mary to Wiliam G. Humphrey 2-1-1844
Todd, Nancy M. to Nicholas D. Harding 12-18-1866 (12-20-1866)
Todd, Sarah to William M. Boon 11-19-1866 (11-22-1866)
Todd, Sarah to William Oliver 4-4-1846 (4-5-1846)
Tomlin, Ella to Robert S. Lindsey 10-24-1866
Tomlin, Lyde to Jno. T. Botts 12-1-1868
Tomlin, Margaret C. to John B. Hayley 6-23-1860 (6-27-1860)
Tomlin, Mary Lou to James M. Houston 2-16-1870
Tomlin, Nancy E. to James T. Hayley 11-6-1856
Tomlin, Sarah E. to Jos. T. Mann 4-22-1850
Tomlinson, Caroline to James Flaherty 8-31-1846 (9-1-1846)

Tooms, Lucy Ann to Frank M. Walters 12-7-1857 (12-10-1867?)
Toone, Adeline to Wesly Stone 8-30-1844
Toone, Mary A. V. to Thomas P. Marsh 12-26-1842 (12-29-1842)
Toones, Elizabeth F. to John W. Baker 9-16-1867 (9-18-1867)
Totten, Callie E. to Baker C. Springfield 11-23-1869 (11-24-1869)
Townsend, Minerva to John Fennell 5-21-1870 (5-22-1870)
Townzel, Molly Catherine to Charles Thos. Wilkins 5-20-1870 (5-22-1870)
Transou, C. J. to Victor M. Harris 7-6-1858 (7-7-1858)
Trezavent, Virginia L. to William Harrison 8-16-1870
Trezevant, Susie to Walton Watkins 10-17-1871 (10-18-1871)
Trice, Susan (Mrs.) to John R. Murchison 10-4-1869 (10-5-1869)
Truob, Barbara to Melchior Pfyfer 5-30-1868 (6-5-1869?)
Tucker, Alice G. to William B. Edwards 1-28-1867
Tucker, Sarah O. to M. D. Ozier 10-2-1855 (10-4-1855)
Tull, Elizabeth to Craven L. Taylor 11-7-1854
Turley, Irene to James Cobourn 2-24-1857 (2-25-1857)
Turley, Mary E. to Thomas W. Harris 3-24-1842
Turnage, Christinna to Thomas C. Lane 3-4-1852 (3-8-1852)
Turner, Adaline S. to Hudson C. Graves 2-22-1844 (2-26-1844)
Turner, Emeline to Wm. H. H. Kearney 3-20-1866 (3-22-1866)
Turner, Mary Jane to William L. Graves 12-27-1854 (12-28-1854)
Turner, Mollie V. to Phillip Cole 2-1-1868
Tyler, Granada to David J. Williford 1-5-1870 (1-6-1870)
Tyner, Julia Ann to Wynn Shelton 11-7-1850
Tyner, Sarah R. to William H. Watson 2-4-1843 (2-10-1843)
Tysen, Margaret (Mrs.) to James Allen Taylor 9-14-1869 (9-16-1869)
Tyson, Mary J. to Leroy C. Gillispie 10-28-1845 (11-1-1845)
Tyson, Sarah to Charles W. Cate 12-16-1845 (12-10?-1845)
Underwood, Lucy Jane to Samuel Cloud 5-13-1858
Upton, Mary to Thos. G. N. Smith 12-7-1854
Upton, Matilda to Shevarts Hurst 10-31-1842 (10-4?-1842)
Ursery, Elizabeth to Joseph Teddleton 8-9-1867 (8-10-1867)
Ursery, Jane to Alsey Jordon 11-20-1845 (11-27-1845)
Ursery, Sarah A. to Thomas G. May 10-31-1855 (11-1-1855)
Ursery, Susan M. to William B. Johnson 8-2-1855 (8-9-1855)
Usery, Lucy to James C. Bradford 10-5-1844
Usery, Mary E. to John W. Usery 9-24-1870 (9-27-1870)
Usery, Sarah to William Johnson 1-13-1848
Utley, Sue to Andrew Taylor 9-14-1870 (9-15-1870)
Vail, Emma to Joseph W. Duffey 7-?-1871 (7-28-1871)
Vail, Jane to John Robinson 1-22-1848 (1-23-1848)
Valentine, Charity to William Burton 3-23-1854
Valentine, Martha Ann to Saml. H. Weatherly 11-13-1866
Valentine, Sarah Frances to John Thomas Connor 12-22-1856 (12-23-1856)
Van Pelt, Susan A. to Fountain P. Young 12-9-1862 (12-11-1862)
Vance, Rhoda to Murdoch M. Murchison 11-7-1852
Vandouser, Mary to William A. Bruce 11-25-1862
Vann, Bolsoa to Osias Wade 7-30-1855
Vann, Rutha Ann to John M. Smith 10-15-1858
Vann, Susan A. (Mrs.) to Horace H. Hutchings 6-22-1858
Vanpelt, Sarah Jane to Henry A. Thomas 2-7-1850 (2-8-1850)
Vantreese, Rhoda to William Dickerson 11-19-1864 (11-20-1864)
Vantrence, Jane to James Alford 3-9-1841
Vantrice, Sarah to Richard M. Davis 12-20-1842 (12-29-1842)
Vanzandt, Mary Ann to William Osgen 12-26-1842 (12-27-1842)
Vault, Sarha L. (Mrs.) to John G. Granger 10-14-1867 (10-15-1867)
Vaulx, Catherine G. to Lewis B. Shapard 7-24-1860
Vaulx, Mary Eliza to Alexander C. Robertson 11-11-1852
Vaulx, Matilda E. to Charles N. Gibbs 6-5-1850
Ventreese, Frances to Marcus S. Bledsoe 3-15-1856
Verser, Lizzie C. to Young F. Marley 5-19-1857 (5-20-1857)
Verser, Lucy A. to John Connor 12-1-1856 (12-17-1856)
Verser, Margarett to William H. Cleaves 3-8-1843
Vevely, Jane D. to Benj. F. Mills 8-8-1866 (8-16-1866)
Vick, Amanda to William L. Anderson 4-29-1848
Vick, Octavia A. to James A. Dusmuke 11-16-1854
Vick, Sarah S. (Mrs.) to Joel Rushing 2-2-1858 (2-3-1858)
Vick, Sarah T. to John W. Sykes 8-28-1866
Vincent, Nancy to Stephen Harbert 7-20-1840 (7-23-1840)
Vincent, Sarah A. to Edward Davie 1-14-1869 (1-21-1869) *
Vinson, Caroline to William Chisum 1-3-1848
Vinson, Elizabeth H. to L. H. Ware 1-20-1846
Vinson, Elizabeth to Jesse B. Branch 10-6-1842

Vinson, Mary to Philip Northern 12-4-1841
Vinson, Nancy A. to James Henderson 8-14-1855 (8-16-1855)
Volentine, Emeline to Samuel Burton 6-5-1855
Volentine, Mary J. to James Weatherly 11-7-1860
Volentine, Mary J. to Joseph F. Connor 12-12-1868
Waddell, Mary Ann to John M. Sanders 9-11-1856
Waddle, Lidia to W. R. Towell 12-23-1839 (1-7-1840)
Waddle, Martha Jane to William H. Sanders 12-12-1840 (12-14-1840)
Waddleton, Elizabeth to Patrick Sauls 1-30-1843 (2-2-1843)
Wadley, Mary Jane to William W. Layn 3-10-1856 (3-16-1856)
Wadley, Paralee to William W. Baily 8-18-1855 (8-19-1855)
Wadlington, Euphania to John F. Price 1-19-1870
Waggoner, Amanda M. to Francis M. Whitworth 3-16-1854
Waggoner, Martha to Josiah Hodges 5-2-1844
Waggoner, Mary G. to Wm. J. Sykes 11-20-1866
Wagoner, Paralee to John F. Johnson 5-13-1862 (5-14-1862)
Wagster, Josephine to William S. Robinson 10-8-1867 (10-10-1867)
Walden, Roenna M. E. to James L. Todd 8-2-1848
Walker, Charlotte to Nimrod Estes 6-1-1841 (1-3-1842)
Walker, Elizabeth (Mrs.) to George Hardee 5-23-1868 (5-24-1868)
Walker, Hannah to Saml. S. McElwee 1-27-1855
Walker, Liuisa? to Volentine Walker 11-1-1870 (11-2-1870)
Walker, Luzinda to Thomas J. Slocum 7-23-1857 (7-27-1857)
Walker, Mary F. to James W. King 1-15-1857 (1-18-1857)
Walker, Mary Jane to William J. (Dr.) Drake 5-3-1859
Walker, Neely Ellender to William Walker 8-8-1846 (8-9-1846)
Walker, Otey to Valintine Walker 1-18-1850 (1-20-1850)
Walker, Rebecca to Theo. Arnold 8-27-1839 (9-4-1839)
Walker, Sarah M. to E. C. Robards 4-16-1867
Walker, Susan to Robert Mann 7-29-1844 (7-31-1844)
Wallace, Eliza Catharine to Wm. Thomas Byrd 8-28-1867 (8-29-1867)
Wallis, M. J. to William L. Amos 12-2-1867 (12-5-1867)
Walls, Louisa to Charles H. Nelson 10-14-1856
Walsh, Dinebia to Frank B. Hamilton 11-18-1869
Walsh, Mary F. to A. Hamilton Burkhead 1-28-1869
Walsh, Sarah A. to Council B. Mayo 2-1-1870
Walston, Lucy Jane to Henry M. Sexton 7-4-1866 (7-5-1866)
Walters, Martha Ann to Wm. Martin Longmire no date
Ward, Lucy Ann to Samuel M. Fry 12-23-1848 (12-26-1848)
Ward, Martha J. to Augustus B. Goodin 10-3-1848 (10-5-1848)
Wardlow, Mary to Edward (Capt.) Pendergrast 7-25-1862
Warlick, Cynthia J. to William G. Smith 1-18-1848
Warlick, Emma C. to Joseph E. McDonald 10-3-1859 (10-6-1859)
Warlick, Laura to Theophilus Bond 4-1-1852
Warmoth, Sarah A. to William R. Lewis 3-17-1852 (3-18-1852)
Wat, Wilmouth J. to Cyrus E. Mathis 10-30-1844
Waters, Delia C. to John Donelson 1-13-1849 (2-13-1849)
Waters, Mary C. to Hugh N. Anderson 1-30-1845
Watkins, Elizabeth I. to P. Shivers 2-3-1840 (2-6-1840)
Watkins, Hepzhibad to John P. Lane 12-17-1844 (12-19-1844)
Watkins, Nannie J. to Jesse R. Phillips 12-2-1869 (12-7-1869)
Watkins, Nannie J. to John W. Willoughby 6-27-1867
Watkins, Tabitha L. to Robert H. Cox 10-19-1866 (10-21-1866)
Watson, Eleanor to Alfred B. Gooch 5-19-1841
Watson, Jane to William M. Graves 12-3-1838
Watson, Julia to Thomas A. Crews 3-14-1855 (3-15-1855)
Watson, L. Melinda to Stephen Dyer 10-5-1848
Watson, Lucretia W. to John P. Brooks 9-20-1845 (9-25-1845)
Watson, Margaret C. to Washington T. Exum 12-11-1854 (12-13-1854)
Watson, Mary E. to Burwell Blackman 9-8-1846 (9-10-1846)
Watson, Nancy to Daniel R. Allison 6-29-1843
Watson, Sarah J. to Alexander H. Cathey 2-9-1853
Watt, Louisa F. to Miles J. Sloan 11-14-1861 (11-17-1861)
Watt, Mary M. to Nicholas Nivell 2-2-1842 (2-3-1842)
Watt, Nancy N. to James McClure 9-22-1846
Watt, Paralee to Alexander Kimble 2-8-1850
Watt, Parmelia T. to Shephard B. Hicks 8-15-1848 (8-20-1848)
Watt, Susan to Samuel Farmer 9-14-1846
Weaks, Elizabeth to Benjamin F. Vantreese 9-29-1852
Weatherly, Elizabeth C. to George W. Day 10-28-1856 (10-30-1856)
Weatherly, Margaret to John R. Paisley 9-17-1857 (9-29-1857)
Weathers, Elizabeth Ann to David H. Jones 1-15-1867
Weathers, Narcissa to William J. Derryberry 7-19-1869
Weaver, Cyrena Jane to James G. Mays 6-24-1859 (6-28-1859)
Weaver, Frances H. to Andrew Patrick 12-29-1862 (12-30-1862)

Weaver, Martha to James R. Ledbetter 11-3-1841
Weaver, Mary C. to Wilson Cooper 9-12-1853 (9-15-1853)
Weaver, Nancy G. to Archibald S. Rogers 2-20-1849 (2-22-1849)
Webb, Alpha to Montgomery Anderson 1-10-1844
Webb, Barthinia S. to James E. Whyte 7-22-1847
Webb, Caroline to Silas Lassiter 9-8-1860 (9-9-1860)
Webb, Elizabeth A. to Thomas H. Lee 9-16-1853
Webb, Fanny H. to George L. Smith 11-8-1853
Webb, Mary Elizabeth to Nathan H. Whitlow 11-1-1854
Webb, Mary F. to Henry J. Elliott 2-5-1868
Webb, Mary Jane to Janes Valentine 9-8-1853 (9-11-1853)
Webb, Rebecca to James W. Keaton 12-14-1859 (12-24-1859)
Webb, Sallie to Cit L. Bell 3-8-1871
Webb, Wethly to Norman Webb 12-7-1843
Weir, Ann B. to Donald D. Weir 2-14-1842 (2-15-1842)
Welch, Amelia to Wily Thom 11-26-1838 (11-29-1838)
Wells, Margarett A. L. to Johns R. Neely 10-29-1845 (10-31-1845)
Wells, Nannie E. to Lacy L. Brown 11-28-1866
Welsh, Jane to Murphy G. Holt 12-28-1843 (1-4-1844)
West, Bettie to William Dodson 10-10-1871 (10-11-1871)
West, Seleta to Elias W. May 7-24-1838
Westerbrook, Margaret E. to Daniel C. Johns 11-26-1840
Wethers, Lyde to James S. Smith 1-19-1870 (1-20-1870)
Wharton, Mattie to James G. Reid 11-6-1866 (11-8-1866)
Wheeler, Missouri P. to Edward Talbot 9-26-1870 (9-27-1870)
Wheeler, Susan to Harbert Joyce 4-14-1845
Whiley, Louisa to Jacob Dickson 3-13-1868 (3-15-1868)
Whitaker, Martha to Nicholas Greener 2-22-1862 (2-23-1862)
White, Annie C. to John D. Wilhelm 8-28-1866 (8-30-1866)
White, Delia to James C. Gooch 2-22-1869 (2-28-1869)
White, Eliza to Wallace Newman 10-30-1844
White, Frances E. to Henry F. Sowell 12-30-1869
White, Harriet M. to Robert T. Webb 10-31-1860 (11-1-1860)
White, Mary A. to George H. Hawson 2-11-1869
White, Mary Ann to Raleigh Hammers 7-4-1859 (7-5-1859)
White, Mary Elizabeth to Anail Watson 7-1-1854 (7-2-1854)
White, Nancy E. to Charles R. Belote 8-31-1854
White, Sarah Elizabeth to Elisha J. Crawford 8-7-1866
Whitenton, Mary F. to John I. Brown 11-16-1869
Whiteside, Axelina to Everett G. Piercy 7-28-1847 (7-29-1847)
Whitesides, Eudora to William H. Cox 10-23-1866
Whitington, Emeline to James B. Wilson 8-22-1843 (8-23-1843)
Whitlow, Emanda E. to George S. Williamson 2-11-1871
Whitlow, Nancy S. to Jacob E. Vanhook 11-19-1844
Whitlow, Phinela to James R. Cole 2-17-1842
Whittington, Frances Ann to Christopher C. Harris 2-10-1848
  (2-14-1848)
Whittington, Laney to Barney King 9-29-1856 (10-16-1856)
Whittington, Mary Jane to Joseph M. Dalton 10-13-1842
Whitworth, Ann Elizabeth to Rounsville Williams 12-28-1859
  (12-29-1859)
Whitworth, Louisa to Richard Hargis 12-23-1857
Whitworth, Margaret C. to George Waggoner 4-26-1861
Whitworth, Mary G. to Joseph Warner 9-4-1856 (noncomeatibus)
Whitworth, Mary G. to Stephen B. Waggoner 12-23-1856
Wigg, Susan L. to Laurence McCafflin 5-5-1870
Wiggins, Emely to Hardin Jones 7-18-1838
Wiggins, Hannah T. to Thomas G. Mullins 9-10-1862 (9-11-1862)
Wiggs, Caroline to Loi R. Wiggs 10-1-1840
Wiggs, Martha E. to William D. Harper 2-13-1845 (2-27-1845)
Wiggs, Mary I. to Ryland Chandler 5-17-1838
Wiggs, Sarah E. to George T. Shelton 12-20-1859
Wiggs, Susan S. to Alexander Howell 8-3-1854
Wilhelm, Josephine to John W. White 9-8-1866 (9-9-1866)
Wilie, Mary J. to Berry L. Spring 12-18-1860 (12-19-1860)
Wilie, Mary W. to Jas. B. Cunningham 9-7-1869 (9-9-1869)
Wilie, Susan A. B. to James H. Buntin 2-8-1870
Wilkes, Martha N. C. to James W. Bond 1-16-1856 (1-22-1856)
Wilkes, Mary D. to John E. Pearson 11-7-1852 (11-10-1852)
Wilkins, Catherine E. to Young Bradford 4-3-1860 (4-5-1860)
Wilkins, Charlotte E. to Henry Matlock 12-31-1855 (1-1-1855?)
Wilkins, Margarett to William Baker 7-28-1846
Wilkins, Mary Ann to James H. Bryant 4-9-1852 (4-16-1852)
Wilkins, Nancy (Mrs.) to Solomon D. Ford 11-30-1860
Wilkins, Sarah to Andrew Kilpatrick 8-16-1842 (8-18-1842)

Wilkinson, Jane to Simon Beal 12-25-1843
Wilkinson, Nancy E. to Marcus Rickman 8-21-1841 (8-23-1841)
Willett, Mary E. (Mrs.) to Rufus N. Binkley 2-18-1869
William, Dilly to Moses Medlin 8-14-1867 (3-10-1870)
Williams, Alevia W. to James H. Young 6-16-1857 (6-21-1857)
Williams, Amanda Jane to Nathaniel Britt 8-26-1857 (8-27-1857)
Williams, Amanda to William Teague 8-27-1846
Williams, Ann Z. to Martin Shaw 8-3-1846
Williams, Carolina A. to Samuel S. Sykes 4-10-1848
Williams, Ciddy Ann to Elisha Jackson 11-30-1859 (12-8-1859)
Williams, Clarkey Ann to Alex P. Rector 5-21-1870 (5-22-1870)
Williams, E. K. to Solomon W. Vanhook 1-25-1871
Williams, Elizabeth Ann to Robert N. McClellan 11-20-1842 (12-1-1842)
Williams, Elizabeth to Gibson Whittington 8-20-1840
Williams, Elizabeth to John Ellington 5-17-1838 (5-18-1838)
Williams, Elizabeth to Peter Ford 1-3-1852 (1-7-1852)
Williams, Elizabeth to Reuben Daughby 9-9-1839
Williams, Emma to Cecil Fleming 1-29-1870 (1-31-1870)
Williams, Feriby F. to Ezekiel B. W. Hobbs 10-16-1848 (10-17-1848)
Williams, Fidelia E. to Nathaniel Perry 12-31-1868
Williams, Henrietta to John E. Ohara 12-3-1861 (12-5-1861)
Williams, Jane to Thomas Vantreese 1-31-1855 (2-1-1855)
Williams, Jennie to Wm. L. Harris 5-7-1870
Williams, Kate (Mrs.) to Jesse Mark 6-25-1870 (6-26-1870)
Williams, Laura L. to Colen M. Patterson 11-26-1868
Williams, Louisa to Elisha Jackson 1-20-1846 (1-28-1846)
Williams, Mariah to Hugh Montgomery 12-6-1843 (12-7-1843)
Williams, Martha C. to David W. Johnson 2-14-1859 (2-15-1859)
Williams, Martha Ione to W. B. Richardson 10-1-1842 (10-6-1842)
Williams, Martha to Matthew G. Bobbitt 12-14-1846 (12-15-1846)
Williams, Mary A. to Daniel S. Lacy 4-14-1858 (4-15-1858)
Williams, Mary Ann to Wm. A. Vantreese 12-8-1866 (12-20-1866)
Williams, Mary E. to William B. Wallace 3-28-1848
Williams, Mary Jane to Everett Wallace 7-28-1857 (7-30-1857)
Williams, Mary to Felix Johnson 6-26-1861
Williams, Minerva to Ruben K. Stephens 11-2-1870 (11-3-1870)
Williams, Nancy to Everett Carey 11-11-1841 (11-12-1841)
Williams, Nancy to Vincent L. Pendergrast 11-13-1866 (11-14-1866)
Williams, Nancy to William Richars 8-15-1842
Williams, Nannie E. to Frank B. Winfree 2-28-1871
Williams, Parmelia to James F. Randolph 10-8-1859
Williams, Peninah to Allen Bryant 4-15-1850 (4-18-1850)
Williams, Pernetta E. to Josiah S. Robertson 9-28-1867 (9-29-1867)
Williams, R. Caroline to David Hoad 7-2-1859 (7-3-1859)
Williams, Rosa Ann to William J. McKenna 10-11-1848 (10-12-1848)
Williams, Rowena Eliza to Barham Perry 8-27-1869 (9-1-1869)
Williams, Rowena to Wm. R. Ellington 9-21-1869 (9-29-1869)
Williams, Sallie M. to Henry H. Swink 5-23-1871
Williams, Sarah Ann Elizabeth to Felix Josiah Hall 12-13-1856 (12-14-1856)
Williams, Sophronia to B. B. Rankin 12-31-1860
Williams, Susan (Mrs.) to Thomas J. Cobel 9-7-1867 (9-10-1867)
Williams, Susan M. to John W. C. Hendron 2-1-1841 (2-3-1841)
Williamson, Callie to Geo. E. Campbell 10-18-1871
Williamson, Caroline E. to Clement P. Fitz 9-3-1849 (10-3-1849)
Williamson, Clementine C. to Wm. McMillin 2-2-1869
Williamson, Eliza to William D. Wilson 9-3-1842 (9-4-1842)
Williamson, Fannie to John A. Metcalf 3-3-1858 (3-7-1858)
Williamson, Hannah to Elisha Altom 4-16-1849 (4-6?-1849)
Williamson, Mariah to John Mickum 9-18-1847
Williamson, Mary E. to Jno. W. Sykes 1-10-1871 (1-11-1871)
Williamson, Mary E. to William J. Robinson 4-30-1850 (5-1-1850)
Williamson, Mary I. to Floridore A. Keelen 4-8-1861
Williamson, Melissa A. to Robert J. Ruffin 4-24-1856
Williamson, Nancy (sen.) to Robert C. Neely 9-14-1858
Williamson, Rebecca C. to Henry Rosser 8-15-1870
Williamson, Sarah A. to John W. Tiner 11-24-1859
Williamson, Sarah F. to David Reid 10-3-1849 (10-10-1849)
Williamson, Winnie to Charles N. Johnson 9-24-1867 (9-26-1867)
Willis, Elizabeth C. to Frank A. W. Burton 10-31-1844
Wilson, Amanda T. to James R. Burrow 2-?-1845
Wilson, Delphina E. to James L. Cooper 12-7-1861
Wilson, Elizabeth to Anderson Edwards 4-22-1841
Wilson, Julia A. to Joseph W. Exum 9-18-1867 (9-19-1867)

Wilson, Lucinda to William H. Edwards 1-28-1846
Wilson, M. Callie to Jno. F. Fanville 2-22-1869
Wilson, Malinda to Allen Hill 1-25-1840
Wilson, Martha A. D. to James J. Baker 12-14-1847 (3-26-1848)
Wilson, Mary C. to Henry W. Wynkoop 6-3-1862
Wilson, Mary C. to Robert M. May 3-31-1866
Wilson, Mary M. to Robert Jones 11-20-1852 (11-25-1852)
Wilson, Miria L. to William A. Compton 1-5-1853
Wilson, N. C. to D. W. Harston 12-29-1860
Wilson, Nancy to Noah Dickson 12-16-1847
Wilson, Rosalie A. to John E. Boykin 11-6-1855 (11-7-1855)
Wilson, Sarah A. to Emmet T. Morgan 7-27-1858 (8-10-1858)
Wilson, Sarah Ann to Benjamin F. Transee 10-4-1847
Wilson, Sarah C. to Hamner King 9-6-1858 (9-8-1858)
Wilson, Susan to George A. Lunsford 2-19-1861
Wilson, Wm. A. to M. J. Paisley 2-2-1854
Winfield, Elenora L. to Michael Doble 1-29-1870
Winfrey, S. P. to Geo. A. Moxey 9-18-1866 (9-19-1866)
Winslow, Lenora (Mrs.) to Thomas Fesmire 10-6-1869 (10-14-1869)
Winston, Ann E. to Robert I. Bryan 12-17-1867 (12-19-1867)
Winston, Sarah F. to William W. Weatherly 12-15-1858 (12-5?-1858)
Wise, Sarah Ann to William H. Greer 7-2-1850
Wiseman, Mary A. (Mrs.) to George W. Chappel 2-22-1870
Witherlington, Elizabeth to Harmon Reddin 12-28-1839
Withers, Lydia C. to Ransom Burns Hicks 10-8-1861 (10-9-1861)
Wittman, Margaretha to Louis Eppinger 4-25-1861
Wittman, Matilda to Edward Iffland 6-29-1869 (7-1-1869)
Womack, Mariah A. to Francis W. Campbell 12-19-1859 (12-20-1859)
Womack, Sarah A. to Robt. D. Anderson 3-10-1868 (3-20-1868)
Wood, Bettie D. to C. A. (Dr.) Chapman 12-17-1866 (12-18-1866)
Wood, Elizabeth to John Oliver 9-24-1838
Wood, Florida E. to Thomas W. Walker 8-23-1858 (8-25-1858)
Wood, Melissa Ann to Robert Weatherly 11-13-1866
Wood, Sarah J. to William T. Landers 12-17-1869 (12-19-1869)
Wood, Susan to Benjamin Neal 11-21-1846 (11-23-1846)
Woodard, Mary to Has. Chamberlin 1-3-1842
Woodard, Zelpha to Aaron W. Woodard 3-12-1838 (5-20-1838)
Woodfolk, Allia G. to Thomas F. Lane 11-11-1871 (11-12-1871)
Woods, Armanda Jane to Matthew S. Bryant 10-4-1847 (9-6-1848)
Woods, Martha to Jeromiah P. Wood 5-27-1868 (5-28-1868)
Woods, Mary A. to Andrew D. Woods 2-14-1870 (2-15-1870)
Woods, Mary Ann to Drury Johnson 12-13-1851 (12-14-1851)
Wooley, Christain A. to John T. Smith 7-19-1858 (7-21-1858)
Woolfolk, Artie to J. L. Williams 12-6-1870 (12-7-1870)
Woolfolk, Ellen to Thos. B. Utley 11-3-1868 (11-4-1868)
Woolfolk, Mildred A. to William A. W. Davie 4-5-1869 (4-7-1869)
Woollard, Sarah (Mrs.) to Benj. Marion Spencer 7-6-1869
Worl, Mary to Thos. P. Snowden 12-24-1838
Worley, Clara A. to Marmaduke Y. Harston 12-30-1845 (1-1-1846)
Worrell, Elizabeth to Halsted Butts 11-18-1850 (11-20-1850)
Worrell, Mary J. to James T. Thompson 2-31-1852
Wrenn, Mary Ann to William G. Haltom 2-19-1839
Wrenn, Sarah E. to Henry H. Brown 5-23-1842 (5-26-1842)
Wright, Candis to Gray Rodick 1-20-1840 (1-22-1840)
Wright, Louisa C. to John H. Hudson 1-31-1848 (2-3-1848)
Wright, Martha to Lytle Newton 1-7-1858
Wyatt, Mary to Lorenza D. Cash 4-4-1843 (4-6-1843)
Wyley, Terrissa M. to Wiley F. Blackard 12-22-1855 (12-24-1855)
Yarbrough, Arlesia to Nathan Parlow 8-15-1870 (8-18-1870)
Yarbrough, Martha Mahalda to James R. Butts 8-23-1870 (8-25-1870)
Yarbrough, Sallie to Simon A. Collins 9-12-1870
Yarbrough, Tempie A. to Paul T. Harris 11-12-1866 (11-15-1866)
Yates, Monian to Julian Tarver 12-17-1867 (12-18-1867)
Yerout, Margarett to Clark L. Stone 2-15-1842
York, Eliza Jane to John T. Buchanan 8-22-1866 (8-26-1866)
York, Elizabeth to Callin Hays 12-25-1847 (12-28-1847)
York, Loset M. to Thomas Black 2-21-1843
York, Mahilda G. to Robert P. Dunnway 12-28-1847 (12-30-1847)
York, Mary C. E. to Ephraim J. Lee 6-1-1858
York, Mary Jane to Isaac C. Stephen 10-29-1839
Young, Drucinda E. to Richard S. Pitts 12-18-1855
Young, Eliza to Jno. T. Fowler 2-28-1871
Young, Elizabeth to George Jones 4-11-1840
Young, Jane to Hardy Dean 2-11-1843 (2-14-1843)
Young, Julia A. F. to Archibald McMillan 10-23-1856 (10-26-1856)

Young, Lucy to Marcus Bledsoe 3-20-1850 (3-21-1850)
Young, Margaret to John J. Brasfield 8-17-1850 (8-22-1850)
Young, Martha J. to Chas. W. Carter 1-27-1862 (1-28-1862)
Young, Martha L. to Francis A. Bond 12-3-1850
Young, Mary Ann to Burtis Lunsford 5-27-1843 (6-8-1843)
Young, Mary E. to Lewis L. Cox 11-10-1869 (11-11-1869)
Young, Mary Jane to Winston Ellington 6-6-1859 (6-8-1859)
Young, R. E. to John G. Key 11-10-1868 (11-12-1868)
Young, Susan E. to John S. Haltom 9-24-1853 (10-6-1853)
_____, America to Andrew Caradine 12-16-1846
_____, Emily to Thomas M. Graves 1-29-1844 (2-1-1844)
_____, Martha to Richard Johnson 1-30-1847
_____, _____ to David Nolen 1-30-1847
_____, _____ to Wm. C. Robinson 6-26-1867

www.ingramcontent.com/pod-product-compliance
Lightning Source LLC
Chambersburg PA
CBHW081341090426
42737CB00017B/3240